the basic basics
KITCHEN HACKS AND HINTS

Best known in Britain as an entertaining and innovative TV chef, New Zealand born Glynn Christian began food broadcasts on London's LBC radio and BBC TV's Pebble Mill at One in 1982 and made over 1000 live broadcasts. He appeared three mornings weekly on BBC TV Breakfast Time and made the first TV food series shot abroad.

His UK journalistic career includes writing weekly for *The Sunday Telegraph* for four years for which he was nominated for Glenfiddich Food Writer of the Year, *Elle* magazine, where he was the original food editor, and work for *OK, House and Gardens, Gardens Illustrated*, as well as being the original cookery and food presenter on QVC Shopping Channel UK and then senior presenter on TVSN, Australia. He is the author of over 25 books mainly about food and cookery which include his best-known *REAL FLAVOURS—the Handbook of Gourmet and Deli Ingredients*, which was voted Best Food Guide in the World. Nigel Slater called it 'one of the only ten books you need'; Tom Parker Bowles says it is 'as important to the kitchen as a sharp knife'.

Glynn helped found The Guild of Food Writers and is the only food writer given a Lifetime Achievement Award from within the UK food industry, by the Guild of Fine Food, 2008 Great Taste Awards. He co-founded the iconic Mr Christian's Provisions on Portobello Rd.

He now lives in Battersea, London.

the basic basics
KITCHEN HACKS
AND HINTS

350+ amazing tips for seasoned chefs and aspirational cooks

Glynn Christian

GRUB STREET • LONDON

Published in 2021 by
Grub Street
4 Rainham Close
London
SW11 6SS

Email: food@grubstreet.co.uk
Web: www.grubstreet.co.uk
Twitter: @grub_street
Facebook: Grub Street Publishing
Instagram: @grubstreet_books

A CIP catalogue record for this book is available from the British Library

ISBN 978-1-911667-10-0

Printed and bound by Finidr, Czech Republic

CONTENTS

1

LIQUID ASSETS

MARTINI MAGIC

Freeze favourite olives and add
to straight-up martini cocktails.
They'll keep the drink ice cold
without dilution. And then
be delicious.

Choose a thick slice of frozen
lemon if you prefer a twist.

Freeze pearl onions for a Gibson.

G&T PERFECTIONS

A goblet-shaped glass will
enhance the G&T experience
by trapping and enhancing
aromas, whereas a straight-sided
glass allows them to disperse

Preserve the coldness of the
drink longer and avoid dilution
of the gin by first chilling the
glass with ice cubes and then
pouring out any melted water.

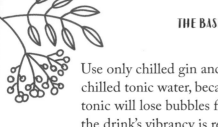

Use only chilled gin and then chilled tonic water, because warm tonic will lose bubbles faster and the drink's vibrancy is reduced.

FRUIT ICE CUBES
To keep cocktails and soft drinks cold without diluting, freeze sliced lemon, lime or orange, cubes of melon, water melon, peach, whole cherries, grapes, raspberries, blue berries and more, and then use instead of ice cubes.

WATER ICE
Chill wine and champagne faster by using a mixture of ice cubes and water; it's quicker than just ice and will reach higher up the bottle.

FRUITY SUMMER WINE
Create happy faces and colourful tables with goblets of fruity red, rosé or white wine chilled by frozen berries or cubes of fruit. No dilution plus extra flavour and at least you might eat something.

NOT SO COSY
Use a tea cosy only when there are no tea bags or tea leaves in the pot. Tea brews, draws or mashes best in cooling water. A cosy keeps the temperature up and this extracts the bitter tannin content sooner than it should.

THE CUCUMBER GIN AND TONIC
Serve a single slice of cucumber in gin and tonic to transform it; once tried you'll never go back to lemon or lime.

TWO FOR TEA

Use a second, warmed teapot if you don't take out the bags or leaves once the tea is brewed. Pour the perfect tea into that and yes, this is when to use a cosy. The second pot was common right up until the 60s and there were even newspaper ads and infomercials in cinemas to remind people. Then came tea bags, the greatest advantage of which is that they may be removed when the brew is right.

COLD TEAS

Make a concentrated base for crystal-clear iced tea by brewing at least four tea bags overnight in 300 mls/½ pint cold water; using hot water makes it cloudy as it cools. Drink as is over lots of ice or dilute with sparkling water, fruit juice, especially pineapple, or with white wine and sparkling water for a Tea Spritzer. Sparkling white wine is especially good with Rose Pouchong or Earl Grey tea.

TEA OFF

Control your caffeine intake from tea by heading East through the day. Assam has the most, followed by other Indians except for fragrant Darjeelings, and then it's Ceylon/Sri Lankan or Kenyan. China Blacks have less caffeine than those, followed by Oolongs and then Green tea to gentle you into the night.

SHARP WARNING

Use lemon to counteract bitterness only in harsh, low-grade teas. Used in higher grade teas, lemon destroys the finesse and fragrance you have paid for.

COFFEE GROUNDINGS

Pouring boiling water onto ground or instant coffee destroys the finest of the fragrant oils that give the best flavour.

Pour less-than-boiling water from a height onto instant coffee or ground coffee; this cools it on the way down and also aerates the mixture.

Ignore advice that ground coffee should not be refrigerated. Tightly wrapped in its bag and stored in an airtight container, it will be fresh for weeks.

Freeze ground coffee tightly sealed and it is good for months, some say five months. Spoon out what you need and return to the freezer.

Using frozen coffee grounds means their temperature cools water that is too hot.

Get higher with Robusta coffee beans, which have a much higher caffeine content than Arabica beans, but a coarser flavour. Robusta beans are more likely to be used to make instant coffee, so this is commonly more stimulating than brewed coffee. Important to remember when following hacks to make super-caffeinated whipped coffees.

INSTANT WHIPPING I

Create Korean or Delgado whipped coffee with equal quantities of instant coffee, white sugar and water, which can be iced, ambient or hot: one or two tablespoons of each are a good starting point. Beat for three or more minutes to form a thick foam that peaks like meringue.

Serve over hot or cold milk, including nut milks.

Top cocoa or hot chocolate to make mocha heaven.

Pile onto brownies, chocolate or other cakes.

Finish ice-cream sundaes.

Heap onto sparkling water to make coffee soda like no other.

INSTANT WHIPPING II

Serve Greek frappé as a less caffeinated whipped coffee, a drink that's even found made to order in bars. In Corfu, three versions differ according to sweetness:

→ Straight (*sketos*) 1–2 teaspoons of instant coffee and no sugar.

→ Medium (*metrios*) 1–2 teaspoons of instant coffee with two teaspoons of sugar.

→ Sweet (*glykos*) 1–2 teaspoons of instant coffee with four teaspoons of sugar.

Combine your choice with 2–3 tablespoons of water and shake to create a stable foam. You can also use a milk frother or a milkshake maker. Pour over ice cubes in a tall glass, adding water, sparkling water or milk to taste—perhaps a mixture.

Fool frappé-heads into thinking you are part of the head-high gang by using de-caffeinated instant.

DOUBLE PLUNGING

Plunge a cafetière immediately after pouring on the water and then return to the top, which ensures the grounds are evenly wet and will brew fully. Then brew less time than you would usually do.

SKIMMING THE TOP

Froth only skimmed milk because it makes firmer frothed milk for hot coffee; it is protein not fat that makes the foam. Even made with a hand beater rather than in a dedicated foam-producer, skimmed milk will hold its shape better than full milk.

DROP SHOTS

Drop a square of high cocoa-solids chocolate (70%) into espresso for a maxi-mocha. Trending high cocoa-solids milk chocolates add creaminess.

EGGSACTLY

FLOATERS AND SINKERS

Check egg freshness in a bowl or jug of water. Fresh eggs lie on the bottom, those that stand tippy-toe are OK, any that float should be discarded.

SHELL BE RIGHT X 2

Boil eggs direct from the refrigerator without cracking their shells by starting in cold water. When the water boils, cook them your preferred time.

If your eggs are room temperature, they won't crack if you prick both ends of the shell with a needle before putting into gently boiling water.

NAILED IT

Wet your fingers if long acrylic nails make it tricky to pick up eggs or to take them from a carton.

QUELLING QUAIL EGGS

Keep quail eggs warm to peel easily. Cook and then almost cool in running water. Roll over a worktop to crack the shells and then put back into warm water so that seeps under the shells. It's letting the membranes get cold that makes shelling difficult.

HARD FACTS

You'll try harder to peel hard-boiled very fresh eggs.

Crack the shells of hard-boiled eggs while they are cooling under running water; do this easily by vigorously shaking the pan. This avoids a black ring forming around the yolk and usually makes shelling easier.

Use a pasta server to move slippery eggs after shelling.

NET RESULTS

Fry shelled hard-boiled eggs in olive oil and create a golden, webbed net around each.

Dip into spice mixtures, like cinnamon, cumin and salt, or coriander and salt, or garam masala and salt. Chopped parsley or fresh coriander, too.

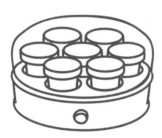

NIGHT EGGS

Simmer eggs in their shells at least eight hours, or overnight, and both whites and yolks develop melting tenderness. These are even better if fried as above once shelled.

Add onion skins to the water, which will lightly colour the eggs.

Spices or herbs in the water will scent the egg; you get a bigger flavour if these are regularly changed for fresh ones. Serve the same spices and herbs in any dip for the eggs.

SIMULTANEOUS SERVICE

Start and finish fried or poached eggs for a crowd at the same time: first break the eggs into a bowl and then tip them into the pan all at once.

PRE ORDER

Poach eggs in advance and remove from the water. When reheated in water or fried, they will not cook more but stay the same liquidity.

BEATING RETREAT

Eggs for meringues and soufflés should be at least two days old and four or five is better, as the whites of very fresh eggs do not give the best volume or texture.

3

BAKING STUFF

COOL HANDS

'Hot hands' make it impossible to rub butter into flour without it becoming a paste rather than crumbs, so:

→ Freeze the butter and grate it into the flour. By the time it is rubbed in, it will only just have thawed.

→ Rub the butter and flour together high over the bowl and let it drop back from that height; this keeps heat out of the bowl and the crumbs cool as they fall.

BETTER BUTTERING

Grate frozen butter onto anything about to be baked, rather than dabbing and dotting unevenly. Keeps hands clean, too.

EVEN PIECES

Mix only three-quarters of dried fruits or nuts into a cake mixture. Add the last quarter of the dry ingredients into the remaining batter when about two thirds through transferring to the baking tin, because that portion usually has fewer fruits mixed in.

DON'T DROP IT

Spoon cake batters into baking tins for a lighter result. Pouring cake mixes bounces out some of the air you have incorporated, especially from sponge mixtures.

SWEET SPOONING

Avoid honey and time waste by dipping a spoon quickly into oil and draining or running under hot water before spooning out honey, liquid or creamed.

NO MUFFIN SECONDS

Spoon muffin mixtures into tins or paper cases with a single blob. A second spoonful can make muffins heavy.

SCONESENSE

True scones never contain eggs.

Scone mixing should be done with a table knife and then never rolled but patted into shape.

Cut with sharpest blade possible, so edges are not smeared and scones can rise fully.

Round and fluted cutters must be sharp and deeper than the mixture is thick, so the edges are not smeared, which inhibits rising.

Ideally, preheat and flour the baking tray and shape the scones on that.

Transfer baked scones to a cooling rack and leave them alone to keep crustiness, cover with a clean cloth for soft scones.

Pull hot or cold scones apart rather than cutting, which smears and flattens the light texture.

FLAT OUT

Spread the top of fruit cake mixtures towards the sides before baking, leaving a depression in the centre, and you are more likely to get the admired flat surface.

FLAT IN

Screw baking parchment into a ball before lining a tray. When it's flattened it stays like that rather than curling.

MAKING MATCHES

Make a shallow cut from top to bottom before slicing a cake horizontally prior to adding a filling. Replace the layer or layers exactly by aligning the cut. Otherwise, insert a cocktail stick above and below where you slice across and realign those.

HOT RELEASES

Release a reluctant cake that has cooled too long in the tin, by holding it over gentle heat, which will melt butter or other fat on the base. Not a problem if you have lined with baking parchment.

COCOA FLOURING

Use cocoa powder instead of flour when preparing a baking tin for a chocolate cake. No white smudges on the cooked cake and the flavour will be heightened, too.

SHINY ICING

Aim a hair-dryer at a freshly iced cake, which will slightly melt and shine the surface. Practise on left-over icing because too much heat makes the icing melt and run.

FIRST SLICE EASE

Cut a neat first slice of any pie, tart, flan, quiche, whatever, that's baked and served from a dish with sides:

→ Fold a doubled piece of aluminium foil into a wedge shape slightly narrower than an ideal serving and put in before the pastry. The piece must be long enough to fold up the inside of the pan and over the lip. Bake the usual way.

→ To serve the first slice, cut just outside the edges of the foil wedge and then use the tab over the edge to lift it.

REALLY WHEELY

Use a pizza wheel rather than a knife for more control when cutting shallow tarts and flans.

ROLL OVER

Transport pastry to dishes by rolling it lightly around a pin and then unrolling directly above the baking tin or pan.

LUMPING TO LIKE IT

Use a small lump of pastry to push pie crusts firmly into the bottom of the tin and into any fluting, ensuring sharp edges and no puncturing.

BLIND LEADING

An easier way to use beans or other weights when blind-baking is to keep them in an ovenproof roasting or baking bag, much easier to distribute evenly over the pastry and to remove, and you can use the same roasting bag many times.

Otherwise, to ensure a pre-baked base is cooked through and that the edges stay upright, make a thick circle of crumpled cooking foil and arrange this close to the upright crust.

FIRMER BOTTOMS

Brush a still hot, blind-baked pastry case for anything savoury with lightly whisked egg white and let this set before adding the filling.

For something sweet, spread lightly melted chocolate onto a blind-baked pie crust, defending it from attacks from the filling and adding a surprise.

PIES TO GO

Choose short crust for the base and flaky or puff pastry for the top of any pies to be eaten in the hand because this gives a firmer crust that's easier to hold. Especially useful outdoors, whether for sweet or savoury, and *de rigueur* for a bacon and egg pie.

PROPER TARTS

Use a bulb baster rather than a spoon to fill individual tartlet cases, making it easier not to overfull or spill.

FREE-FORM ESCAPE

Avoid conventional fruit pies and present an open-topped galette instead. Roll pastry to a circle, top with sugared fruit leaving a wide edge and then turn the pastry to cover as much or as little as the filling as suits. Apple, peach, pear, pineapple and soft berries are the usual fillings.

QUICHE ME SLOW

Experience real Quiche Lorraine by filling only with a thin scatter of chopped green (unsmoked) bacon, perhaps with a little leek, and a custard of eggs and cream: one egg to every 150 ml. Blind baked pastry and then bake

slowly at less than 180° C/350° F. What happened to the British savoury tart? That was where spinach and salmon and cheese once went.

NO WHEY TO GO

Avoid baked egg-custard mixtures splitting into curds and whey by never cooking above 180° C/350° F. This is why these should be cooked in pre-baked cases, because the mixture cooks and sets before pastry cooks through but *see Portuguese Egg Tarts, page 22.*

SWEET TIMES—OR NOT

Judge cooking times for an egg-custard mixture by whether it is sweet or savoury.

The sweeter the mixture, the longer to set: a salty one sets faster.

FLOCCULATE ME

Move scrambled eggs very slowly with a broad spatula as they cook, so you encourage large soft clouds, a process known as flocculation.

PORTUGUESE TWISTS

Identify an authentic Portuguese Egg Tart (*pasteis de nata*) by checking for a swirl on the base of the pastry, made by doing the following, which creates the unique flower-like flaky upper edge:

→ Roll up puff pastry and slice into thin circles.

→ Lay each circle on an individual tart tin and push the pastry into the base by swirling with your thumb and thus forcing the edge to stand up exposed.

→ Fillings must be very sweet, so they do not split at the high temperatures needed to make the edges separate into frilly flowers.

PAVLOVA STEPS

Authentic Antipodean Pavlova has a thick, marshmallow centre and crisp crust, made by adding cornflour and vinegar to beaten egg whites and sugar. Without those two ingredients it's 'just a bloody meringue, mate!' A topping of strawberries and passion fruit on whipped cream was the norm but now kiwi-fruit rules.

Control the otherwise free-form shape of a Pav by drawing around a plate on baking paper and piling within the circle.

CHEESECAKE CHEAT

For something faster and lighter than cheesecake, mix two parts of whipped cream with one part of crème fraîche or plain or flavoured thick yoghurt. Leave it alone for an hour or so and their acid thickens the cream.

CRÈME BRÛLÉE CHEAT

Make the above, put into ramekins (over raspberries?) and strew with muscovado or stronger-tasting molasses sugar, which will liquefy when you refrigerate it for an hour or more. No crust to crack but a rum-flavoured topping without a grill cracking your porcelain ramekins or blistering your skin.

CRUSTY THOUGHTS

Instead of digestive biscuits for a cheesecake crust, crush Italian amaretti for something original, sweet, chewy and very almondy.

Crumble dark chocolate digestives rather than plain ones and leave them slightly rough, so there are definite pieces of chocolate. Or add chopped chocolate.

And don't forget ginger biscuits, but include finely diced preserved or candied ginger.

SHINING IN

Use baking foil with the shiny side on the inside. If this is outside, it reflects heat and extends cooking time.

DONE FOR

Push a strand of uncooked spaghetti into a baking cake to check if it is done. If wet mixture is seen when it is withdrawn, it needs longer. A fine skewer or thin knife can also be used.

CRACKED IT

Repair a cracked cheesecake while still warm by surrounding it with a wide strip of doubled foil, doubled cling film, muslin or ribbon, pulling that tight

enough to close the crack and then securing firmly with a bulldog clip.

Or ignore it and cover with lightly crushed berries or a sweeter jam, especially cherry.

CRUMBLING SOLUTIONS

Get the crumble type you prefer, both better made by hand.

For crunchy crumble with buttery lumps, rub together equal weights of flour and butter, without making an even texture, and then stir in the same weight as the butter of sugar, white or demerara. Strew unevenly and without pressing down.

For a sandier crumble, use twice the weight of flour to butter, rub together to make an even texture and then stir in the same weight of white or demerara sugar as of butter. Spoon on rather than sprinkle and do not pat down.

DECONSTRUCTED CRUMBLE

Bake the first crumble mixture on a flat tray until brown, crisp and separate. Serve with separate bowls of cooked fruit and of custard or cream and let everyone make the balance they like best. No more sludgy layers of undercooked crumble.

ROLLING ON

Roll flaky and puff pastries with short, sharp strokes. Long strokes can force air bubbles out of the layers.

PASTRY ROLLS

Forget pastry sticking to work surfaces:

→ Wrap cling film over a cutting board and secure it underneath. Dust lightly with flour.

→ Put baking paper or waxed paper over and under pastry and roll like that.

PASTRY PARTICULARS

Add flavour and interest to pastry as you roll, particularly to flaky and puff:

→ Sprinkle on sweet spices or grate orange, lemon or lime directly onto the pastry before you make the first turn.

→ Strew savoury spices, whole or ground, like fennel or cumin seeds, garam masala, baharat etc: good combined with orange zest. Add herbs, especially, rosemary, oregano and mint, dried or fresh.

A PROPER JOB

Thinly slice and layer rather than chop ingredients for a true Cornish pasty: beef, potato and swede; some like a little chopped onion but salt and plenty of pepper are musts. NO CARROT.

The number of crimps, top or on the side, is debatable, but should be at least 20.

WINE NOT

Instead of a rolling pin, use a full bottle of chilled white or rosé wine, which will keep the pastry firm; wrap it first in cling film to protect the label.

EXCESSIVE USE

When you have excess pastry hanging over a baking tin, cut off the untidy edges with kitchen scissors, because using a knife is liable to stretch the pastry.

Tuck excess pastry under the edge to make a double layer, which can then be pressed with a fork or crimped. Easier and more reliable than cutting off and adding a circle of leftover pastry to the rim.

UNDERCUT

Slice away excess pastry from a cooked blind-baked shell from inside to outside, or you will break away the crust and pieces will fall inside.

THE REST OF IT

Avoid pastry shrinking by planning your baking so the pastry can rest and chill before cooking, at least 30 minutes in a refrigerator.

ANGLE POISE

Slice choux buns and eclairs at an angle from the top down towards the opposite side, so the filling doesn't squeeze out when you bite; easier for decorating, too.

DECORATOR'S PLATES

Cobweb pastries, cake and pie slices:

→ Lightly flood a small plate with cream, thin custard or a fruit coulis; add a central blob of something contrasting and use a teaspoon to draw radiating lines from the centre to the outside. Serve the sweetness centrally on this.

→ Make a comma or apostrophe; place blobs of whipped or thick cream, custard, fruit coulis or thicker fruit or vegetable puree onto the serving plate. Point the tip of a teaspoon through the blob and then quickly draw out, curving as you do. Add extra drama by dripping a contrast into the centre and starting the teaspoon in that.

SAVING YOUR DOUGH

RAISING THE STAKES

Bread-dough and cake mixtures are raised by one of three different ways of creating bubbles within the mixture:

Baking powder: this is a mixture of chemicals invented in the mid-19th century. It works only in the presence of heat, as in an oven, and does not need gluten to work, so can be used with flours other than wheat.

Baking soda, also called bicarbonate of soda or sodium bicarbonate: do not confuse with washing soda, which is sodium carbonate. This is activated by mixing with an acidic liquid, like buttermilk or yoghurt. The action is immediate and means the dough must be mixed swiftly and put into the oven as soon as possible. Works best with wholemeal or white wheat flour.

Yeast is a live enzyme that ferments when mixed with flour and water, creating carbon-dioxide bubbles of elastic gluten that aerate or leaven wheat flour and some others. It cannot leaven a flour that does not contain gluten. Available in several forms:

→ As fresh or compressed fresh yeast.

→ As dried yeast granules, some types of which can be mixed directly into dough without being first activated.

→ As sourdough, which is a portion of previously made dough and known as a mother or starter.

→ As natural yeasts in the air, which will ferment a mixture of flour and water and then become a new starter giving different flavour characteristics according to the location it is made.

SODA, SO GOOD

Test baking powder for freshness by dropping a little hot water onto a teaspoon of it, or by stirring two teaspoonsful into a cup of hot water. It should fizz. Cold water won't give a result.

WHEN YEAST GOES WEST

Sugar should only be used to activate dried yeast; it inhibits fresh yeast and should be mixed only into the flour mixture.

Salt also inhibits yeast and should not be incorporated into any activating mixture but mixed only into the flour blend.

BREAD QUICK SMART

Make soda bread in minutes, serve it within the hour. Although traditionally made with wholemeal flour, plain white flour makes a lighter loaf that is often more enjoyed.

Mix flours to make your own, including oat or barley flour.

You do not need to stretch gluten by kneading, instead mix lightly with a table-knife blade and knead only once or twice out of the bowl to even up the dough.

Put onto a preheated baking tray in a free-form circle then cut a deep cross two-thirds into the loaf and get it into the oven as quickly as possible, because baking soda works the moment it mixes with an acidic liquid.

White flour needs less soda than wholemeal and too much can add an unwelcome flavour. One teaspoon for 500g white flour or a scant two for 500g of wholemeal are good starting points to establish your preferences.

Soda bread does not, and should not, include baking powder or cream of tartar/tartaric acid; these make it a scone loaf.

SODA SO GOOD
Try plain yogurt as an alternative to traditional buttermilk in soda breads. Soured cream or crème fraîche give softer, sweeter loaves.

MEASURED THINKING
Remember the world uses two fluid measurements:

→ The UK and Australian pint is 20 fl oz/600 ml: half that is a cup measurement.

→ The USA, South Africa and New Zealand pint is 16 fl oz/500 ml: half that is their cup measurement.

SLICED BOTTOMS
Turn a very crusty loaf onto its side to cut, and your knife will more easily cut the tough bottom crust.

PULLING POWER

Never cut a hot or warm bread roll—and don't do it to cold ones either. This smears the inside and flattens it back to dough—and is an insult to the baker. Pull them apart, to protect the texture and make eating more pleasurable too. It's ok to insert a knife point to start off.

GARLIC BREAD

Slice a baguette lengthwise to make garlic bread, rather than into almost-slices. The butter is unlikely to leak so there is even less reason to wrap it in foil, which nastily steams and softens the bread. Let it cool to warm before slicing.

TWISTER SAVINGS

Keep bagels, buns and sliced bread fresh and neat by twisting the top of the wrapper tightly and then folding the excess back over and down around the remainders. Tidier and space-saving, too. Could also be used on other wrapped products.

CRUMBS

Slice off tough bottom crusts before making breadcrumbs and the result will be more even and better coloured.

NO-NEED

Forget kneading bread made with 100% wholemeal flour, as the wheat germ inhibits yeast action and you get a heavier loaf.

MONKEY AROUND

Amuse everyone by making Monkey or Pull-apart Bread next time you bake. Best done in a mould, add the dough in lumps, brushing the top of each with butter or olive oil and any other flavours that occur, sweet or savoury.

NOT STRAIGHT

Cut angles into baps for bacon or sausages, rolls for egg or any other salad, kaisers for ham or salami or any other filling. Slice at an angle from one side of the top towards the opposite base. Fillings and sauces don't squash out and they look much more generous.

SPACE OUT

Make even more space in angle-cut rolls by pulling out a little of the bread. Keep the crumbs in the freezer.

Hide delicate buffalo milk mozzarella slices under the tomatoes but a better idea is only to add them after baking.

Strew on dried oregano for the elusive true taste of pizza.

PIZZA SLICES

Use twice the usual yeast content to make bread dough as the base for genuine Neapolitan deep-dish pizza in a roasting pan or cake tins. Plenty of olive oil underneath and tinned tomatoes with all their own juices, lightly crushed. Then the usual suspects and much more olive oil.

EAST-WEST PIZZA-NAANS

Use hot, billowy naan bread instead of rice as a base for curries, dhals or meat stews and topped with fresh herbs and plenty of black pepper. Or do the same with a crisped pizza base.

Smear just-warm naan bread with crème fraîche or soured cream, top with smoked salmon and fresh basil leaves, perhaps also with a little black or white truffle oil, if you can forget the flavour is not real.

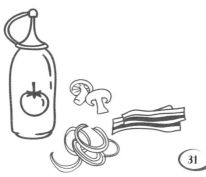

5

FISH AND NO BONES ABOUT IT

FRESH SIGNS

Ensure these when buying
fresh fish:

→ The smell should be of salt
   or fresh water; nothing
   ammoniacal or strong.

→ Eyes should be bright and bulgy.

→ Gills must be bright red
   and not brown. Scales must be
   firmly attached.

FISH WAYS AND MEANS

Steam/poach fillets in one
or two old-fashioned but
forgotten ways:

→ Between two plates over boiling
   water. Butter, seasoning, perhaps
   some herbs but no liquid other
   than a splash of medium-dry
   white wine or white vermouth.
   The microwave does the same
   thing more simply and without
   steam in the kitchen.

INCHING

Bake fish gently using this broad guide: 10 minutes per 1 inch/2.5 cm thickness plus 10 minutes.

SKIN CONDITIONS

Skin a fish fillet from the tail end. Make a small incision through the flesh to the skin at the very end of the tail and then flatten the knife between the skin and the flesh. Grab the skin end behind the knife and then move the skin sideways to and fro while easing the knife forward. Blunter knives work better than sharper.

→ Poach fish in milk rather than water and use the milk to make a sauce: use water only as a last resort, even if it is highly flavoured, because so much fish flavour is left in the water. Heavily smoked or artificially coloured fish is best cooked in water, which should then be discarded.

→ Leave a whole salmon overnight in the poaching liquid to ensure moistness.

BOWLED OVER

Detect the pin bones in a side of salmon by first running the back of a knife over the flesh from tail to head end.

Then lay the salmon side skin-side down over a bowl and the arching will make the bones more obvious. Use tweezers.

SMALL BONES

Debone sardines and other small fish before cooking. Once gutted and cleaned, spread the fish belly down and press firmly from head to tail along the spine. Turn the fish over, and the skeleton should come out in one piece but double-check for left overs.

SALMON CATCH

Mix a tin of salmon with crushed salt crackers (Ritz, Saltines etc.), season with grated lemon zest, chopped parsley, a press of garlic and a little mayo. Leave 30 minutes for the biscuits to soften, shape into a patty and fry to heat through.

SMOKED SALMON PIE

Layer well-flavoured smoked salmon between thin pancakes, smeared with soured cream flavoured with a breath of horseradish, lemon zest, parsley and black pepper—at least four layers topped with a fifth. If it's for adults, sprinkle gin lightly, too. Leave several hours, expecting most filling to sink into the pancakes and hold everything together. Cut into wedges as perfect hand-held picnic fare but just as good with salad as a first course or light main. Slight sweetness in the pancakes is a good thing.

BELLY-STUFFED FISH

Gut fish by slicing along the spine rather than opening the belly. Snip the spine behind the head and at the tail, carefully cut around both sides of the rib cage, remove this and then the guts and gills.

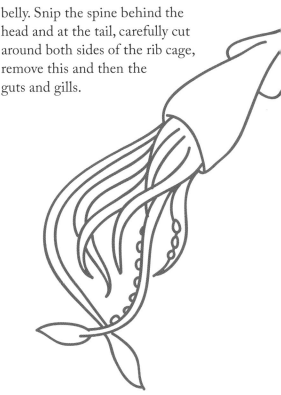

Season and stuff the interior, knowing it will not spill out during cooking and you can serve astonishingly whole fish without bones, serving in neat slices that include both sides and the stuffing.

KIPPER TIES

Eliminate (most) kipper smells by traditional jugging, putting them head down in a tall jug and filling that with boiling water. After five minutes, pour away the water and then slide out the kippers. Use a deep covered saucepan if you don't have a suitable jug.

RACKING UP

Barbecue fish between cake racks tied loosely together. Use tongs to turn them over.

SAUCE SOURCES

A little sweetness enhances white fish tastes, so add lemon *and* butter, or lemon *and* cream and wine, rather than just lemon juice.

Thus, use a medium-dry white wine to make sauces for fish, never a dry one; that is what you should drink too.

Finish cream sauces for fish with a few drops of sweet wine—even rich ports or a PX sherry, unless you use too much.

ROLL CALL

Roll flat fish fillets, especially sole, with the flesh side outwards

because there is a ligament that pulls the flesh into a curve when cooked; if done incorrectly the fillet will unfurl messily.

LESS LEMON

Zest lemon directly over smoked salmon rather than flooding with juice, to give a fresher flavour and better appearance; you will actually taste the salmon.

BEGONE!

Hiding the smell and flavour of stale or less-than-fresh oysters or caviar was why raw onion, shallots, spring onions and their mates were once served with them, especially after WWI. Or to make flaunting public consumption of them possible for people who simply didn't like them. The smell of raw onion was part of the plan to mask the palate, egg dulled the palate.

With today's better transport and refrigeration we should taste these rare treats naked:

→ Serve oysters unaccompanied, perhaps with a little lemon juice or grated lemon zest—no, absolutely no—onion, shallots, vinegar or chilli sauce.

→ Chew oysters at least once— otherwise what is the point of spending that money?

→ Be especially respectful of the finer flavour spectrum of the rare, flatter-shelled native oyster.

→ Cook or heat only coarser flavoured rock-oysters.

→ Touch caviar with no metal other than gold as they will interact to change its flavour: otherwise use bone, wood, semi-precious stones or plastic. Then, eat caviar by the unsullied spoonful or you'll never know what the fuss is about.

→ Accompany those spoonsfuls with unsalted butter on high-quality white bread or on warm unsweetened brioche.

MUSSEL MUSCLE

Double-check raw mussels are safe to eat, even when from a reliable source. Discard all that will not close before cooking and any that are broken. After cooking, don't serve or eat any that remain closed. Just to be sure.

6

BIRDS IN THE HAND

WISH AWAY

Remove the wishbone from roasting birds to make carving stress free. Before cooking, lift the neck skin and use a very sharp knife to cut around and then sever the wishbone. Leave it in place if you like but flick it away before carving. Especially good advice for Christmas turkeys and geese but for family chicken dinners, too.

GETTING ABREAST

Make carving and serving large turkeys faster and neater by removing each side of a cooked and rested turkey's breast meat in one piece:

Cut through the skin either side of the central breast bone and down to the carcass, then use a sharp pointed knife to cut the breast away from the bone and slice it off at the bottom. Cut into thick slices, which look great on the plate. Lots of gravy.

BUTTERFLY SAVING

Save at least 20% cooking time by butterflying your bird, small or large.

Cut either side of the backbone and remove.

Turn the bird over and spread the sides and then press down on the breast bone to break and flatten it.

Roast or grill, turning just once.

GETTING STUFFED

Stuff poultry under the skin or in the neck but NEVER in the cavity, as this can stop the inner bones cooking through and transfer food poisoning to the stuffing, which might be undercooked anyway. Stuffing or forcemeat was once only cooked under a spit-roasted bird or baked in balls around it.

DESTRUSSING

Remove all trussing from poultry before roasting and pull legs away from the body without breaking the skin.

Trussing was used to ensure spit-roasted birds turned evenly but means heat cannot get to the thickest part of oven-roasted birds, making it likely you overcook the breast while waiting for the legs to be done.

STOCK ANSWERS

Make richer stocks from poultry bones by first browning them. Roast or grill them carefully but deeply, or do this in a big saucepan, turning regularly. Cover with water and simmer at least two hours, with or without vegetables; add bay leaves and herbs only for the last 10–20 minutes. Strain and then use to cook rice by the absorption method or as a soup base.

Or reduce, cool and freeze in cubes as a handy addition to sauces, soups and gravies.

SAUCE SOURCES

Create super sauces for poultry by reducing cooking juices and then stirring in Boursin cheese, either the herb or the black pepper version.

DUCK IT

Ensure pan-fried or grilled duck breasts are tender by resting longer than you would a steak —at least 10 minutes. DON'T cover with cooking foil. Then slice at a very acute angle for the best look.

FRUITY RELATIONS

Serve more than orange sauces with duck and poultry:

→ Stir sliced fresh cherries into hot buttered rice and flavour lightly with ground allspice.

→ Do the same with sliced dates or micro-roasted almonds or walnuts, perhaps both. Torn parsley or coriander, too, of course.

→ Cook cranberries with orange zest and a little orange juice until they pop; add sugar only now or the skins will toughen.

→ Pan-fry thick slices of fresh pineapple in butter until the surfaces start to caramellise and then grind coarse black pepper onto both surfaces. Cook for a few minutes more so the pepper releases its full aromas. Perfection with duck.

→ Purée and strain raspberries, add roasting juices and then heighten with cider vinegar to make a sweet-sour flavour. Heat gently or the colour and flavour will dissipate. Very good with pheasant or grouse and a barley pilaff.

→ Flavour a sharp apple purée with a mix of orange and lemon zests, or with lime zest alone.

→ Purée canned red plums and cook on to thicken with a cinnamon stick, mace, several bay leaves and red wine. Finish with judicious additions of either brown sugar or citrus juice, maybe both.

→ Soak fresh, pitted dates in cream or PX sherry. Put into hot gravy at the last moment, or heat a little in the microwave and serve separately. Grate on lime zest for added intrigue.

MEATING OF MINDS

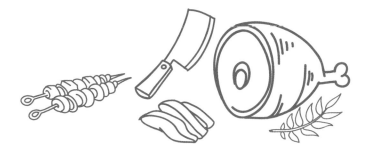

COLOUR STEAKS

Steak will not colour well if the surface is wet. Dry both sides with kitchen roll immediately before cooking, so it browns fully. This also applies if you have used a marinade.

OIL-FREE STEAK

Do not smear steaks with olive or other oil, as most kitchen extractors cannot cope with the resulting smoke; anyway the high heat denatures the oil and changes its flavour. A properly hot pan will give excellent colour to a steak with a dry surface.

JUDGE THE PERFECT STEAK

Bring steak to room temperature before cooking. Cook over high heat without flipping until you see the first drops of red liquid appear. Turn and cook until the same thing happens.

This gives medium-rare steak and you'll soon learn to judge how much juice appears before you choose to flip and serve, thus making the steak more or less done.

Do not press a steak with any instrument while it is cooking as this compacts and toughens the meat.

Do not use a splatter guard as it creates steam and toughens steaks. Instead, use a wire sieve as the height of the mesh above the food prevents the steaming caused by the closeness of a splatter mat.

Remove to a warm plate, season and then rest about ten minutes before serving, according to thickness.

Do not cover while resting as this creates steam and can toughen the meat.

GRATER GARLIC

For bigger garlic flavour on steak without burning it, slice garlic thinly and smear onto steak and leave there as it comes to room temperature. Scrape off before cooking but save and tip back into the grill-pan juices after the steak is removed. Cook quickly without browning and pile onto the steak.

LADLE MEATBALLS

Make small, even meatballs by pushing a pasta ladle into minced meat mixture and scooping off the amount that pops through the hole in the middle.

FLAVOUR STAKES

Season steak with salt and pepper only after cooking and while resting.

Dribble on excellent extra-virgin olive oil or add a knob of flavoured butter after cooking and while resting.

CHOP OR FORK

When you don't have a rack small enough to fit into a roasting pan, criss-cross chopsticks or inverted large forks to keep your ribs, roasts or birds off the base.

NO SPLAT

Lessen cleaning up splattered fat by covering unused burners or elements during cooking with an easily cleaned metal baking tray or secured kitchen foil.

COOL HOT STUFF

WHAT'S THE DIFFERENCE BETWEEN CHILLI AND CHILI—OR CHILE?

Chilli and chillies with two 'l's rhymes with Hell, a reminder these are Hotter than Hell, and that these are the proper words for the fruit, whatever its size, colour or heat. Chilli powder should mean only ground chillies.

Chili with one 'l' should mean a cooked dish containing chillies, such as chili con carne. Chile is a variation of chili.

Chili dishes are often fiery but otherwise banal because ground chillies have been mis-labelled and used instead of big-flavoured chili compound or powder.

Chili powder or compound should include cumin, oregano and garlic. That's the right, robust flavouring for a chili. Or a chile. Add other spices like turmeric or coriander and it becomes a curry.

WHERE'S THE FIRE?

The pale inner ribs of a chilli have most of the heat from capsaicin oil and the seeds have almost none.

A purple blush in the ribs indicates a high heat value.

Easiest removal/control is to slice from top to bottom and then remove both ribs and seeds with a sharp melon baller.

It's worth wearing rubber gloves.

BEER AND WATER DON'T QUENCH CHILLI OR CHILI HEAT

If your mouth is too hot, absorb chilli oils with rice or bread, otherwise, eat another fat, like milk, cheese, soured cream, yoghurt or butter, which will combine with and dilute the chilli oil. Drinking water, beer or wine flushes the chilli oils directly into your stomach and bowels and then …

ADDICTION RESULTS

Capsaicin oil in chillies burns the tongue, which the brain registers as injury and so it creates feel-good serotonins. That feeling is equivalent to a drug-high and explains why so many experience chilli-hot food as gratifying, whatever it tastes like.

Like all euphoria-producing drugs, the more you consume chillies, the more you need to equal the first sensation, BUT you have been creating scars on your tongue, which hide apparent damage, so you need increasingly more and more but taste less and less.

Using more chillies is common as palates age, but you are further blinding your tongue to the full pleasures of food, of fine wines, great whiskies, opulent ports and yes, even bread, butter, tea and coffee. Or cake.

IT'S NOT SO HOT ABROAD

Don't think it is authentic to copy the chilli-heat you experience abroad. That level of heat is NOT what the locals' life-long damaged tongues experience, so you are right to ask for or to use less.

⇒ TASTE TIPS ⇐

Replace chilli
with strong explosions
of flavour:

Very coarse black pepper

Roasted black peppercorns

Zest of lemons, limes or oranges

Roasted cumin seeds

Ground cumin

Cubes of acidic aged cheese

Fresh rocket

Fresh watercress leaves

Salt-preserved lemons

———————

9

IN A STEW

KNOT FULL

Learn how to tie a butchers' knot, so you can make beef, pork and other roasts neatly shaped and thus cook evenly—you'll find many other ways to use this skill. Practise on a wine bottle, jam jar or can.

Slip string under the meat with a longer length on top and a shorter one protruding underneath.

Hold the two lengths between the thumb and forefinger of your left hand with the long one on top.

Loop the shorter length from under the meat under, over and back across the long length and then through the hole that is created. Pull the long length to tighten. Add another loop or knot for extra security.

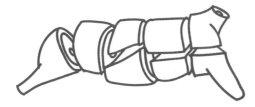

BROWN STUDY

Brown meat for stewing with no flour to get maximum colour and flavour; browning with seasoned flour mainly colours the flour and that adds little useful flavour.

FLOUR POWER

Stir flour for thickening a stew into the precooked vegetables you are adding, like properly browned onions or leeks: at least a tablespoon per litre of liquid for a medium to thin texture.

BROWNED NOT BURNED

It takes 40–45 minutes for 500 g/1 lb of onions to sweeten in butter or oil over very low heat. Turn up the heat now and the onions caramelise adding true heritage flavour.

Brown before they have sweetened and you carbonise, so curries, stews and casseroles will never taste like grandma made— she knew to put the onions on and then to walk away.

SWEETENING

Sweeten onions faster in the microwave. Cooked covered, with no added oil, butter or fat, which makes them more likely to burn.

SIZE MATTERS

Cut meat for stews at least 50% bigger than you want on the plate, as cooking shrinks meat and thus looks mean when served.

CONNECTIONS

Choose meat for stews that has connective tissue and gristle rather than fat-free single muscles, as these are what give voluptuous mouth feel. Chuck and shin and brisket are best and the combination of any of these is recommended.

EXPENSIVE NOT

Avoid single muscle meats for stewing, like rump or sirloin. Whatever you do, they will always be dry in the mouth.

MIXING IT

Make a mixture of chuck and shin for the most succulent stews. Using just one of these is good but not as good.

BULB LIGHT

Lighten *and* darken garlic content by cooking a whole unpeeled bulb of garlic in a stew, prepared by slicing off enough of the top to expose the individual cloves. The dish will be lighter in garlic than if you added the same amount peeled and chopped.

For those who want more, squash the custardy garlic from the skins onto the plate.

WELL-RESTED MEAT

Rest meat after roasting, grilling, frying or barbecuing. Each method contracts flesh and forces juices towards the surface. Resting allows the flesh to relax and then to reclaim and reabsorb the moisture. If you don't rest meat, it will lose moisture when cut—a sure sign—and that means toughness and less flavour.

RESTING TIMES

No-one expects meat to be boiling hot and roasted meat and poultry stays hotter than you think, giving plenty of time for cooking sauces and vegetables without fuss or rush.

Turkey or goose will still be very hot 45 minutes after it comes from the oven.

Rest steaks and chops in a warm not hot place for 10 minutes or more.

Roasts can wait 30 minutes or more.

So can chickens.

Rest game birds for 10–15 minutes.

MOIST TESTS

Rest meat roasts and roasted birds long enough so you do not see steam rising when you first carve, as this moisture should have been absorbed.

Making a puddle of liquid when cutting or carving means you have done this too soon.

NEVER FOILED AGAIN

Never cover cooked meats and poultry with a tent of foil because you create a steamy atmosphere and if water drips back it will dissolve flavour and soften any crispness.

Foil tents are an unnecessary modern expense invented by foil manufacturers. We managed without foil in castles to cottages for thousands of years.

HAMBURGERS AT HOME

Make even-sized patties (and fish cakes, too) by shaping with a biscuit/cookie cutter or in a deep screw-top lined with cling film.

Put chips of ice in the middle of a hamburger patty to keep the centre pink while you grill burger-brown outside.

Toast and generously butter hamburger buns—that's the original way. Floury, chewy bap-style buns work better than the soft sweet ones from burger chains.

STACK 'EM HIGH

Understand what made the original hamburgers so popular by stacking the buttered, toasted buns with plenty of lettuce (crunchy iceberg is favourite), plus modern caramelised grilled tomato rather than fresh, maybe roasted zucchini or red-pepper slices. And plenty of ketchup and mayo—aioli perhaps? And mild mustard or pickles— even a fruit chutney. In New Zealand, sliced beetroot is mandatory and sometimes grilled pineapple is, too.

MINCE MATTERS

Cook red-meat mince in a sauce a long time: it's made from tough cuts and so needs at least 45 minutes, longer is better. This includes meatballs particularly; a Bolognese sauce takes at least 90 minutes—*see opposite for the crush test.*

FLAVOUR SMELLS

Prepare mince by first frying with nothing else until it has lost all excess moisture and is starting to brown. It then smells of its origins, beef, pork, or lamb, and that dryness means each morsel will then absorb whatever flavours you add as stocks, sauces, finely chopped onion, herbs and spices and so on.

CRUSH TEST

Test a morsel of cooked mince against the roof of your mouth with just tongue pressure. It will disintegrate when properly tender.

DIFFERENT COURSES

Surprise by serving Yorkshire Puddings as puddings. Bake them over a little stewed fruit: rhubarb or apples are particularly good. Sprinkle with sugar before serving and then put ice cream into the hollow. Think of them as crisp, misshapen pancakes.

10

THE VEGGIE WAYS

Judge for yourself the advantages and myths about cooking vegetables.

MICROWAVING
This is optimal for flavour and health benefits, even Government websites say so. Fresh or frozen, the microwave steams away some of a vegetable's internal moisture, concentrating its goodness and flavour—no essentials are dissolved and wasted into cooking water. Add a little water only when cooking a large amount of root vegetables.

As we age and our taste buds diminish in ability, the microwave rewards us with greater flavour as well as important better nutrition. It's safer, too, especially in older households; no pans of boiling water and the microwave obediently turns itself off.

Anyone who says microwaves take the life out of vegetables has overcooked them or incorrectly microwaved them in water. Probably both.

ROASTING AND GRILLING

Increasingly popular, roasted or grilled vegetables offer excellent nutritional values plus the added bonuses of concentrated flavour and some caramelisation. Do this faster and save energy by first lightly microwaving and then tossing in a little oil before putting into the oven or under a grill.

STEAMING IN BAMBOO

When food is steamed in bamboo baskets Asian-style, it sits on a plate or round of paper in the basket. The bamboo absorbs most water vapour, so little or nothing condenses and then falls onto the food to dissolve flavour and nutrition on its way back into the boiling water. Any that does is collected on the plate or paper. A very close second to microwaving.

Note that flavouring steaming water is pointless as steam does not carry flavours.

STIR-FRYING

Any liquid in stir-fried recipes is served with the dish and so stir-frying is very close to both microwaving and bamboo-steaming in the nutrition it returns.

STEAMING IN METAL

The Western way of steaming in and on metal is little better nutritionally than boiling, except for texture. Water vapour condenses inside the lid, falls back onto the food, dissolves the invaluable vitamins and flavour compounds and then drains these into the steaming liquid—easily seen and smelled. Great if you use that liquid, but most people do not.

BOILING

Nutrition and flavour are seriously compromised by being dissolved into the water. Compare the taste of a boiled vegetable and a properly microwaved one and you will astonish yourself at how lively the latter is.

11

VEGETABLES MATTER

SUN SINS

Sunlight speeds up the deterioration of harvested vegetables, yes, even organically grown. This is why markets and open displays outside shops are not that good an idea unless the produce is shaded. And this is why supermarket vegetables can be a better choice nutritionally, especially if also chilled.

CORNY WORDS

Judge sweetcorn cobs are ripe when the silk tassels at the top have turned red-brown.

Cook corn cobs in their outer husk leaves for best flavour whether boiling, grilling, microwaving or barbecuing, but first, pull them back, remove the silk, and then stroke the husks back into place.

Remove the silk with a light bristle brush or by wrapping rubber bands around your fingers and brushing with that.

Remember fresh corn gets less sweet the longer it has been picked and tougher the longer you cook it. Native Americans walked to collect corn cobs but ran home to cook them.

COOL CUCUMBER

Poach arcs of cucumber to look like jade:

→ Peel and slice a cucumber in half lengthwise, then scoop out the seeds using a teaspoon. Cut evenly into semi-circles about 2 cm/¾" wide and poach a few minutes until you see a slight colour change and then run under very cold water and they will turn transparent.

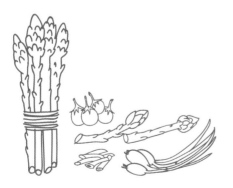

→ Use cold in salads, serve hot with butter or in a cream sauce, the way Georgians and Victorians did.

→ Poach thin slices until softening, cool completely in running water until bright green and translucent; use these to decorate a skinned, poached salmon or trout. Aspic to cover.

ONION CHOPS

Easiest way to chop onion is to peel it, cut a thin slice from the bottom so it sits neatly and then cut across the radius almost to the base a few or many times, according to the size of chopped onion you want. Then, slice in half, top to bottom, sit on a flat side and slice down, again according to the size you want.

TEARLESS ONIONS

Putting an onion into the freezer for 10–15 minutes will reduce its ability to cause tears.

PERKY PEPPERS

Keep stuffed peppers upright when baking by standing in large muffin tins.

SKINNY DIPPING

Tomatoes, peaches and other fruits will skin more easily if you cut a cross on their bottoms before covering with boiling water.

WIN ONE

One spear of microwaved broccoli has the nutrition of five cooked by boiling or steaming. Excellent way to trick kids who think they've won by eating only one.

SLAW RIDES

For finely sliced cabbage, cut in half and then use a vegetable peeler for thinner, even strips for coleslaw, salad or pickled cabbage.

SAUCY BEINGS

Ban 3-bean salads but do puree one can of beans with olive oil and feta cheese to make a sauce for another colour of beans: pureed chick peas surrounding red or black kidney beans perhaps.

VEGETABLE BUBBLES

Reboil vegetable stews containing unpeeled vegetables, like ratatouille, after 24 hours, which is the only way to kill yeasts that develop since the first cook; otherwise they will ferment and spoil the dish.

NOT ANY OLD RICE

Look for aged basmati rice, the only rice that improves by the year. Specialist suppliers have as many vintages and styles as a vintner. Cook by the absorption method or the nuances of flavour will be thrown out with the cooking water.

BARLEY PARLEY

Cook barley as a pilaff instead of rice:

→ Roast or fry in butter or oil until golden then cook with three parts stock or water to one of barley.

→ Great with fattier roasts and super with game birds.

OVER-BAKED POTATOES

Get more pleasure from baked potatoes by over baking them, creating a thick, crisp and savoury skin. Pierce but do not oil or butter the skins, as that can prevent crispness. After an initial burst in the microwave, bake at 200°C/400°F/gas 6 or more for at least an hour.

Cut them almost in half the second they come from the oven or the skin will soften, essential advice for all baked potatoes.

BEAN POISONED

Boil soaked red-kidney beans hard for at least 10 minutes during cooking or they are toxic. It's best to do the same to all dried kidney beans but canned ones are safe to eat as they are with no further heating.

BLOW OFF WINDS

Never cook soaked beans or lentils in water in which they have been soaked, because the wind-producing elements are still in full force.

SALT SENSE

Don't add salt or salted meats when cooking soaked beans until after they are tender. Doing so keeps the skins tough.

OLD SALTS

Accept that tongues become less sensitive with age. Using chilli or mustards to create mouth-feel increases the problem—*see Cool Hot Stuff on pages 47–48* for better ideas.

SALTING MYTHS

Salt does not change food and 'bring out the flavour'. Salt stimulates taste buds to taste more fully, but as each person has a different number of taste buds, Super-Tasters need no salt and Slow-Tongues need a lot to get the same taste but risk tasting more salt than food.

It is impossible to tell another mouth how much salt it needs.

BITTER LESSONS

Balance bitterness in food or drink with acidity, as in using lemon in harsh black tea. Sweetness has no counter-active effect on bitterness.

BAG AND BOTTLE

Keep cut herbs and all greens fresh and crisp for ages by sprinkling lightly with water, then putting them into a large freezer bag (a plastic carrier bag for large amounts).

Invert in the refrigerator with plenty of space within to create a hydrating atmosphere. Works better and for longer than storing cut herbs in water.

Store smaller amounts in screw-top bottles.

GREEN REFRESHMENT

Refresh tired green salads leaves, spinach, cabbage or other leafy vegetables by sprinkling lightly with water and storing for at least 30 minutes as above.

INSTANT SPAIN

Purée frozen ratatouille to make an instant gazpacho soup: if it's too thick purée in canned tomatoes and/or peeled cucumbers. Extra olive oil of course.

DEFROST COLD

Defrosting food in a dish or bowl slows the process as cold air is trapped by the container. For faster results, stand on a rack or flat plate.

CHUTNEY AND PICKLE SOURCES

Make chutney with fully ripe fruit: make pickles with barely ripe vegetables.

Choose any vinegar that is at least 5% acetic acid; sweeten with dark or white sugars.

Grind in spices for darker results; tie whole spice in muslin for a lighter colour.

Leave chutney and pickles at least two weeks before using— and as long as two years.

SALAD DAZE

Make old-fashioned salad cream for potato or other salads by whisking as you add in order: 1 egg, 400 g (approx.) sweetened condensed milk, 1 tsp mustard powder, 75 ml milk and 60 ml white wine, cider or tarragon vinegar. Leave to thicken for 10–20 minutes. Add capers, horseradish—whatever.

12

PASTA PECULIARS

DUMP THEM

Add gnocchi to meat or vegetable stews to make mini-dumplings. Cook no longer than recommended or they disintegrate.

DULLER IS BETTER

Find dull-looking pasta that has a rough texture you can sense with your teeth, like natural pearls. That's because it's been extruded and shaped traditionally through bronze dies, leaving a coarse surface. Seek the word *bronzato* or similar on packs.

The rougher surface of bronze-extruded pasta absorbs more of any sauce or dressing, combining the two before it gets to your mouth. Shiny pasta extruded through plastic can't do this.

HOLEY PASTA

The hole in a pasta server is the perfect measure for a single serving of dry spaghetti.

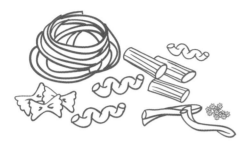

NON-STICK PASTA

If your pasta sticks together after cooking it's because you have not cooked it in enough water. Dried pasta absorbs 1½ times its volume of water, so a ratio of 1 litre of rapidly boiling water to 100 g dried pasta is a minimum and much more is better; increase the water proportionally for more pasta. Salt very well.

CALM WATERS

Adding oil to pasta cooking water does not solve the sticky problem. A touch of oil is added to prevent foam spilling out of the pot and this is where the confusion began. Cook in plenty of water to prevent pasta sticking together; oil on water does not do it.

SAUCING TIME FOR PASTA

Wait a few minutes before saucing cooked and drained pasta until most steam has stopped rising, which means the rough surfaces of bronze-extruded pasta (and to a lesser degree the smoother surfaces of plastic-extruded types) have dried and will then absorb much more sauce.

Do this naturally when drained pasta is piled on to a serving plate and the sauce is added to the middle but mixed only when served at the table.

THAT PASTA COOKING-WATER THING ...

Forget the idea of stirring pasta-cooking water into a pasta sauce. Nowhere in Italy does this as a matter of course, except if a regional sauce has reduced too much, which is unlikely because thicker is better. Wouldn't you rather add more of an ingredient already there rather than diluting with salty, floury water?

GETTING IN TO SHAPE

Choose a pasta shape according to the sauce:

→ Rugged, lumpy sauces with bits of vegetable, seafood or meat are best with shaped pasta, so there are cavities and folds and tubes to hold the pieces as you catch them on your fork.

→ Smooth pastas like fettucine and spaghetti were created to go with smoother sauces and work much better with bronze-extruded pasta that has been allowed to steam dry before being mixed with the sauce—some will be absorbed into the pasta rather than puddling on the plate.

Shapes that are both basically smooth but are hollow tubes can do both, like penne.

Ridged or grooved shapes can do for most sauces, especially grooved penne rigata or bigger penne regine.

MAC 'N' PIZZA

Pimp macaroni cheese by baking it topped with everything except the crust that makes a favourite pizza: tomato, mozzarella, salami, black olives, olive oil, dried oregano, whatever. Outstanding outdoor food, hot or cold. Fabulous for fireworks.

13

MICROWAVE MARVELS

Think of your microwave as a steamer and you'll never be disappointed with floppy results—it can't do crisp unless it's vegetables, spices and nuts.

MICROWAVE BASICS

Microwaves work in the presence of water, oil and sugar and the more there is of one or all, the faster they work.

Microwaves penetrate about 2.5 cm/1 inch according to density. They do not cook from the inside out but cook the penetrated thickness all at once:

other methods rely on the heat being transferred from the outer surface.

Recommend a microwave for the kitchen of older cooks, because it is obedient, safely switching off when told to do so.

VEGGIE STUFF

Vegetables are cooked in a microwave by the steam-heat of the water they contain; as this is released it concentrates the flavour and nutrition.

Cook vegetables, including frozen vegetables, with no added water but covered with pierced or folded back cling film. The exception is large quantities of root vegetables, especially potatoes, but only add a little water.

Or cover food to be microwaved with a plate, serving side down, and when it's ready you'll have a hot plate to use.

Frozen vegetables are processed within hours of harvesting, giving a freshness nothing in

shops or supermarkets can equal. Sometimes the varieties frozen are not the best tasting but the superior nutrition is always there.

BAN BACON SCUM

Cook bacon slices between absorbent kitchen paper in the microwave and never see excess moisture, scum or fat again. Works even better with dry-cured bacon, quickly giving crisp, golden fat.

Timing depends on thickness of bacon and microwave power, so start slowly.

MORE MICRO-HACKS

Cook porridge in minutes, while you are in the shower— it won't boil over or burn unless instructed to do so.

Roast nuts without added oil. They cook all through for greater flavour and texture; arrange in a circle on a plate, cook uncovered in bursts of a minute or more, mixing and rearranging from time to time. Life changing.

Peel and roast chestnuts marvellously: cut a cross through the pointed top of each and microwave six to eight for a few minutes until you see the cross opening. Allow to cool a little while you process the next batch. They peel best when still warm, hence the small batch method.

Micro-roast black peppercorns as above, a little or a lot. Doubles your repertoire, giving extra depths of flavour to everything from eggs and sandwiches to curries and stews.

Micro-roast cumin seeds and use as sprinkles to add texture and flavour bursts to salads, sandwiches, roasted or grilled vegetables, cheeseboards and more.

Heat curry powders and masalas with no added oil for cleaner, clearer flavours.

Make best-ever mashes faster by microwaving starchy potato in chunks with a few tablespoons of water (the only time you do this). Remove the film and the potatoes are ready to mash—no need to dry them further.

NOTHING STEAMY

One of the greatest ways to make Christmas Day and Christmas pudding even more welcome is to banish steamy Christmas kitchens by microwaving your pudding on the day. Nine minutes at Medium is the same as two hours of steaming over water for the average pudding size. Most bought ones have microwave steaming times if you look and home-made ones do just as well.

Microwave other steamed puddings to save hours and eliminate steamy kitchens.

BUTTERING FAVOUR

Brandy and rum butters should not be served with Christmas pudding; they are meant to go with mince pies.

SAUCY I

Best and most traditional sauce for Christmas
pudding is a light vanilla custard, made
lump-free in the microwave, flavoured with
orange zest and/or a splash of such as Cointreau,
Triple Sec, Grand Marnier or Mandarine
Napoleon, but be creative.

SAUCY II

Make thickened sauces, custards and more
in the microwave faster and with no lumps.

SAUCY III

Microwave a caramel sauce
in minutes, but with care:

Put sweetened condensed milk in a deep bowl
and microwave a minute at a time—there's so much fat,
sugar and water it happens very fast.
Watch without fail, whisking after every minute or so,
being careful to keep your fingers away from
the sauce. Depending on the power you use, this can take
only a few minutes or up to ten, each one of them rewarded.

Make it more voluptuous by stirring in cream or salted butter.

Be cool and when it's well cool, stir in salt flakes
(like Maldon) or muscular crystals to make proper salted
caramel—you have to be able to taste salt or it's just caramel.

When almost cold, stir in roughly chunked dark
chocolate or/and micro-roasted nuts.

14

WOK'S WHAT

SHAPING UP

Pre-heat woks until smoking without oil or any other ingredients. This also helps build a non-stick surface.

Stir-fry using the entire wok surface because it heats evenly all over.

That's because a wok's shape is the form that sheet metal takes naturally when placed directly

over flames, as also seen in the Indian Karahi.

It is impossible to get the correct amount and style of heat over a normal domestic gas flame unless you are cooking for one. If cooking substantially for two or more you are likely to be stewing rather than stir-frying, so should use something flat bottomed.

Get true wok-burn flavour by:

→ Fiercely heating the wok completely empty and

→ Lightly pre-cooking ingredients in the microwave, so they are hot all through when added. Many an Asian cook living out of their home country knows this.

Add flavouring liquids to a hot wok by pouring them around the wok above the food, so they run down evenly. This ensures they are hot before being stirred into the ingredients and are incorporated evenly.

Preserve your wok's non-stick surface by rinsing quickly while still hot, using no detergent or soap, and then wiping dry.

SMOKING THE WOK

Smoking food in a wok is an ancient Chinese thing to do and is a wondrous way to add flavour and excitement without having to own a smoking hut. It can be used two ways:

→ Hot-smoking, which cooks food at the same time as it smokes. Fish is the best choice, especially such oily ones as mackerel and salmon.

→ Flavour smoking, which adds a smoked finish to already-cooked food, including duck or chicken breasts, belly of pork, ham or bacon joints, sausages, and vegetables including baby potatoes, thick sliced sweet potatoes or squash and tomatoes. It's a great joke to smoke shelled, hard-boiled eggs because they look as though they still have brown shells and no-one knows until they pick them up, and then drop them because they are soft.

Start by lining a wok and its cover with foil, shiny side up. Then mix together 125 g/4 oz rice or barley with 50 g/2 oz of black tea leaves, which can be very ordinary, so use nothing special or scented. Put that mixture into the base of the lined wok.

Add a metal rack and put the food on that, leaving plenty of space for smoke to circulate.

Put the lid on tightly. Wet a couple of tea towels, wring

them out and then twist them. Use these to seal the wok; the smoke smells delicious but is permeating and will make everything smell if it escapes.

For Hot-smoking:

→ Put the sealed wok over maximum heat for ten minutes. For big amounts of food and food in big pieces, reduce the heat to low for another five minutes. For food in small pieces, remove from heat after ten minutes. In both cases, leave sealed for at least ten minutes, to allow the smoke to settle. You can leave the wok sealed up to an hour and the food will still be warm and moist.

For Flavour-smoking:

→ Put the sealed wok over maximum heat for ten minutes and then remove and let stand at least ten minutes.

The only thing you might do wrong is to over smoke and that's quickly learned. Counter act it by serving with something acidic, like soured cream or yoghurt, citrus juice or a dressing that includes vinegar.

Otherwise ignore versions that put sugar in the mix, which adds nothing but acridity. Neither does adding alcohol or herbs do anything detectable. However, a flavoursome sawdust or wood chips, such as camphor wood, sandalwood, hickory, cedar or manuka can substitute for a third of the tea leaves. Using only wood is likely to be too strong.

15

FRUIT PICKS

BERRY BEST FLAVOURS

Enjoy sweeter more fragrant strawberries, raspberries and blueberries by serving at room temperature. Store them in the refrigerator but remove well before you eat—you'll probably add less sugar too.

PROPER STRAWBERRIES AND CREAM

Recreate the old-fashioned way to enjoy strawberries and cream:

→ Cut hulled strawberries into halves or large chunks, and pour on cream that is thick and liquid or that has been whipped only until lollopy.

→ Add caster sugar, stir a couple of times and then leave an hour at room temperature, or four in the refrigerator but then allow to come back to ambient.

The cream and juices make a pinky-streaky sauce and the flavour seems to double.

Disturb the streakiness as little as possible when serving but keep puddling when you eat.

A little orange-flower water, rose water or jasmine essence adds aromatic magic. So does finely chopped preserved ginger. Or a little of a liqueur mentioned below.

THE HULL STORY

If you must wash strawberries, do this before hulling, that is removing the green top, or you risk dissolving some of the juices and flavour.

MUSH-FREE MARINADES

Macerate strawberries and other berries only in a liquid thicker than their natural juices; soaking in thinner wine or orange juice dilutes berries' natural juices and results in slushy berries with mushy skins but sweet liqueurs or dessert wines have the texture that avoids this.

Slightly sugar strawberries and then add only enough wine, orange juice, champagne or liqueur to make a clingy syrup. An hour at room temperature or much longer in the refrigerator, and then add a little more of the liquid just before serving if you must.

LIQUEURS FOR STRAWBERRIES

Choose these liqueurs to drink with, to marinate or to flavour cream for strawberries: Cointreau or Grand Marnier (orange), Crème de Cacao (chocolate), Parfait d'Amour (vanilla-ish), Cassis (blackcurrant), Frangelico (hazelnut), Galliano (vanilla-herbal) and white or green Crème de Menthe (mint).

BRANDIED FRUITS

Use intense, unsweetened fruit brandy (*eau de vie*) very discreetly to punch up fruit desserts at the last minute. *Poire Williams* on raspberries; *framboise* on grilled peaches, *Calvados* on baked pears or apples or on a Tarte Tatin.

FRUIT PUDDLES
Grill or bake pear, peach or nectarine halves in which there is a little dark sugar. Before serving, add a puddle of sweet liqueur *framboise* (raspberry) or *Poire William* to pears, *fraises des bois* (wild strawberries) to white peaches/nectarines. Etc.

BLACK IS BACK
Pep up strawberries with freshly ground black pepper. It works. With sugar, of course.

MINT-FRESH
Mint mingles excellently with strawberries, fresh or as crème de menthe, especially in cream, in ice creams and mousses and in berry marinades. So good in a sorbet.

MIDDLE-EAST FLORAL MAGIC
Make raspberries taste even more of themselves with splashes of rose water, distilled from fresh roses. Use discreetly, especially in a freshly sieved coulis; raspberry with rose water is one of the best sauces for strawberries. Ever.

Enhance strawberries spectacularly with orange-flower water, distilled from orange blossom, especially in accompanying cream or sprinkled on with a little sugar.

DOUBT THE DOUBTERS
Think of roses when you taste rose water, not soap. Unsophisticated palates often describe rose water as tasting like soap. Wrong. Soap is hoping to emulate roses and rose water - and usually comes off badly. Such a sensual ingredient.

FAMILY FAVOURITES
Boost apple pies and sauces with a little rose water. Apples and roses belong to the same family, and so reliably give a genuine heritage flavour, especially with a buttery pastry and extra butter plus cinnamon on the sliced apples. It's what Shaker communities used to bake.

STRAWBERRY FAVOURS

Favour strawberries with red rather than pink or white flesh, for these are the tastiest. Autumn is traditionally a good time for them but supermarket favourite Murano is a summer bonanza, as is the more delicate but wondrous Mara des Bois, which has wild strawberries in its genetics.

BIRD-FREE STRAWBERRIES

Grow the creamy-white and intensely aromatic variety of small, Alpine 'wild' strawberries, *fragraria Vesca*. Birds ignore them, so you get the full crop. Just a few will scent a fruit salad if you let it sit awhile.

RASPBERRY SURPRISE

Rely on the surprising culinary friendship of raspberries and pears. Raspberry coulis with pears, *framboise eau de vie* on grilled pear halves, or pearly pear sorbet with nuggets of raspberry sorbet to mine inside.

RHUBARB SHAPES

Keep rhubarb's shape and better tastes by cooking without added liquid. Then, stir it into strands if you want and they will not be watery.

Roasted, microwaved or in a saucepan, cut into big chunky lengths, sprinkled with sugar and cooked gently until tender.

Top results come from cooking with orange zest, chopped preserved stem ginger or darkest muscovado sugar.

Adding fresh mint is more original, especially for ice cream.

Top your muesli, add to yoghurts, make a fool or an ice cream.

Use the firm chunks or strips for a Millennial-style deconstructed Rhubarb Crumble—*see page 23.*

REMEMBER THIS?

Blend rhubarb and strawberries to make a very old country-style combination, giving a spectrum of flavour from acid to sweet. Works well in ice cream, or make rhubarb crumble and serve with proper strawberries and cream— *see above.*

BANANA-NO

When a banana is ripe, the skin makes no noise as it is peeled.

A greener, more bitter-tasting banana is better for colon health and helps absorb calcium, if you can stand the noise.

CURTAINS FOR JAM

Test if jam or marmalade is at setting point with a wooden spoon or spatula.

Tip so the edge is pointing down and the liquid can run off. It's done if the jam collects and creates a curtain before dropping, rather than dripping off in blobs. Yes, there are other ways but this works.

FLOATING JAM FRUIT

Wait to bottle for 10 to 15 minutes after cooking jam or marmalade, which allows the mixture to settle and distribute fruit and peel evenly.

Stand hot, recently filled jam jars on their lids if fruit or peel floats to the top. You might have to turn them several times as they cool before you get even distribution.

If the tops and lids are not absolutely clean you will have trouble opening the jars.

SHARP PRACTICE

Get more citrus juice these ways:

→ Roll a lemon or other juice fruit on a firm surface, which breaks down inner membranes.

→ Microwave until warm but not hot.

→ Cut into quarters rather than halves when using a citrus press.

CITRUS TIPS

Cut off the end of a lemon, lime or orange when you want only a small amount of juice, rather than halving. Squeeze through the hole and then seal that with cling film.

16

PUDDING IT RIGHT

DESERT DESSERT

Soak mixed, dried fruit in orange, apple or pineapple juice, with or without a few teaspoons of orange flower water; in the Middle East, where this is called *koshaf*, they would use just water but these are better. Leave 24 hours or more at room temperature or two days in the refrigerator, turning lightly from time to time. The fruit will swell and their sugars exchange to make a syrup—leave at room temperature longer if this has not happened.

Eat small amounts, with or without buttery or gingery biscuits. A perfect snack to have in the refrigerator at Christmas and other holidays.

Bake in or under pastry in a pie: layer with clotted or whipped cream in millefeuilles or eclairs.

SIMPLE ICE CREAM

Create an infallible ice cream faster and that doesn't need to be beaten while freezing. Whisk together approximately even volumes of VERY cold sweetened condensed milk and double (heavy) cream: a 397 g of condensed milk and 300 ml of cream or a 170 g tube of condensed milk and 150 ml cream. It will thicken almost as much as whipped cream alone.

Flavour with vanilla or other extracts, or with the ideas below: alcohol will inhibit freezing.

RE-FLAVOUR ICE CREAM

Melt ice cream slightly and then quickly swirl in something wonderful; serve at once or refreeze. Don't mix enthusiastically or you will lose the air in the ice cream. Try:

→ Lightly crushed raspberries and/or strawberries with a little sugar, orange juice liqueur or flower water.

→ Frozen Fruits of the Forest mixture.

→ Frozen tropical fruit mixes meant for smoothies—chop smaller.

→ Crumbled Christmas cake or pudding, moistened with a very little sherry, rum or brandy; good in chocolate or coffee ice cream as well as in vanilla.

→ Chopped nut brittle, peppermint rock, liquorice all-sorts.

→ Turn cornflakes in butter and brown sugar, cool, crumble and mix in.

ICE-CREAM SCOOP

Forget the interminable faff of freezing hands while scooping individual ice-cream portions. And always have an individual serving ready.

Divide almost frozen home-made ice cream into muffin or cup-cake papers. Freeze on flat trays or in muffin/cupcake trays. Save space when frozen by wrapping individually in cling

film and storing in a zip-lock freezer bag.

Pre-portion bought ice cream by softening only slightly, then proceeding as above.

Make both special with a little fruit or chocolate sauce at the bottom of each—or some microwave caramel—*see page 75.*

FLAT SCOOPS

Flatten the top of each scoop of ice cream against the pack or other surface, and, when it is released onto pie, pudding or cake, it won't slide off.

PIED MERINGUES

Spread meringue mixture right to the edges when topping a pie or it will shrink and weep.

CRÊPES!

Make pancakes thick and crêpes thin.

WHITE OUT

Remember white chocolate is not really chocolate because it is the fat expressed from cacao pods and includes no cocoa solids.

SUCK IT AND SAVE

Freeze chocolate in (big) bite-sized squares; suck a piece when you crave chocolate and then it takes long enough to melt on the tongue for you to feel you have eaten much more.

SAUCY CREAMS

Strain creamy sauces, including custard, through a sieve for smoother textures.

17

CHEF STUFF

TASTING THE DIFFERENCE

Know the difference between 'tastes' and 'flavours'.

Tastes are correctly only sweet, sour/acidic, salt, bitter and umami.

Everything else is flavour, a combination of these tastes plus many other aromatics.

We complicate this by saying we 'taste' food but that verb is a confusion, because you are tasting flavours as well as tastes. Got it?

TASTE DIRECTIONS

Work out how your tongue registers tastes by remembering which part of the tongue is most likely to taste what. Although most of the mouth registers all tastes, we are more likely to get a stronger reaction in particular areas.

SUGAR: the tongue's most sensitive area for detecting sweetness is at the tip of the tongue.

SALT: most likely to be tasted on the side of the tongue.

ACID: towards the sides of the tongue.

BITTER: at the back of the tongue, a final warning before swallowing, because many bitter foods are also poisonous.

UMAMI: the savoury taste is experienced in most parts of the mouth.

Eating must gratify the mouth before it does the stomach. We chew to mix in saliva, an important pre-digestive aid. As that happens, our mouth should be flooded with sensation and flavour, gratification that sates mouth hunger. If mouth hunger is not satisfied, because you swallow too quickly, or if fats and oils insulate the tastebuds from taste and flavour, the mouth will crave more and so you eat more than the stomach needs to be satisfied.

The answer is only to eat foods that bite back with flavour – and then you'll eat less. Bite back does not mean chilli-hot food, which are as bad as bland, because the mouth has little chance to detect what else is there so you eat more than you truly need.

FEED BOTH HUNGERS

Understand why you eat more bland food than you need, and why you eat less of a food that bites back in the mouth yet gratifies both mouth hunger and stomach hunger.

THE CRUNCH

Use semolina for a crunchy crust to vegetables. Turn cooked potatoes in it lightly before putting into the hot roasting pan and do the same to oil-tossed vegetables you are about to roast.

HEADY RELIEF

Relieve summer headaches by including a sprig of fresh rosemary with tea brewing in a pot.

CHOP AND CHANGE

Chop parsley and other herbs without making a mess by snipping with scissors in a deep cup or mug.

Or use a pizza cutter on a board.

SOUP FIZZICALS

Pour a little sparkling wine or champagne into the middle of chilled soups just as you are serving, for super-chic foam without fuss.

MORE LEMON

Get more juice from lemons, oranges, limes and grapefruit by microwaving 10–20 seconds according to size; they should be warm rather than hot, which would change the flavour.

NO COTTAGE SHEPHERDS

Know the difference. Shepherd's pie should be minced lamb, and cottage pie should be beef. Both are made best with leftover roasted meat with plenty of gravy mixed through.

GREATER AS GRATINS

Bake any vegetable dish better with a gratin topping to finish. Sprinkle breadcrumbs evenly over cooked vegetables or vegetables in a sauce, with or without pasta included. Grate butter over the crumbs for a light flavour or sprinkle on olive oil for a Mediterranean twist. For something bolder, grate hearty cheese on to either or as a singular choice. Bake until heated through and the breadcrumbs are browned and crisp. Mix finely zested orange, lemon or lime peel, garlic or chopped herbs into the crumbs, too, especially fresh coriander, which keeps much of its tang.

TOASTED ENOUGH

Get enough toast under your eggs, your baked beans, your full English. Toast two slices, cut them diagonally and then arrange the four pieces with the pointed ends meeting in the middle—a plate of toast.

MELBA SINGS

Make your own thin Melba-style toast. Toast slices the usual way and when cool split horizontally. Reverse these, so the toasted sides are together, the uncooked sides now outside, and toast again like this.

FRIED RIGHTS

Make tastier fried rice by spreading cooked rice to dry on a baking tray, ideally overnight, so it will then absorb the soy sauces and other aromatic flavourings when frying.

BEST LADLE HACK IN THE BOOK

Use the bottom of a soup ladle in a sieve to strain or purée anything. It's much faster than the tiny tip of a wooden spoon, you can use more pressure and you get far greater yields. Brilliant time saver and more profitable, too.

COLD FACTS

Give the proper time to marinades for flavours to exchange and improve:

→ Ignore advice to put something to marinate in the refrigerator for an hour or so, as nothing will happen.

→ Calculate that one hour of flavour exchange at room temperature takes four hours in the refrigerator.

ZEST FOR

Zest lemon, lime or orange directly over and close to where you need the flavour or you lose the fine spray of oil that has most flavour.

Don't grate direct onto a chopping board as this absorbs the oils.

Harvest vital but usually wasted citrus oils after grating by rubbing the outside and inside of the grater with one of the dish's ingredients, such as flour from a mixture, and then incorporate.

CUBE IT

When you want citrus flavour but not the zest, perhaps when baking, scrub the rind of an orange, lemon or lime with a sugar cube and then crumble it to use.

HIGH SALT LEVELS

Salting by hand from a good height above food isn't cheffy show-off but ensures it falls evenly; salting too close can mean salty surprises.

GERM-FREE GARLIC

Avoid garlic-smelly chopping boards by sticking a garlic clove onto the point of a sharp knife. Pull away the skin and then flake the flesh finely with a vegetable peeler directly into or onto where you want. The thin slices melt into sauces and are less challenging when served raw in, say, a potato salad. Perfect start to true aioli.

You'll also slice around the central germ, avoiding its usual bitterness.

SQUARE UP TO PARMESAN

Cut Parmesan or Grana Padano or a great Cheddar into small cubes rather than grating, especially for pasta. Instead of it disappearing, it will constantly surprise the palate with full-flavour hits of what you have paid so much to enjoy.

CHEESE SAUCE

Reduce cooking liquids, especially from roasting chickens, and while warm whisk in Boursin garlic-and-herb cheese to make an immediate creamy sauce.

OIL-FREE SALADS

Eliminate the oil and taste more of the salad by tossing instead in a very little gin, which gives great mouth feel and a slight bite, too. A little lime or lemon zest adds spritz. Especially good on salad leaves used as garnish.

DASHING VERMOUTH

Keep a bottle of dry white vermouth handy. A dash or much more of its high herbal flavours instead of wine adds magical lifts to risotto and pilaffs, to vegetable dishes, fish sauces and cheese or pasta sauces.

THE ART OF THREE

Make any meal look unexplainably better by serving only odd numbers on the plate. One sandwich or three, but not two. Three or five ingredients in a salad, not four or six. Meat and two vegetables, not three, although a sauce can make up the odd number. The rule of three also works when arranging flowers, displaying objects, stacking books, planting out … everywhere.

POPPING WILD

Create new textures and tastes by popping wild rice. Heat a little oil in a heavy-based saucepan, swirl in wild rice, cover and leave over medium heat, shaking the pan from time to time. They won't pop as loudly as corn, or become cloud-like but will butterfly and swell a bit. Flavour lightly with salt, pepper, perhaps a garlic or herb butter. Great as a snack, or stirred into soup, and Canadians mix them into meat balls and call these porcupine.

SET IT RIGHT

Don't try to set fresh pineapple, papaya or kiwi fruit in gelatine because enzymes prevent this happening. Use only canned pineapple or papaya and forget kiwi fruit.

Vegans and vegetarians will find agar-agar has even more problems and won't set chocolate.

MILKING THE BAY

Flavour milk or cream with bay leaves, an old-fashioned taste that lifts runny or baked custards, ice cream, crème brûlée, even a trifle.

Excellent with baked apples, apple pie, summer berries and in a sophisticated trifle.

TEMPER, TEMPER

Stir more of any or all herbs and spices originally used into long-cooked curries, casseroles or stews just before serving to refresh and add savour. It's called tempering and that's the real purpose of garam masala.

GARAM MASALA

Use garam masala properly to temper spiced dishes, that is sprinkled on or stirred in at the last moment to refresh and enhance the differing flavours of cooked spices.

Use Western-style to create gentler dishes as it is fragrant and usually contains little chilli.

Give the mixture a quick burst in the microwave to release the fragrance of the spices without dulling or burning them in oil.

BOUQUET BALLS

Instead of tying fresh herbs for a bouquet garni, trap them in a tea-ball infuser. Great for crushed spices when tempering, as above.

HEATING CURRY

Heat spices before curry mixes and masala before fluids are added or they are added to something already cooking.

Fry in a little oil until the fragrance is released but it's less fuss to do this in the microwave.

It's what you should do before adding to rice for a kedgeree, to mayo for Coronation Chicken or to butch up a weakling curry.

SAFFRON SCENTS

Don't add saffron strands directly to cooking liquids, as you don't get full value. Pour on boiling water and let soak at least 30 minutes and then add both the strands and the brilliant brew.

BLACK PEPPER EXTRAS

It takes only five minutes of cooking for the bright and fragrant heat of freshly ground black pepper to oxidise and lose its virtues, so:

→ Stir freshly ground black pepper into hot dishes just before serving and it lifts fragrance and flavours magically.

→ Roast black peppercorns to double your culinary repertoire. The microwave does this best —*see page 73*—and you might make several caches, some lightly roasted, some darker. The complicated smoky flavours are transformational on everything from a tomato sandwich to smoked salmon, a chicken gravy to oxtail stew or a vegetable, vegetarian or vegan stir-fry. No new recipes to learn, just a new flavour to add to what you already do.

CHOCOLATE BITES

Add an intriguing square of dark chocolate per serving to any sauce rich in tomatoes and spices. This includes chili con carne. Be sparing, you might not need that much.

Use a little cocoa powder instead of chocolate to add to tomato and spice-based sauces but it will be bitter if you use too much.

Dutched cocoa dissolves more easily and is less bitter.

BAKED-BEAN CAN DO

Add a few slugs of rugged red wine to canned baked beans for extraordinary results. Let simmer a while.

Also add whole lightly crushed garlic cloves in their skin, a bay leaf, a dash of Worcestershire sauce—even chunks of meaty Polish or other cooked sausages, like chorizo. Grind on and stir through black pepper. With sourdough toast for breakfast or lunch, or bubbling beside a barbecue.

STOCK CONTENT

Speed up defatting of hot or warm stock by:

→ Dropping in ice cubes to which the fat will adhere.

→ Floating on pieces of kitchen paper, which absorbs the fat but leaves the stock.

SERRATING PASTRY

To cut filled pastries—custard squares or profiteroles—use either a serrated bread knife or, better, an electric knife and with almost no pressure. The filling won't end up as a border.

FILO STACKS

To get maximum crisp but light pastry layering, bake stacks of buttered or oiled filo-pastry shapes direct on a baking tray. Make individual serving sizes or big squares to sandwiches' hot fillings and take to table as Fly-Away Filo Pies, savoury or sweet.

EDIBLE BOWLS

Make small edible bowls for chili, mayonnaise salads or green salads by dipping the bottom of a soup ladle into pancake batter up to the rim, and then holding the ladle to the same level in hot oil until the shape is cooked and brown. Repeat.

Flavour the batter highly with spices, citrus zest or garlic if you don't mind it browned.

NEW PICKLES

Follow the trend and serve pickled vegetables and fruit the new way, lightly soaked in a fragrant vinegar or genuinely sharp verjuice. Slice them fresh and thinly and choose such special vinegars as chardonnay or champagne, cider or tarragon, sherry vinegar or extraordinary Pedro Ximinez, the richest, darkest of all, ideal for any fruit to serve with something chocolate. A couple of hours is maximum or you will ambush the fruit or vegetable flavour and compromise its texture.

LEFT IS RIGHT

Serve food on the left side of anyone seated, the professional way for centuries, so you do not risk knocking a wine glass or getting bumped by a diner reaching for wine.

BUT remove plates from the right side, when there is less risk of spillage. Reverse it for seated left handers.

POURING DOWN

Only pour wine on the right side of a diner, so you do not invade their space by putting an arm across them.

18

KITCHEN STUFF

SPACE MAKING

Put a chopping board over the sink to make more prep or serving surface available.

Create extra counter space by putting a chopping board over a pulled-out drawer BUT, do make sure the drawer is stable and not pulled out too far.

SECURITY MEASURES

Avoid annoying curling of cutting boards by standing on an edge to dry rather than lying flat.

Anchor an unsteady cutting board or mixing bowl by sitting it on a damp, folded cloth or cloths of the same dimensions.

Non-slip shelf lining paper can be used over and over.

NOT A THICKY

Avoid curdling when mixing liquids by always pouring the thicker into the thinner.

WOODEN YOU KNOW

Sweeten wooden chopping boards when rinsed and dry using one of two ways. First is to rub cut lemon onto the surface. Second is to make a paste of baking soda and water, leave for several hours and then rinse.

NON-STICK NO

Use a non-stick spray on non-stick pans and you risk creating a sludgy crust that is difficult to remove. Why would you?

UNSTICK YES

Remove a burnt-on crust in a saucepan by simmering hot water and a dishwasher tablet or boiling up with plenty of detergent.

CAN MUST DO

Clean off the dangerous food collected between the serrated disc and the cutting wheel of can openers to avoid potential for food poisoning. Drip on a little bleach and then run folded kitchen paper through the mechanism until clean and dry.

Or regularly put into the dishwasher.

SILVER SERVICE

Use kitchen foil and baking soda (bicarbonate of soda/sodium bicarbonate) to clean silver fuss-free and without metal loss:

Line a deep bowl or baking tray with kitchen foil dull side up, shake in a thick layer of baking soda; proportions are not exact but be generous. Put in silver spoons, forks, silver-handled knives making sure each on is touching the foil and then cover with very hot water. It will foam up at first but when subsided keep an eye out until the cutlery looks bright. Remove, rinse, dry and buff.

You might need to do it twice or double the amount of soda but the silver will not be damaged.

Big or complicated pieces should be wrapped in foil and covered with the above solution, perhaps in a deep bowl.

FLYING TACKLES

Tackle fruit-fly problems with a small bowl of honey, syrup or jam covered by cling film but with a slight amount folded back. The greedy pests will find their way in but not out. Or …

BASIL AMBUSH

Set a basil plant beside a fruit bowl to deter fruit flies and other problems.

Plant or pot plenty of basil close to outside eating areas and put a pot on the table to ambush all flying annoyances, including mosquitoes.

MORE SODA TO DO

Place a saucer of baking soda (sodium bicarbonate, bicarbonate of soda) in your refrigerator and it will absorb unwanted smells.

Sweeten tainted plastic storage containers by soaking in a strong baking soda solution.

TOOTHSOME SILVER

Use a dry toothbrush to remove dried cleaning powder from ornate silver. Please!

SILVER OCCASIONS

Wrap little-used silver or silver plate in cling film and it will not tarnish between uses.

SAUCY SHINES

Clean and polish copper or brass with ketchup, brown sauce or tomato sauce. Leave five minutes or so and then wipe off, rinse and shine.

Use baking soda (bicarbonate of soda, sodium bicarbonate) and a little water to remove small spots, rubbing with little pressure.

Or mix three parts of citrus juice, lemon ideally, to one part of salt. Apply with a soft cloth when the salt is dissolved.

Make a dip for big pieces with one-part vinegar to three parts water and two tablespoons of salt

to every litre of liquid. Boil this up and then dip.

COPPER MINDING

Apply a fine film of light oil to protect clean copper or brass.

CLEAR VIEWS

Combat and reverse cloudy glassware from the dishwasher in hard-water areas by using twice the amount of dishwasher liquid or tablets. The clouds are residual minerals left because the washing medium couldn't cope with the amount in the water.

BLOWING HOT AND COLD

Ignore temperature controls on your oven or ovens as they can vary up or down by 10 or more degrees. Buying an oven temperature gauge is the best guarantee of baking success.

SHARP PRACTICE

Protect your fingers and knives stored in drawers by inserting the tips into thick slices of used wine bottle corks or a blob of Blu Tack, children's modelling clay or plasticine. A wall-mounted magnetic rack is a better idea.

DRIP CONTROL

Avoid sticky olive and other oil bottles and unsightly labels caused by drips and drizzles by stretching a sweat band above the label. Easy to chuck into the washer when it gets dirty.

Stop jugs dripping after pouring, whether water, milk, sangria or juices, by putting a dab of butter or firm margarine on the lip, which will catch them before they fall.

JAMMED JARS

Open difficult jam, pickle and other jars the old-fashioned way by using a solid wooden door. Open the door widely and put the cap into the space between the door's edge and the frame. Close the door onto that as tightly as you can, and then twist the jar with your free hand. Keep the jar tilted up a little, to avoid sudden drips or floods. It might help first to run the cap under hot water.

GETTING A HANDLE

Rest your thumb along the top of a kitchen knife handle and pointing towards the tip. That's the professional way and gives more power and control than having your index finger there, which can get painful when it is flexed backwards if you press hard.

BLADE RUINERS

Stop slapping an expensive kitchen knife onto a steel sharpener while held horizontally, which can make dents in the blade or chip it. You tend also only to sharpen the central portion. Do what the best butchers do:

→ Hold a sharpening steel vertically for best sharpening, even better if the tip is firm on a tough surface or chopping board.

→ Start with your knife at 45 degrees (half a right angle) and then tilt the knife closer to the steel by half the remaining space and then by half again.

→ Then stroke the full length of the blade from top to bottom of the steel, using both sides of it. You sharpen the entire blade from the handle to the tip. MUCH safer, too.

DISHWASHER HEALTH

Knives including table knives should be put into a dishwasher with the blade down, a safety measure however they are made. This also stops water getting into the handle if the blade has a tang that is separate from the handle, which can lead to rot or the harbouring of germs.

NO PRESSURE

Do not use pressure when cutting and slicing but let a sharp knife do the work. Use light, long strokes, back and forth, using all the blade length. You'll cut through anything easily, even fresh bread, and fragile foods hold their shape.

GETTING EDGY

The sharper the knife the safer it is, because you use less pressure and do less injury if you slip. When a knife is blunt you push harder and if it slips that means any wound is deeper.

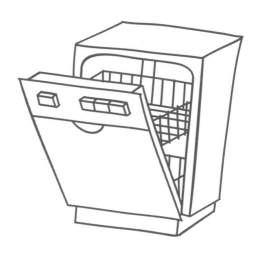

BIGGER IS BETTER

Choose a bigger, sharper knife over a small, lightweight paring or peeling knife, the favourite but awkward choice of many domestic cooks. Bigger knives give more control and their weight contributes to ease of cutting without you adding pressure.

KNIVES OUT—I

Cut fist-sized mozzarella or small bocconcini on an egg slicer. They are too rubbery for most knives and knife skills. Ditto button and small mushrooms. Saves much time.

KNIVES OUT—II

Use Nylon fishing line or non-flavoured dental floss to cut goats' cheese logs or sticky cheeses without squashing them. Slide a long length of either under the food, cross the two ends over the top, pull in opposite directions and the line or floss will cut from bottom to top.

SINK NOT

Protect ceramic sinks from cracking when cleaning heavy pots by first lining with folded wet newspaper or by laying down as many wooden spoons as you have—buy some if you don't.

19

40 FLAVOUR HACKS

Amazing affinities that put you miles ahead but take only baby steps. Here 1+1 = 3 or more—and there are others throughout the book.

ANGOSTURA BITTERS IN FRUIT SALADS.

AVOCADO AND HONEY: works where sugar does not in mousses, ice creams.

APPLE PIE WITH ROSE WATER: a heritage Shaker thing to do.

BACON AND MAPLE-SYRUP: with or without waffles.

BAY LEAF AND CREAM OR MILK: for liquid or baked custards.

BANANA AND CRUNCHY PEANUT BUTTER: but you knew that, right?

THE BASIC BASICS KITCHEN HACKS AND HINTS

BLACK OLIVES AND ORANGE ZEST: a little chili compound, too, or dried oregano.

BLUE CHEESE WITH VOLUPTUOUS GOLDEN DESSERT WINE: yes, not just Stilton, not only sweet red port.

BLUE CHEESE WITH RUNNY HONEY: especially with soft blue cheese and further enhanced with lime zest.

BRANDY OR RUM BUTTER WITH SWEET POTATOES: of course.

BRIE AND FRESH PEAR: unbelievable.

BRIOCHE (UNSWEETENED) WITH CAVIAR: the richness and texture work better than soggy toast; unsalted butter here, too. If you make them, add saffron.

CABBAGE WITH COARSE BLACK PEPPER: masses, when hot, drained, buttered and served pronto.

CELERY IN OXTAIL STEW: the secret.

CHOCOLATE AND PEDRO XIMENEZ (PX) SHERRY: for mousses and such.

CHRISTMAS CAKE AND CHEDDAR CHEESE—WENSLEYDALE FOR SOME.

COFFEE WITH ROAST LAMB: a Scandinavian creation.

CRYSTALLISED OR PRESERVED STEM GINGER WITH DATES AND DRIED FRUITS.

DATES AND LAMB: sliced into gravy and with a little mint.

DILL AND BLACK PEPPER: especially with garlic and a chilli to flavour Christmas vodka.

KIWI FRUIT AND PERNOD: a few drops only; extra good with prawns.

LEMON CURD AND MARMITE: honest!

LOBSTER AND BASIL: in brioche, in salads.

LYCHEES AND ROSE WATER: a fascinating sorbet.

MAPLE SYRUP ON BACON AND EGGS: it must be hot.

PASTA AND BROCCOLI: a Montalbano favourite; cook broccoli pieces for the last few minutes with the pasta, serve with olive oil and Parmesan or Grana Padano cubes.

PEANUT BUTTER AND CARAMEL: anywhere, especially muffins and brownies.

PEAR AND RASPBERRY: anyway you want it, hot, cold, iced, sweet or savoury.

PINEAPPLE AND GIN: beyond mysterious; don't add heat because gin's flavour is highly fugitive.

PINOT NOIR DRUNK WITH ROAST DUCK: counter-intuitive, but.

POTATO AND WHITE TURNIP: mash white on white with cream; called Alabaster.

PRAWNS WITH PX SHERRY: add a little to melted butter or into mayonnaise.

RASPBERRY JAM WITH CHEDDAR CHEESE: in sandwiches.

ROASTED CUMIN SEEDS ON TOMATOES: sandwiches, salads, pizza, anywhere.

RUM AND VANILLA: a background for chicken stews, foreground for muffins or icing and fillings for bigger cakes.

SMOKED SALMON AND MILD HORSERADISH: perfect sandwiches and snacks and doesn't hide the taste as lemon juice does; lots of black pepper, too.

STRAWBERRIES AND BLACK PEPPER: must be fragrant pepper and coarsely ground.

SWEDE AND CREAM SHERRY: a magical mash.

TOMATO AND ORANGE: especially as mixed juices.

WATERMELON AND FETA CHEESE: perfect salad, especially with mint or basil leaves.

INDEX

Liverpool Studies in European Regional Cultures 1

Culture, Tourism and Development:
The Case of Ireland

socio-economic development should, in the first instance, lie with the region itself, and superordinate bodies should primarily play a facilitating role.

The contributions in this first volume in the series address the full spectrum of issues identified here, with particular reference to tourism development. Future volumes will deal with individual aspects of regional cultures in the context of economic and social development. The series is intended to be used with courses in cultural resource management, which are specifically geared towards local and regional development groups, but will, hopefully, be of interest to a wider readership.

As the series editors, we would like to thank Robin Bloxsidge of Liverpool University Press, who was most supportive of the idea from the very start. Special thanks are due to Sarah Stamper for braving the tremendous task of 'tidying up' the manuscripts in addition to her full-time job of keeping the Culture and Tourism Research Unit 'ticking over'. Without her, we would have missed more than a few deadlines.

We would also like to extend our thanks to Holger Beyer, Treasurer, and Helmut Kinny, Secretary, of the European Society for Irish Studies, whose financial and administrative support made it possible to bring the authors together for a workshop in 1993, hosted by the Department of Geography, St Patrick's College, Maynooth, whose efficient organisation and generous hospitality can only be highly commended.

Finally, we would like to acknowledge the vital support of Professor Patrick Buckland and the Institute of Irish Studies at the University of Liverpool, which provides the home for our research unit, and resources to produce this series.

Ullrich Kockel
Máiréad Nic Craith
(Series Editors)

Contents

Contributors

Proinnsias Breathnach
Department of Geography, St Patrick's College, Maynooth
David Brett
College of Art, University of Ulster, Belfast
Anthony Buckley
Ulster Folk and Transport Museum, Cultra, Holywood
Lewis Clohessy
Department of Environmental Resource Management, University College Dublin
Sarah Drea
Department of Geography, St Patrick's College, Maynooth
Patrick Duffy
Department of Geography, St Patrick's College, Maynooth
John Feehan
Department of Environmental Resource Management, University College Dublin
Desmond Gillmor
Department of Geography, Trinity College, University of Dublin
Mary Kenney
Sociology of Development Research Centre, University of Bielefeld
Moya Kneafsey
Culture and Tourism Research Unit, Department of Geography, University of Liverpool
Ullrich Kockel
Culture and Tourism Research Unit, Institute of Irish Studies, University of Liverpool
Gearóid Mac Eochaidh
Development Officer, Community Connections, Blacklion, Co. Cavan
Jeanne Meldon
An Taisce, Dublin
Máiréad Nic Craith
Culture and Tourism Research Unit, Institute of Irish Studies, University of Liverpool
Mary O'Flaherty
Department of Geography, St Patrick's College, Maynooth
Bernadette Quinn
Service Industries Research Centre, University College Dublin
Mary Tubridy
Natural Resources Development Centre/Éigse Ltd, Trinity College, University of Dublin

Culture, Tourism and Development: A View from the Periphery

ULLRICH KOCKEL

INTRODUCTION

Over the past decade or so, tourism has been heralded as the fastest growing 'industry', and consequently a suitable panacea for peripheral regions with little potential for growth in manufacturing. Although the expansion of international tourism has slowed down since the late 1980s, positive growth rates are forecast well into the twenty-first century. Not surprisingly, then, tourism, especially the overseas market, has been targeted as a major growth sector in development strategies for peripheral regions.

Within this planning framework, the promotion of 'heritage'—which has emerged as something of a buzz-word since the 1970s—has become a key concern. In many countries, especially those, like Britain, where economic progress has been less than impressive, a 'heritage industry' has emerged which

> not only ... absorbs considerable public and private resources, but ... is expected more and more to replace the real industry upon which the country's economy depends. Instead of manufacturing goods, we are manufacturing heritage, a commodity which nobody seems able to define, but which everybody is eager to sell (Hewison 1987).

While the analysis underlying such sarcastic portrayals of the 'industry' has come in for well-justified criticism (Morris 1991), it does make a number of valid points:

- definitions of heritage are notoriously non-specific and therefore flexible in the way they can be interpreted;

Ullrich Kockel (ed), *Culture, Tourism and Development: The Case of Ireland*, Liverpool University Press 1994, 1-14.

-    since heritage is commonly regarded as a vital component
     of regional identity, its treatment as a commodity has
     immediate and potentially severe implications for the
     cultural fabric that forms the backcloth for development,
     leading, in the extreme case, to alienation of local people
     from whatever is supposed to be their heritage; and

-    pushing 'heritage' as a panacea replacing manufacturing, or
     indeed any other industrial sector, as <u>the</u> motor for growth,
     creates an artificial situation of regions basing their
     economy on a single activity, which exposes them to
     structural crisis in the long term, as the decline of port-
     based city economies since the 1960s aptly illustrates.

In its recent development plan for 1993-97, Bord Fáilte, the Irish Tourist
Board, emphasises the concept of 'sustainable tourism'. This notion implies
a managerial approach to cultural continuity and change. Any assessment
of the concept must, therefore, pay particular attention to the cultural
background and impact of tourism, directing the focus of discussion on the
potential which tourism based on regional cultural resources offers for
endogenous development, that is, development strategies directed—or, at
least, decisively informed—by local and regional interests.

REGIONAL CULTURE AND ENDOGENOUS DEVELOPMENT

Much of contemporary development research, especially in the English-
speaking world, proceeds from a global, 'world-system' approach. The
inherent deficiencies of this approach have been highlighted by, among
others, the Bielefeld School of development sociology, who have pointed
out that such an approach fails to come to grips with the level at which
decisions are made, namely the local and regional. Stöhr's (1986) definition
of development as enhancement of 'human capabilities on the basis of their
respective historical, societal, and natural conditions' supports the rejection
of a purely global viewpoint, by emphasising regional cultural identity and
territorial political participation as factors which conventional policies with
their focus on factor mobility have frequently inhibited (Kockel 1993).
Regional cultural identity becomes crucial as a factor for endogenous
development, and a catalyst for both 'cooperation [*sic*] among diverse

2

interest groups ... and for the retention or recuperation of initiative and creative personalities' (Stöhr 1986). Such development depends equally on 'the degree of freedom allowed from above and demanded from below' (Brugger 1986). It follows from Stöhr's point that the strength of these demands is eventually a function of regional identity, which is ultimately rooted in the culture, history and environment of the region.

The study of 'culture', however defined, is the key subject of anthropology, but while anthropologists have shown considerable interest in development issues in a Third World context, their attention to European regions has, in this respect, been rather limited. Boissevain (1989) has observed that anthropologists

> have been notorious for ignoring the planters, missionaries, and colonial officers active in the communities they describe... Must tourists be added to this list?

In the same essay, he points out some of the problems anthropologists ought to address more clearly:

> Agricultural land and scarce housing is sold to tourists to the detriment of the traditional economy and lifestyle. ... Traditional art and rituals are commoditized, hence, packaged and sold to tourists as airport art, fake-lore and 'authentic' ceremonies.

A recently published volume of essays on Ireland (O'Connor and Cronin 1993) seeks to address these issues from an interdisciplinary perspective, and there is a now a growing number of publications addressing specific aspects of the problematic.

This new wave of interest is symptomatic of an increasing predicament recognised by researchers, although this recognition has not necessarily, as yet, reached the level of policy making.

The present volume is a contribution to this growing debate. It is the first in a new series, *Liverpool Studies in European Regional Cultures*, produced by the Culture and Tourism Research Unit at the University of Liverpool's Institute of Irish Studies. Details of the work of the Unit are given in the Appendix. The main geographical focus of this work is on the island of Ireland, viewed in a comparative European context.

3

This comparative perspective is shared by many of the contributors to this volume, who refer to the experience of regions outside Ireland where appropriate. In the same spirit, I consider three peripheral European regions which have ventured to utilise tourism potential as a means of augmenting economic development prospects, starting my exploration with regions on Europe's eastern periphery before turning to Ireland, as the main subject of this book, and identifying, as I go along, some of the major issues which are dealt with in more detail by the other contributors.

EASTWARD PERIPHERIES: KARELIA AND ESTONIA

Taking some basic questions from a study of Karelia, which has pursued a highly 'self-conscious' course of integrated regional development since the early 1960s, and considering the tourism strategy of post-independence Estonia, I shall turn to a brief review of the Irish case. The comparison proceeds from key characteristics shared by the three regions: they belong to Europe's rural periphery not merely in an economic sense, but also in a geographical one; accessibility, therefore, constitutes a major constraint on the potential volume and commercial viability of tourism development; and their regional cultural base is not only distinctive, but highly differentiated internally.

North Karelia

The multi-layered similarity between Ireland and Karelia—or, indeed, Finland as a whole—is exceedingly obvious, and it seems rather surprising, therefore, that no rigorous comparative study of these two regions has been attempted to date. As Rizzardo (1987) observes,

> [t]he three Karelian identities …—that of the North, that of the South, that of the expatriates—… exist to recall the troubled past of the Karelian people and their constant desire to achieve cultural autonomy.

The strong parallels between Ireland and Karelia could, indeed, hardly be described in more striking terms.

It must be pointed out here that, like so many other cultural regions in Europe, Karelia has been divided by a state boundary imposed by interests external to the region itself. The South, having been annexed by the Soviet Union, and still being part of the Russian Federation, has suffered the same oppression of regional culture as other 'Republics' within the Soviet empire which delighted in colourful displays celebrating cultural differences at festive events in Moscow while, at the same time, quelling any expression of such differences in the regions themselves. It is only recently, therefore, that the region has been able to initiate policies of its own that address questions of culture and development, including tourism.

North Karelia, in contrast, has experienced substantial development initiatives for some thirty years. In the absence of an elected regional authority, public sector institutions have mediated between central government and the municipalities. This lack of a regional parliament has in no way diminished the vitality of a Karelian regional identity. However, the exploitation of this cultural identity as a resource for tourism has created a situation which has been recognised as problematic:

> The picture of North Karelia offered to tourists emphasises ... the beauty of the landscape, the proximity of the border, the people's affinity with nature, Karelian traditions and the Orthodox religion. The summer theatres produce Karelian plays, the summer restaurants and the market place serve Karelian pastries. The problem of the identity of North Karelia as a tourist area is that it is becoming commercialised, stereotyped and conservative (Rizzardo 1987).

This stereotyping of regional culture, what Boissevain (1989), with reference to Malta, described as 'fake-lore', is not unique to Karelia, nor indeed to tourism development.

Scandinavian anthropologists have developed the concept of 'cultural fixation' to explain how, under certain social and economic circumstances, selected cultural icons are conserved, with their meaning reduced to a stereotypical badge of identity. Even historical events like, in the Irish case, the Battle of the Boyne, or the Shutting of the Gates of Derry, can be contrived in this way.

Recent years have seen an unprecedented growth in the number of local museums and so-called heritage centres especially in peripheral regions. There are obvious parallels to be drawn with the *Heimatbewegung* in

Germany during the nineteenth and early twentieth century (Klueting 1991); amongst other things, this resulted in a large number of local history museums most of which suffered, albeit for quite different ideological reasons, from the same overemphasis on the 'local' as many of their present-day counterparts on the periphery, whose search for items that highlight particularly local characteristics 'involves the danger that local museums may be harnessed solely to serve tourism, which can mean the neglect of qualitative development' (Rizzardo 1987).

Industrialisation has failed the periphery, and the negative externalities of 'remote control' have raised the awareness of local resources across the regions of Europe. Promoting the service sector, and tourism in particular, has been identified as a suitable alternative strategy for endogenous growth. However, in many cases this has led to a gradual destruction of two of the most important local resources, scenery and culture, as the emphasis of development projects has been placed on quantity rather than quality. In their attempt to catch up, economically, with the core regions, peripheral regions have followed economic models constructed for industrial society in its prime without questioning their suitability in different circumstances, and have thus damaged the very resources needed for their own economic development. With regard to North Karelia, Rizzardo (1987) has raised the big question: 'How can a window be opened ... to the world without destroying a region's special characteristics?'

Estonia

In 1992, not long after regaining independence, the government of Estonia gave special priority to tourism as part of a strategy to overcome the country's current economic problems. Like South Karelia, Estonia had suffered severe restrictions under Soviet rule. The freedom to promote tourism-oriented activities was limited, and many picturesque landscapes especially along the coast and on the islands were used for military purposes, thus being not only 'off limits' for tourists as well as locals, but exposed to serious environmental damage.

Prior to 1939, Estonia had a long tradition of tourism, centred precisely in those areas which were most heavily affected by Soviet military activity. In the inter-war period, there was a semi-state body which coordinated tourism development. This organisation published a magazine under the title

Loodushoid ja Turism (Nature Conservation and Tourism)—an indication that policy thinking in Estonia at the time was comparatively advanced, recognising the vital link between tourism—based economic development and resource conservation, which the more western parts of Europe have only recently rediscovered.

History and culture are recognised by planners in Estonia as important factors in international tourism. Even under Soviet rule, the country had a certain, however small, share in this large cake:

> For the tourists from the East, Estonia has always been their own version of 'The West'. For the tourists from the West, Estonia has represented a slice of medieval European culture (Ehrlich and Luup 1993).

Present policy is informed by a healthy pragmatism; while history and heritage are acknowledged as important resources for tourist development, it is noted that '[i]n addition to our rich historical and cultural heritage we also have our everyday activities to carry out'.

This echoes the concern expressed by the participants of an Inter-Regional Cultural Tourism Exchange Forum, held in Hull/England and Brielle/ Netherlands, in February 1994, that in cultural tourism development, where the people themselves are, in a sense, the main tourist attraction of a region or locality, it is for them to decide how much of their culture they wish to share with the tourists. It also reflects a different strategy for cultural tourism, and one that has been successfully pursued in Karelia:

> Cultural development in North Karelia has recently been directed towards promoting regional events which stress cultural quality and professionalism ... The repertoire of these events is not based on the Karelian culture but is characterised by originality, which gives it a distinct identity also in the eyes of tourists (Rizzardo 1987).

Such a strategy, carefully planned and competently followed through, may offer a viable alternative to the all too common cultivation of the quaint without surrender to the dreaded globalisation of culture.

At present, some 90% of tourists visiting Estonia stay in the immediate vicinity of the country's capital, Tallinn. This is largely a result of Soviet tourism development policies, which concentrated facilities of international standard in the city, while, for example, Estonia's second biggest city, Tartu, was completely closed to foreigners. In the process of opening up and developing the country for tourism, attractions like the Song Festival will play a major role. The origins of the Song Festival date back to the period of National Awakening in the nineteenth century, and it offers the potential for a skilful blend of traditional culture and modern originality which appears to be working well in North Karelia.

THE WESTWARD PERIPHERY: IRELAND*

As in North Karelia and, to a lesser extent, Estonia, the tourist season in Ireland is relatively short by international standards. However, like the other two regions, Ireland draws a substantial revenue from the tourist trade, making tourism a key sector of the national economy. Since the 1980s, the composition of this income has changed dramatically. Over the period 1987-91, the share of the North American market dropped from 32% to 18%, while the share of the mainland European market increased from 21% to 36%. Considering that over the same period, total overseas tourism revenue, in 1991 prices, increased from £572 million to £865 million, these figures suggest a significant shift in the nature of Irish tourism, away from the predominantly 'roots-searching' North American market towards more diverse mainland European markets whose combined share in the overseas tourism revenue increased by almost 260%. Family links with Ireland are only a very minor attraction for European tourists, and this has obvious implications for the tourism product. Bord Fáilte (1992) noted that

> car touring is the single most important activity, with enjoyment of scenery being the main motivation, closely followed by visits to historic monuments and attractions.

The main attractions listed by Bord Fáilte are practically the same as for Karelia and Estonia:

---

* "Ireland" throughout the text refers to the Republic of Ireland only.

- superb scenic landscapes;

- a quiet island with a relaxed pace of life;

- a distinctive heritage and culture;

- the absence of mass tourism.

The report continues by spelling out, in some detail, a strategy for what is termed 'sustainable tourism'. This strategy is very much a response to pressures from the local level, where the non-monetary impacts of tourism are most directly felt.

Local issues

The strategy has been criticised from different angles—local, regional, and national—as insufficient to achieve its declared targets. These targets are described as follows (Bord Fáilte 1992):

- environmentally sustainable: product development should preserve and, ideally, enhance the quality of the environment;

- economically sustainable: concentration of initiatives on developing viable tourism enterprises, and diminishing obstacles to growth (seasonality, low profitability, poor access transport, limited product range etc.);

- socially sustainable: creation of a considerable number of new jobs, and laying the foundations for future growth.

In principle, one could have few quibbles which such high aspirations. However, their realisation requires the careful balancing of inevitable trade-offs, and the firm acknowledgement of potentially negative externalities associated with even the noblest intentions. A significantly extended season, or improved access transport, to take but two examples, will most certainly produce detrimental effects on the natural as well as the social environment at the local level, and these need to be taken into account at the planning stage, as later amelioration invariably demands a vast commitment of scarce resources which ought to be used for other purposes.

9

Ullrich Kockel

Ethnographic research projects on rural and cultural tourism, carried out during 1990-93 at the Institute of Irish Studies, Liverpool University, have shown that, despite an indisputable air of economic depression, in many West of Ireland communities there is also a very keen understanding of the development context, and of the initiative required to 'turn the tide'.

Tourism in general tends to create primarily lowly paid work for local women. High rates of female emigration have long been a problem in the rural West of Ireland, and the policy makers—being predominantly male—therefore regard the provision of employment opportunities for women as crucial. However, if these 'opportunities' are mostly low-grade, lowly paid jobs, they will do little to stem emigration.

From a cultural perspective, economic benefits are only part of the context of such developments. At the applied level, community participation is a far more important concern, since it determines and reflects the extent to which the image of the region that is represented to the visitor is grounded in actual cultural experience. This is particularly apparent in the case of Heritage Centres, which have been set up all over Ireland in recent years. While Heritage Centres are, in a sense, more dynamic than a conventional museum, the danger of 'musealisation'—that is, the detachment of objects and experiences from their real-life context—remains; only, whereas in the museum the focus has been on cultural objects of the past, in the Heritage Centre it is more often than not on the dynamics of the display facilitated by present-day technology and know-how. Thus Heritage Centres may, in actual fact, tell the visitor considerably more about modern technological gimmickry than about the culture and history of a community. That is not to say modern technology should not be utilised to its full potential; but the purpose of the display should be the story told, rather than the techniques used in telling it.

This raises another important issue, which is closely related to the problem of 'musealisation': that of 'fixation', a process I referred to earlier. Heritage Centres, like museums, by their very nature accelerate the process of fixation. Composition of a display requires selectivity with regard to objects and images, and a degree of economy with the guiding narrative, to avoid 'overloading' the spectator. Displays are, therefore, necessarily reduced representations. There is no easy way out of the dilemma. Telling a story from different angles, as in the recently opened Famine Museum, is one possibility, but its use is limited to specific events or practices. Other options still need to be explored. One possibility, which would particularly serve the local community itself, but also enhance the attraction of Heritage

10

Centres for the tourists, would be to retain for these Centres some of the dynamic of old-fashioned museums. In many Heritage Centres, there is an internal dynamic in the display which itself never changes; museums, in contrast, change their displays in frequent intervals, allowing dynamic interpretation of their representations. This, of course, requires considerable skills on the part of the curators, who have to link different, more or less continuously changing displays by means of an accessible, non-abstract narrative. There are many training courses preparing local people for the accommodation and catering sectors of tourism development. Similar courses aimed at cultural resource management are few and far between.

PRELIMINARY EVALUATION

There are a number of lessons to be learnt from the comparison sketched out here. For the present purpose, I shall only pick out and highlight a few. While they share significant structural characteristics, the three regions have had very different experiences with tourism development. All three of them are now eager to promote heritage-based tourism as a major growth sector.

The experience of Karelia suggests that regional identity need not be grounded exclusively in a glorious past and traditional culture, but may equally be based on excellence in a field of contemporary international culture. Estonian tourism policy reminds us that, while history and folk culture are important as resources for tourism, the fixation of selected aspects of heritage has an ultimately alienating effect, and the exploitation of heritage can only make sense if it is rooted in, and directed by, the everyday concerns of contemporary people. Ireland illustrates, in particular, the need to construct complex narratives of culture and history which, at the same time, remain widely intelligible. The achievement of goals like these depends on the availability of skills, both at the policy level and within local communities, and requires intensive and extensive inter-regional experience exchange and co-operation, to facilitate mutual learning through practice.

THE CONTRIBUTIONS TO THIS VOLUME

The essays in this volume mark a significant departure in this direction. Most of them were initially produced for the first in a series of experience exchange workshops organised by the Culture and Tourism Unit (Quinn's

11

article is based on a contribution to a workshop on 'Ireland and the Single European Market', and an earlier version of this introductory essay was presented at a 'Gateway Europe' conference of local and regional tourism authorities). The purpose of these experience exchange workshops is to bring together academic researchers from different disciplinary backgrounds and research users working at various levels. This aim is reflected in the present collection, with inputs from anthropology, art history, economics, landscape ecology, geography and sociolinguistics alongside contributions from professional planners and local development workers.

The four essays in the first part provide an overview of the context for tourism development in Ireland. Gillmor sets the wider scene by discussing patterns and changes in Irish tourism from the perspective of economic geography. The capabilities and limitations of existing organisations and structures for the promotion of tourism are reviewed by Drea. Employment is a major consideration in tourism policies, and Breathnach analyses the structure and potential of the tourism labour market, with special reference to the siginificant gender divisions in this sector of the national economy. Quinn addresses the changing nature of the overseas tourist market, looking in detail at marketing images used to promote Ireland in mainland Europe.

In the second part, key cultural issues are examined with a view to the necessary conditions for the achievement of sustainable development. Duffy begins by highlighting areas of conflicting interests in the use of cultural resources. Two of the main aspects are then investigated further by Meldon, who discusses the impacts of tourism strategies on the environment, and Feehan, whose contribution concentrates on community development in the context of rural tourism. Kneafsey takes up the current theoretical debate surrounding cultural tourism and the exploitation of heritage, bringing into sharp relief the vital question of tourist-host interaction, which runs as a common thread through the remaining essays in this part of the book. The construction and use of images, already touched upon by several authors, is the main focus of Brett's contribution, which discusses the ideological background and content of the way in which peripheral regions like Ireland are portrayed. From a more applied perspective, representations of heritage are then reviewed with reference to controversial resources. Buckley and Kenney, although not specifically dealing with tourism, discuss educational practice in a museum context, emphasising problems and opportunities of using 'heritage' as a resource in a situation of divided cultural identities, while Nic Craith, highlighting recent changes in the geographical and socio-economic patterns of the use of Irish, points out the potential of tourism to provide fresh hope for the future of lesser used languages in Europe.

Four local case studies continue the focus on the applied dimension in the third part of the book. Tubridy considers the prospects for improving the economic situation of a remote rural district in County Galway through tourism. From a more environmental perspective, O'Flaherty assesses the potential of a coastal area in neighbouring County Mayo to generate greater income from tourist activities through the exploitation of local resources. The experience of 'Community Connections', a locally based cross-border development initiative operating in a situation of extreme economic as well as geographical peripherality, is described by Mac Eochaidh. In the final essay of this volume, Clohessy reviews Dublin's performance as 'European City of Culture', thus reminding us that, while peripheral regions in Europe are predominantly rural, and the (cultural) tourism debate converges almost entirely on these rural areas, there is also an urban periphery with its own specific dimensions, which must not be overlooked.

The debate is ongoing, and—with the opening up of Central and Eastern Europe—is likely to expand as new regions, most of them on the periphery, seek to reap economic benefits from the exploitation of their environmental and cultural heritage through tourism. Planners and development workers as well as academics in these regions take a keen interest in the experience of comparable regions in Western Europe. The essays in this volume offer a critical appraisal of the Irish case. Those involved in tourism development in Ireland look upon Central and Eastern Europe with some apprehension as their country faces increased competition in what has become its second largest market, and potentially the most important source of revenue from cultural tourism. Competition may be a pretty idea for policy-makers sitting comfortably in the centres of economic and political power. For peripheral regions, the opposite of competition—improved inter-regional co-operation becomes a necessity if they are to avoid further marginalisation. Experience exchange workshops organised by the Culture and Tourism Research Unit will continue to provide an interdisciplinary forum for those concerned with social and economic development on the periphery, giving special attention to the sensitive management of cultural and environmental resources. Many peripheral regions already find that these are the only resources which have been left to them as the core regions have expanded. How realistic are the hopes which these peripheral regions attach to the development of tourism? The Irish case affords some sobering insights, but there are also positive signs. And many open questions, too.

REFERENCES

...rstein, J (1989)
Tourism as anti-structure. In Giordano, C, Schiffauer, W, Schilling, H, Welz, G and Zimmermann, M (eds), *Kultur anthropologisch: eine Festschrift für ... Maria Greverus*. Frankfurt/Main: Institut für Kulturanthropologie und Euro-päische Ethnologie, 145-59.

... Fáilte (1992)
Developing Sustainable Tourism: tourism development plan 1993-97. Dublin: Bord Fáilte.

Brody, H (1973)
Inishkillane: change and decline in the West of Ireland. London: Faber & Faber

...burger, E (1986)
Endogenous development: a concept between utopia and reality. In Bassand, ..., Brugger, E, Bryden, J, Friedman, J and Stuckey, B (eds), *Self-reliant*...

... Department of Tourism 1993.

... *The Heritage Industry: Britain in a Climate of Decline*. London: Methuen.

... (ed) ...
... *und Reform: Beiträge zur Geschichte der deutschen*
... *Darmstadt: Wissenschaftliche Buchgesellschaft.*

Kockel, U ...
The ... ... development in the West of Ireland. Reissue, ...

...
... history, heritage and the stereotype in the Scottish borders. In ... and Rees, G (eds), *Regions, Nations and European Integration: remaking the Celtic periphery*. Cardiff: University of Wales Press, ...
Kockel, U and Cronin, M (eds)
Tourism in Ireland: a critical analysis. Cork: Cork University Press.

... (1987)
Cultural policy and regional identity in Finland: North Karelia between tradition
... *Strasbourg: Council of Europe.*

... conditions and a paradigm shift in regional ... In Bassand, M, Brugger, E, Bryden, J, Friedman, J and ..., B (eds), *... Development in Europe: theory, problems and ...*

Tourism Development and Impact in the Republic of Ireland

DESMOND GILLMOR

INTRODUCTION

Tourism is often referred to as the world's fastest growing industry, and is receiving increasing attention internationally in development considerations. This is reflected in the extent to which it figures in the literature, in conference programmes and in development proposals. Such attention is evident in Ireland in recent years, particularly in the extent to which tourism is being seen as a potential remedy for high unemployment.

The impacts of tourism are many and complex, and they relate to economic, social, cultural and environmental influences, both positive and negative. Some of these effects are considered by other authors in this volume. The purpose of this paper is to provide an introductory background by outlining visitor trends, economic and employment contributions, and development plans relating to tourism in the Republic of Ireland.

General geographical analyses of Irish tourism have been written by Gillmor (1985), Pollard (1989), and Ó Cinnéide and Walsh (1991). Pearce (1990; 1992) discussed organisational structures in the industry. Reports oriented towards policy issues included those by the National Economic and Social Council (1980), Government of Ireland (1985), Price Waterhouse (1987), Department of Tourism and Transport (1990), Tourism Task Force (1992) and Bord Fáilte (1992a), together with earlier plans and various other publications by Bord Fáilte.

TRENDS IN TOURISM

Substantial development has occurred since 1960 in the tourist industry of the Republic of Ireland. The trends in the total numbers of visitors to the state (Figure 1) are an indicator of this growth, but they show also that there have been interruptions. The expansion of the industry has been

Ullrich Kockel (ed), *Culture, Tourism and Development: The Case of Ireland*, Liverpool University Press 1994, 17-34.

related to those influences which have contributed to the development of
international tourism in general.

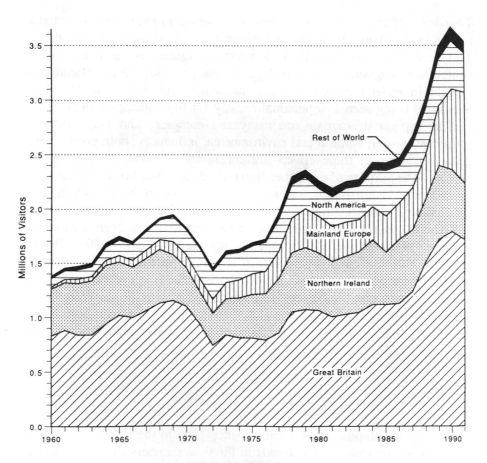

Figure 1   *Visitors to the Republic of Ireland over the period*
1960-1991: total numbers and market sources

These include greater affluence, more leisure time, improved transport, increased population and urbanisation, stronger desires to travel, and greater tourism organisation and promotion. Because of its island location, the introduction of car ferries in the 1960s and developments in air travel were of particular significance in the Irish context.

It is evident that the major setback to the growth of tourism in the Republic of Ireland was that of the period 1969-72, when visitor numbers fell by one-quarter (Figure 1). This resulted mainly from the deterrent effect on potential visitors to Ireland of the terrorist violence in and associated with Northern Ireland. The effects of violence increased for a while in the early 1980s and continue to cause severe harm to Irish tourism. The setback of the early 1980s, however, was related more to the international recession of the time and to the Irish Republic's loss of cost competitiveness because of high price inflation, so that it became a more expensive destination. The difficulties experienced by the industry were even greater than suggested by the downturns in visitor numbers, in that expenditure per visitor fell. This happened to the extent that earnings in real terms in the first half of the 1980s were less than those of the late 1960s. Meanwhile world tourism continued to expand, so that the Irish Republic's share of the global industry fell substantially.

This trend was reversed in the late 1980s as the number of visitors rose rapidly. The increase in external revenue in real terms over the last decade has been 97%, with the real annual growth rate in the second half of this decade being as high as 9%, which exceeded the world average by about one half. Several factors have contributed to this expansion. The government gave a high priority to tourism development, leading to active promotion of the industry and new investment in it, including important European Community (EC) funding under the *Structural Programme for Tourism 1989-1993*. It encouraged liberalisation of air transport, which occurred mainly in 1987-88, so that there were substantially reduced access fares. Tourism prices benefitted greatly from a decline in inflation to very low levels, and there were also reduced VAT rates for tourists. A major influence on visitor numbers was greatly increased return visits by recent emigrants following the escalation of emigration from Ireland in the mid 1980s.

There was a slight decline in the number of visitors in 1991, however, mainly because of recession in the USA and UK markets and the effect of the Gulf War on travel. Improved performance on the home market also is shown by an increase in the domestic market's share of holiday expenditure by residents of the Irish Republic from 25% in 1986 to 48% by 1991.

In 1991, 3.54 million external or out-of-state tourists visited the Republic of Ireland and spent £928 million there. The carrier receipts to Irish air and sea companies in transporting them were £275 million. To these values are added the £10 million spent by day excursionists, mainly from Northern Ireland, to give the total revenue of £1,213 million from external tourism in 1991. The revenue from domestic tourists was £505 million, 29% of the total tourism revenue of £1,718 million.

Substantial changes in the nationality structure of visitors to the Republic of Ireland have occurred over the years (Figure 1). These began to appear in the 1960s but the shifts were accelerated by the recession of the early 1970s. A major feature was the diminished relative role of the UK market. The terrorist violence and political situation strongly discouraged those potential British visitors who were not of Irish ancestry and many Northern Irish residents were more reluctant to travel south. Another influence was the growth in UK travel to more distant destinations, especially on package holidays to the Mediterranean region. The major growth sector has been in travel from mainland Europe. The mainly young visitors from there were less deterred by the violence, the accessibility of Ireland improved with transport development, awareness of Ireland grew with accession to the EC, media coverage and tourism marketing, and the appeal of the type of holiday which Ireland offers increased. Travel from North America rose substantially in the 1960s and has fluctuated since with changing exchange rates and other considerations but with a decline in 1991. The outcome of these trends in visitor numbers has been shifts in the relative contributions of the different markets to total external tourism revenue. This may be seen by comparing the shares of different markets in 1991 with those for 1960 (in brackets): Northern Ireland 8% (21%), Britain 37% (58%), mainland Europe 33% (3%), North America 17% (16%), and other areas 5% (1%).

ECONOMIC AND EMPLOYMENT EFFECTS

It is very difficult to measure accurately the effects of tourism on the national economy but estimates of its contributions to national income, tax revenue and balance of payments give some indication of its role. The contribution of tourism to gross national product in 1991 was estimated to be 7.3%, this being an increase from 5.7% in 1985. Tourist spending filters widely through the economy and calculation of the tourism multiplier is fraught with difficulty, estimates having ranged from 0.5 to 2.1 (Deegan and Dineen 1992), with the value of 0.94, suggested by Henry (1991), having received a wide measure of support. There is a substantial yield to the exchequer through tax revenue, estimated to be 27% of tourist spending and equivalent to approximately 5% of total government receipts from taxes on income and expenditure and social insurance contributions. Tax revenues accruing to the exchequer as a result of tourism in 1990 were about £430 million, while total public sector allocations direct to tourism, including those sourced from the EC, were about £70 million (Tansey, Webster and Associates 1991). It would be even more difficult to calculate other costs to the Irish economy consequent upon tourism.

Total earnings from external tourism in the Irish Republic amounted to 7.3% of the value of all exports of goods and services in 1990. The beneficial contribution to the national balance of payments is greater than this suggests because the import content of tourist spending, estimated at 8%, is much lower than that of expenditure in the economy as a whole. Moreover, leakage of revenue out of the country is further reduced by the predominantly Irish ownership of tourist facilities. Tourism accounts for 60% of the exports of all services. The net contribution of tourism to the balance of payments is a positive one, as the receipts from external visitors exceed by two-thirds the expenditure abroad by Irish residents. The net tourism balance is equivalent to over half of the overall current account balance.

The provision of employment through labour-intensive tourism is the major consideration in promoting the development of the Irish tourist industry. It is estimated that there were about 87,000 full-time job equivalents in tourism in 1991, having increased from 56,000 in 1986. The 1991 value was equivalent to 7.1% of total employment and to 12.6% of that in the service sector of the economy. Over 60% of this is direct employment in servicing tourists, two-thirds of which is in the catering and transport industries, but many sectors of the economy benefit. The total includes also indirect jobs sustained by tourism purchases from other sectors of the economy and induced jobs sustained by the domestic re-spending of incomes arising from these direct and indirect purchases of goods and services. The substantial seasonal and part-time element in tourism employment may be seen to be a deficiency but many employed on this basis are students and housewives who would not be prepared to work full-time and for whom tourism is a valuable income supplement.

Table 1   Contributions of external market sectors to the tourist industry in the Republic of Ireland, 1991

Market sector	Percentage of visitor numbers	Percentage of tourism revenue	Expenditure per visitor
Northern Ireland	14.7	7.8	139
Great Britain	48.4	37.5	203
Mainland Europe	23.8	32.9	363
North America	10.1	16.5	431
Rest of World	3.1	5.4	460
ALL OVERSEAS	100.0	100.0	263

The average economic benefit to the Irish Republic of each external visitor varies by the market source from which they come, the mean expenditure of visitors from outside of Europe being more than three times that of Northern Irish residents in 1991 (Table 1). Amongst tourists from mainland Europe, the expenditure per person was: Germany £397, Netherlands £389, Italy £349, France £338 and other mainland Europe £353. Tourist expenditure is a function of many factors, including length of stay, income level, party composition, accommodation used, method of transport and nature of holiday. The fact that more than half of the time spent by British visitors is staying with friends and relatives rather than in paid accommodation, reflecting their large ethnic component, is one of the reasons why their expenditure level is relatively low.

Accommodation is an essential part of the tourism product and its supply has grown with the industry in quantity and quality. At present there is a problem of oversupply. Although there has been a trend towards higher grade and increasing size of hotel, a predominant feature of accommodation provision is that of the small scale of enterprises. Most hotels are family-owned businesses and a substantial amount of other serviced accommodation is provided on a bed and breakfast basis. Hotels generate more employment than the other sectors but there has been a shift towards self-catering for reasons of cost and independence. About 33,000 people are employed in hotels and guesthouses alone, with three quarters of this employment being directly related to tourism. A high proportion of these are permanent employees but nonetheless a major handicap of the accommodation sector is the seasonality of business. Of all overseas tourists, 50% arrive during the four months June to September, but travel specifically for holiday making is even more peaked.

REGIONAL PATTERNS OF TOURISM

Special importance is attached to tourism in considerations of regional development. Tourism at the regional level is administered by seven regional tourism organisations, for which the current areas of responsibility are shown in Figure 2. These regional shares of tourism revenue and beds in 1991 are shown in Table 2, where they may be compared with those of population at the 1991 Census.

Table 2   *Regional shares of population, tourism revenue and tourist bedrooms, 1991*

Region	Population (%)	Revenue (%)	Bedrooms (%)
Dublin	29.1	22.7	17.6
East/Midlands	17.3	9.8	6.2
Southeast	10.9	10.5	10.8
Southwest	13.7	20.4	23.7
Midwest	10.5	12.6	13.3
West	9.7	14.6	16.2
Northwest	8.9	9.4	12.3

Dublin and the Southwest Region together reaped 43.1% of national tourism revenue. Although Dublin is by far the smallest region in area, it had the leading share of revenue and the second-ranked though lower proportion of beds. Both values were less than the region's share of the total population, and these relationships were even more pronounced for the East/Midlands Region. Conversely, in the Southwest and West especially, but also in the Midwest and Northwest, the shares of population were exceeded by those of revenue and, to an even greater extent, of bedrooms. While Table 2 indicates the relative significance of tourism in the different regions, the magnitude of regional tourism revenue is shown by the sizes of the proportionate circles in Figure 2.

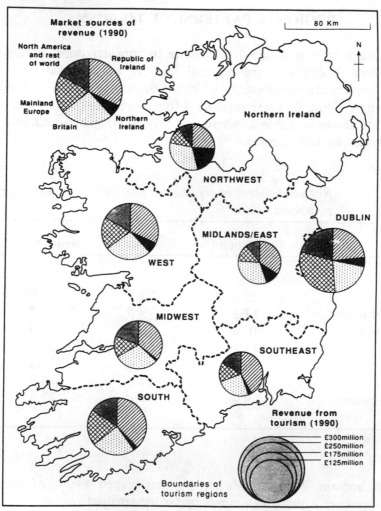

Figure 2   *The regional distribution of tourism revenue and its market sources*

24

Another and more detailed perspective on the spatial pattern of tourism can be obtained by the mapping of tourist bedroom data at the county level (Figure 3). The numbers of officially registered tourist bedrooms in the counties are shown by the proportionate circles and the ratio of these to the resident populations at the 1991 Census by the density of shading. The map reflects the regional patterns already outlined but brings out also some intra-regional variation. Thus the national and regional importance of Counties Kerry and Galway is emphasised and the significance of Counties Clare and Waterford within their regions may be seen.

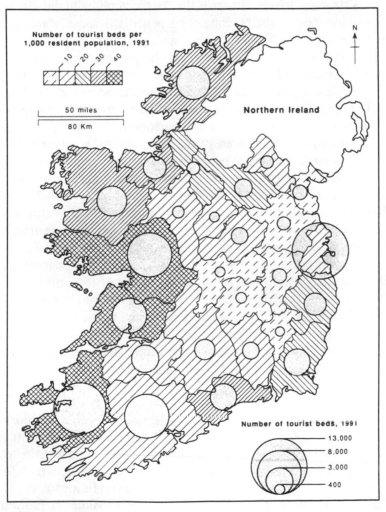

Figure 3   *The distribution by county of registered tourist beds*

The regional table and map together with the county map show that there is a distinct spatial distribution of tourism within the Republic of Ireland. The regional pattern reflects the geographical distributions of the various tourist attractions, the regional levels of development, investment and promotion, and the location of tourist gateways. The pattern would be even more uneven than it is if it were not for the substantial ethnic element that occurs in Irish tourism, which is related more to the distributions of migration sources and of relatives and friends than to normal tourist resources.

Tourism is strongly oriented towards the coastal zone, with the maritime counties receiving most of the revenue. This is partly because of the scenic attraction of the coast itself and the scope which it provides for beach and water-based activities. It follows also from the predominantly peripheral distribution of upland relief and of urban settlement, the latter having historical and cultural features and also accommodation and entertainment facilities. The western part of the country is that which has the greatest appeal to tourists. This results from a combination of its physical assets of a long attractive coastline and extensive upland scenery, together with the character of its human landscape, people and traditional culture.

The largest tourism centres in the west are Killarney and Galway-Salthill. In the northern part of the state, proximity to the border with Northern Ireland has a deterrent influence, affecting especially the northwestern peripheral county of Donegal which otherwise has major tourist attraction.

Major historic sites, great houses and exhibition gardens are more common in the east and south. Eastern regions get a higher proportion of the revenue than they would otherwise have because of their proximity to entry points for overseas visitors. Dublin is the single most important focus for tourists, having 23% of the national revenue and being visited by two-fifths of overseas tourists. This reflects the various attractions of the capital city in addition to it being the country's main international gateway and a centre for business travel. Indications are that Dublin's share of national tourism has increased.

There is some regional differentiation in the market sources of tourism revenue (Figure 2). The facts that the British sector is the one with the lowest variation, and that it tends to be relatively most important in the least popular regions, reflect the large ethnic element amongst British travellers which is drawn less than other tourists towards the main destinations. That the British role is proportionately greatest in the Midlands/East and Northwest regions is influenced by the attraction of the lakes of the

26

northern midland area for British anglers and relative proximity to access routes from Britain. The Northern Irish component is the most localised, one third of it being to the adjacent Northwest, especially Donegal, with the Midlands/East and West also popular. The North American contribution is highest in Dublin and the Midwest, related to air arrival and departure at Shannon and Dublin and to the attraction of the capital city. The appeal of Dublin is most marked with regard to visitors from continental Europe, accounting for nearly a third of its revenue, and their contribution is high also in the Southwest and West. The proportion of revenue derived from domestic tourism is highest in the Southeast, reflecting its relative proximity to Dublin as the main source of Irish visitors and also the attraction of its beaches and relatively sunny climate. The Southwest and West are popular with Irish holiday makers, accounting for two fifths of the revenue from domestic tourism.

The regional impact of tourism is a function of both the spatial pattern of tourism itself and its role in regional economies. Regional contributions are even more difficult to evaluate than those at the national level (Tansey, Webster and Associates 1991). It is estimated that the shares of regional employment attributable to tourism range from about 4-6% in the East and Midlands regions to about 8-11% in the West. The contribution to regional incomes varies from about 4% in the East to about 10% in the Northwest and West. Those regions where tourism is of greatest significance tend to be the regions where levels of overall economic development are lowest and the range of non-agricultural employment opportunities least. This gives to tourism its important regional development dimension, whereby it has a redistributive effect on employment and income within the state. Much of the Midlands region is an exception to this regional development role of tourism, in that tourism is of minor significance despite the economic development needs of the area.

TOURISM DEVELOPMENT PLANNING

Development planning is all the more desirable in tourism because of the need to promote co-ordination within this complex and disparate industry, but this very complexity, in turn, renders the formulation and execution of development planning all the more difficult. The first major contributions to tourism planning in Ireland were made at the local and regional levels in the 1960s and early 1970s. National tourism planning was minimal prior to the 1970s and had been only in the context of the state's general economic programming. The first national tourism plan by Bord Fáilte related to the mid 1970s and since then updated and modified plans have been produced on a continuing basis. The most comprehensive and elaborate development planning was that for the period 1976-80, incorporating a strong spatial dimension through the combination of eight regional plans with the national plan.

A new impetus to tourism development planning began to emerge in the mid 1980s as a result of the official importance being attached to the industry in economic and employment terms. This seems to have been stimulated by the difficulties being experienced by the industry at that time, the search by government for remedies for severe national economic and employment problems, and the publication of a White Paper (Government of Ireland 1985) and consultancy reports on tourism (Stokes Kennedy Crowley *et.al.* 1986; Price Waterhouse 1987). A more positive government attitude towards tourism than had been demonstrated previously was evident in its 1987 *Programme for National Recovery*. This outlined a strategy for the next five years whereby the number of foreign visitors would be doubled, an additional £500 million of foreign tourism revenue would be earned and an extra 25,000 jobs created. These ambitious targets were to be attained through lower access fares, the development of inward air charter traffic, better marketing and the aggressive promotion of investment in the industry. Investment was encouraged by the application to certain tourism enterprises over the period 1987-91 of the Business Expansion Scheme, providing tax relief on venture capital.

Ireland's plans for tourism development were approved and adopted by the EC in 1989 as the *Operational Programme for Tourism 1989-1993* (Department of Tourism and Transport 1990). This involved essentially application of the earlier targets and policies to this period but provided for Community funding of almost half of the planned £300 million investment. It was made possible by the doubling of Structural Funds to promote cohesion associated with the Single European Act. The *Operational Programme* was designed to enable Irish tourism to compete successfully so that it might stimulate the economic growth needed to reduce unemployment and to raise incomes towards EC levels, tourism having been identified as one means of doing this.

While tourism is of major importance in the economy and life of the Republic of Ireland, it was felt desirable that the considerable difficulties which have been encountered should be acknowledged in its development planning. The *Operational Programme* identified the weaknesses of the industry as comprising: deficiencies in the quality and range of important elements of the tourism product; lack of price competitiveness; difficulties in marketing, exacerbated by the negative image relating to the troubles in Northern Ireland; access difficulties and cost associated with the country's isolated location. The peripherality which hinders access has facilitated the retention of some of that Irish individuality appeal which should become even more significant in an increasingly unified Europe. Also, its hindrance of many other economic sectors makes the need for tourism development to increase revenue and employment all the greater.

Policy to date under the *Operational Programme* has been to endeavour to counter the weaknesses in Irish tourism through a fourfold strategy. The primary component is a product strategy designed to provide a better and wider range of tourist attractions and facilities. This focuses on five product themes comprising: active pursuits; passive pursuits; cultural, heritage and entertainment interests; leisure, fitness and health facilities; business travel. It includes human resource training, efforts to reduce seasonality and the development of tourism centres, theme towns and traditional resorts. The other components are a competitiveness strategy to provide better value in terms of price and quality, a promotion strategy aimed at greater penetration of existing markets and entry to new ones, and a distribution strategy to ensure that the product is made readily available to the potential customer through an improved information and reservation network. This more vigorous and better co-ordinated approach on the part of government, Bord Fáilte and the industry is doing much to further the development of Irish tourism, though inevitably progress is affected also by influences beyond the control of any of these agencies.

EC Structural Funds have been the dominant incentive to investment in tourism over the period of the *Operational Programme*, tourism's share of the total allocation to Ireland being 5%. Half of the investment for which the Structural Funds provided support was public and half private. It is estimated that a total incentive package of £235 million led to matching finance of £384 million to produce an investment of £619 million, with an additional investment of £150 million which was not driven by state incentives. Of the total incentive package, 48% came from the European Regional Development Fund, 26% from the national Business Expansion Scheme, 15% from the European Social Fund and 6% from the International Fund for Ireland which relates mainly to border areas.

Commitment to continued development of tourism over the next five years is indicated by the publication in December 1992 of *Developing*

Sustainable Tourism (Bord Fáilte 1992a). Emphasis in this draft development plan for the period 1993-97 is placed on the development of tourism which is sustainable in terms of economically viable tourism enterprises, of enduring employment creation and of environmental conservation. It is suggested that there is the potential to earn a further £450 million in overseas tourism revenue, involving an average growth rate of 8.3% per annum, and thereby to create 23,000 additional jobs. The aim is to increase the economic return per visitor, so that the revenue targets would be attained through a slower growth in visitor numbers, which would have reached 4.45 million by 1997. A further increase of £150 million in domestic tourism revenue is envisaged. Thus by 1997 the total industry would be worth £2.6 billion and support 115,000 jobs. In pursuance of these targets, it is estimated that incentives of £500 million from EC and other sources will be needed to create the economic environment conducive to a total product investment programme of £1,600 million. Additional marketing expenditure of £100 million to promote the expansion of the industry is suggested (Bord Fáilte 1992b).

The strategy devised in *Developing Sustainable Tourism* is specified as having seven key elements which comprise: continued investment in quality; priority to projects which improve seasonality and profitability; development of products of sufficient scale to compete internationally; further expansion of the special interest portfolio; investment in the authentic and natural elements of Irish heritage; creation of a strong rural tourism product; and protection of the environment.

In the implementation of the development strategy, a four-fold framework with a strong spatial dimension is proposed. This is done with the aims of co-ordinating investment decisions and promoting realisation of the full potential of all parts of the state. The four categories of area identified in the plan and shown in Figure 4 are:

(1)   *Tourism centres.* The designation of tourism centres accords with the application of the growth centre concept to tourism, involving the concentration of investment in and around specified centres of 15 km radius that can develop a range of facilities and services and that can evolve into recognisable holiday destinations. A three-tier structure of five major centres (2000+ rooms in all types of approved tourist accommodation), 10 established centres (1000-2000 rooms) and 26 developing centres (400-2000 rooms) is recognised. The major centres, comprising in rank order, Dublin,

Killarney, Galway, Cork and Limerick, have 44% of the rooms. The 41 places in the three categories of tourism centre together account for 85% of the total registered accommodation in the state.

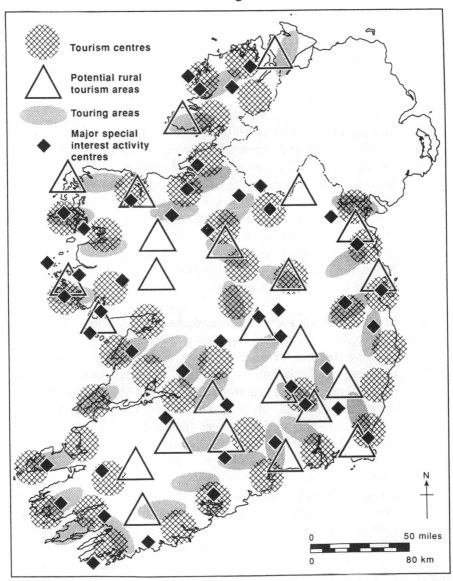

Figure 4   *Tourism area categorisation according to the Bord Fáilte document 'Developing Sustainable Tourism'*

(2)   *Rural tourism areas.* Outside of the tourism centres, many places have the potential for the development of rural tourism, catering for the increasing number of people who seek a quiet holiday in the countryside. Rural tourism tends to be characterised by smallness of scale, community orientation and environmental friendliness. Ireland is well suited to and has considerable potential for this form of development. The number of proposed rural tourism areas is 25, of which 13 are in the West and the Southeast region combined.

(3)   *Touring areas.* The mobility of modern tourists is recognised in the delimitation of 36 areas of considerable natural beauty catering for car, coach and cycle touring. Touring areas are categorised as being coastal, mountain, river valley, lake shore and heritage, though an area may be within more than one category. A further distinction is made between established areas (eg. Shannon, Ring of Kerry, Connemara, Wicklow Mountains, Glen of Aherlow, Lough Gill and Boyne Valley) and developing areas (eg. Cooley Mountains, West Clare, Innishowen, Comeraghs, Lee, Lough Allen and Southeast River Valleys).

(4)   *Special interest centres.* The designation of places offering good opportunities for special interests is a recognition of the need the growing demand for such activities which can be the reason for choosing an Irish holiday. Certain localities have established reputations for particular activities but the desirability of developing clusters of products to aid market penetration is emphasised. The product themes identified, with some examples of special interest activities under each heading given in brackets, are: (a) recreation (angling, golf, cruising, walking); (b) water sports (sailing, surfing); (c) sports (Gaelic games, equestrian sports); (d) nature (bird-watching, ecology); (e) pastimes (crafts, genealogy); (f) lifestyle (shopping, business, health and fitness, language learning); (g) culture (literature, folklore, festivals); (h) heritage (clan rallies, architecture, gardens, history).

Developing Sustainable Tourism is supported by plans for each of the seven tourism regions and these specify how its objectives can be applied within their territories. They and the national plan are the result of Bord Fáilte thinking and of consultations which it had with the regional tourism organisations and other tourism interests at national and local levels. This development plan represents a major input to current discussions as to how the next round of EC Structural Funding to Ireland should be spent. The outcome of these discussions will have a major bearing on the shape which tourism development and its impacts in the Republic of Ireland will take over the next five years.

CONCLUSION

Considerable development and change have occurred in the tourism industry of the Republic of Ireland and future adaptation to evolving circumstances will be necessary. At present much reliance is being placed on the industry to contribute towards alleviating the economic and employment problems of the state. This faith is evident to an even greater extent at local level, in the priority accorded to tourism in community and area development plans throughout the state, as under the EC LEADER Programme. Perhaps the temptation for local communities to regard tourism as the panacea for all their ills is too great. The real potential for tourism varies spatially, and in many places it can be a very important and valuable component in local economic and social development, but the risks and disadvantages associated with an undue reliance on this sector alone are very real.

REFERENCES

Bord Fáilte (1992a)
   Developing Sustainable Tourism: tourism development plan 1993-97.
   Dublin: Bord Fáilte.
Bord Fáilte (1992b)
   Developing Sustainable Growth: tourism marketing plan 1993-97.
   Dublin: Bord Fáilte.
Deegan, J and Dineen, D (1992)
   Employment effects of Irish tourism projects: a micro-economic approach. In Johnson, P and Thomas, B (eds), *Perspectives on Tourism Policy.* London: Mansell, 137-56.

Department of Tourism and Transport (1989)
Operational Programme for Tourism. Dublin: Stationery Office.
Gillmor, D (1985)
Economic Activities in the Republic of Ireland: a geographical perspective. Dublin: Gill and Macmillan, chapter 8.
Government of Ireland (1985)
White Paper on Tourism Policy. Dublin: Stationery Office.
Henry, E (1991)
Estimated Employment and Gross National Product Impacts of 1989 Tourism in Ireland. Paper read to Statistical and Social Inquiry Society of Ireland, Dublin.
National Economic and Social Council (1980)
Tourism Policy. NESC Report 52. Dublin: Stationery Office.
Ó Cinnéide, M and Walsh, J (1991)
Tourism and regional development in Ireland, *Geographical Viewpoint* 19, 47-68.
Pearce, D (1990)
Tourism in Ireland: questions of scale and organization. *Tourism Management* 11, 133-51.
Pearce, D (1992)
Tourism Organizations. Harlow: Longman, chapter 7.
Pollard, J (1989)
Patterns in Irish tourism. In Carter, R and Parker, A (eds), *Ireland: a contemporary geographical perspective.* London/New York: Routledge, 301-30.
Price Waterhouse (1987)
Improving the performance of Irish tourism. Dublin: Stationery Office.
Stokes Kennedy Crowley *et.al.* (1986)
Tourism Working for Ireland: a plan for growth. Dublin: Irish Hotels Federation.
Tansey, Webster and Associates (1991)
Tourism and the Economy. Dún Laoghaire: Irish Tourist Industry Confederation.
Tourism Task Force (1992)
Report of the Tourism Task Force to the Minister for Tourism, Transport and Communications. Dublin: Stationery Office.

The Organisation of Irish Tourism

SARAH DREA

INTRODUCTION

This essay gives an overview of tourism organisation in Ireland, beginning with an outline of the roles of the main actors in tourism development. The essay then looks at some research which has been carried out to assess the effectiveness of the structures currently in place to promote and develop the Irish tourism industry. Finally, recommendations for a new structure are presented, based on these research results.

In order to incorporate regionally based and locally based organisations into the project, the Southeast was selected as a regional level case study, and within this region County Kilkenny was chosen as a local level case study (Figure 5). The Southeast region was taken because it is not in a particularly advanced stage of tourism development, and County Kilkenny was felt to be of interest because it is an example of a relatively successful inland tourism area.

ORGANISATIONS INVOLVED IN IRISH TOURISM

Government departments

Direct government involvement in the tourism industry comes primarily under the aegis of the Department of Tourism and Trade (previously the Department of Tourism, Transport and Communications), which has overall responsibility for the development of tourism. Policy is formulated by senior management within the Department and, occasionally, is initiated by the Minister in line with the development policies of the government. Other government departments whose policies indirectly affect tourism include:

- the Department of the Environment, through its role in the provision of infrastructure, in environmental policies relating to pollution control and in relation to planning;

Ullrich Kockel (ed), *Culture, Tourism and Development: The Case of Ireland*, Liverpool University Press 1994, 35-46.

- the Department of Agriculture, through its role in directing the evolution of alternative land-uses, especially the development of agri-tourism projects;

- the Departments of Labour and Education, through their role in training personnel for the industry.

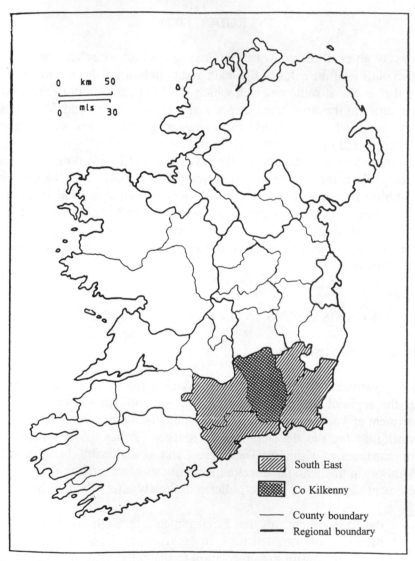

Figure 5   *The Southeast region and County Kilkenny*

Local government involvement in tourism development comes under the brief of the local authorities, who come under the umbrella of the Department of the Environment. They are primarily concerned with the provision of infrastructure and amenities for tourists and local residents alike.

As well as the government departments involved in the industry, a number of state agencies also play a major role in the sector. The most important of these is the National Tourism Organisation—Bord Fáilte— which reports to the Department of Tourism and Trade. The Board is concerned primarily with the implementation of policy formulated by the Department and it is responsible for the overall marketing and development of the tourism industry in Ireland. The Board's functions are concerned with the development of the tourism product, marketing, training of personnel and providing information to visitors.

Regional Tourism Organisations

The Regional Tourism Organisations were established in 1964 by Bord Fáilte to service the tourism needs of individual regions. There is a parallel between the RTOs' functions at regional level and those of Bord Fáilte at national level. The RTOs carry out any tasks which can be more effectively performed at regional or local levels.

Servicing visitor needs is seen as a primary function of the RTOs, and they operate the network of tourist booking and information offices throughout the country. The general function of the RTOs is to stimulate increased local effort in tourism development. They provide a structure which, in theory, facilitates local support of tourism. It must be said, however, that local financial support for the RTOs has been disappointing (Pearce 1990) and hence their heavy reliance on Bord Fáilte to provide the bulk of their funding.

The Office of Public Works

The Office of Public Works (OPW) is responsible for the protection and conservation of the national heritage, which comprises an increasingly important part of the tourism product. Accessibility to heritage sites takes place subject to it being consistent with upkeep and conservation. Tourism is not, therefore, a central concern for the OPW, but it is something which

37

the organisation's individual sites must accommodate. At a number of sites the OPW provides tourist facilities, and its representatives may be actively involved in the promotion and development of tourism at the local level.

CERT

The Council for Education, Recruitment and Training (CERT) was formed in 1963 by Bord Fáilte. Its role is to provide education and training for the personnel of all sectors of the tourism industry, including hotels and catering. Part of CERT's role is to advise the government on manpower and training needs and it organises education and training programmes which implement government policy.

Teagasc

Teagasc, the Council for Research and Training in Agriculture, is a semi-state organisation whose primary function is to provide an advisory service to the agricultural sector. In some regions Teagasc advisers are actively involved in the promotion and development of agri-tourism schemes. Part of their involvement is in motivating local effort and providing a framework within which local groups can work to develop tourism projects.

Private and voluntary organisations

In addition to the public organisations involved in the industry, a number of organisations representing the interests of the private sector exist. Their function is to represent, promote and protect the common interests of their members. In addition, these organisations generally provide essential services for their members and may carry out marketing on their behalf.

Examples of this type of organisation include, in the accommodation sector, the Irish Hotels Federation and, representing the 'Bed & Breakfast' sector, Irish Farm Holidays, Town and Country Homes, and Hidden Ireland (the latter representing those providing accommodation in historic houses). Each of the accommodation organisations has a regional structure, through which individual members can voice their opinions and concerns.

The Coach Tourism Council represents individual private coach companies who are involved in providing transport for incoming tourists. Unlike the accommodation organisations, the Council does not have a marketing function. Part of the Council's role is to liaise with Bord Fáilte on behalf of its members. It also plays a role in keeping its members up to date with coaching legislation from Brussels.

Several of the organisations serving the interests of the private sector are members of the Irish Tourist Industry Confederation (ITIC). Its role is to give a single voice to the Irish tourist industry (Pearce 1990, 144) by acting as a lobbying group to pursue issues of common interest to its members. ITIC only operates at national level, having no regional structure or members. It does not deal with individuals, but with the organisations to which they belong; it deals, for example, with the Hotels Federation, rather than with individual hotels.

At the local level, Kilkenny Tourism Council is one example of an area based organisation which represents the tourism interests of Co. Kilkenny. The principal purpose of the Council is to market Kilkenny as a tourist destination, both at home and abroad.

Graiguenamanagh Chamber of Commerce is another example of an area-based organisation operating at local level in Co. Kilkenny. Unlike the Tourism Council, the Chamber's concerns are not limited to tourism. The overall purpose of the Chamber is to stimulate local development by improving the economic and social life of Graiguenamanagh. In relation to tourism, the Chamber encourages the development of facilities in the town to ensure that the town benefits economically from the level of tourism it is already experiencing through fishing in the river Barrow.

THE SURVEY

The Price Waterhouse Report (1987), which was prepared for the Irish government, pointed out that 'the institutional structures for Irish tourism are critical to the successful implementation of tourism policy'. However, while tourism has been targeted as a key sector for economic growth, little research has, as yet, been directed towards the organisational structures in place to promote and carry out this development.

In order to investigate the effectiveness of the tourism organisational structure, a pilot survey was carried out by means of a series of structured interviews with key actors within the industry. The survey was intended to reflect the diversity of the industry and to be representative of the national, regional and local levels of involvement in the tourism industry. Moreover, it was intended that the public, private and voluntary sectors be represented by the participants.

Table 3   *Survey participants by ownership type and spatial level of operation*

	Private	State	Voluntary	Other	Total
National	3	3	4	1	11
Regional	0	4	1	0	3
Local	6	4	3	0	13
TOTAL	9	9	8	1	27

It proved possible to distribute the survey evenly between the principal types of ownership. The concentration of the private sector at local level bears out the perception that tourism is an industry characterised by small-scale local businesses. In relation to the spatial scale of operation, however, Table 3 implies a bias against the regional level. The apparent underrepresentation of this level can, however, be accounted for by the absence of regional organisations in the industry, although many of the national level voluntary organisations have regional representatives.

Communication and co-ordination were considered to be important factors in measuring the effectiveness of the structure and the interviews focused on the co-ordination of marketing and promotion and interaction for day-to-day operations and policy discussions.

Marketing and promotion

Participants were asked about their marketing operations. A large percentage of participants said they were involved in marketing to one extent or another. It was found that there was a significant amount of liaison with key agencies like Bord Fáilte, the RTO and Kilkenny Tourism Council to co-ordinate marketing efforts. This was particularly true amongst local level operators, although the fact that several of the participants liaise with each of the organisations simultaneously raised questions regarding the effectiveness of liaison and the extent to which liaison actually leads to co-ordination.

Day-to-day interaction

Those interviewed were also asked about the interactions they have with various organisations for the purposes of the day-to-day running of their business. Figure 6 shows the number of interactions between national, regional and local level participants with national, regional and local level organisations.

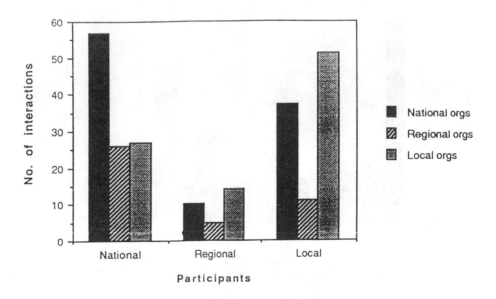

Figure 6   *Day-to-day interactions between tourism organisations*

There was an element of insularity of national level participants' interactions with national level organisations. Local level participants' contacts are also somewhat insular, with the majority of these being with local level organisations. This is as would be expected, since day-to-day concerns would tend to be more closely related to organisations and businesses operating at the same level as themselves.

The extent of national level insularity is much greater than that of the local level and it can be seen from Figure 6 that national level participants have much less day-to-day contact with local level operators than local level participants have with national level organisations. This reflects the local level's need to avail of certain of the services provided by national level organisations.

Regional level organisations do not appear to be the focus of a very high level of interaction with participants, but it should be pointed out that there are far fewer of these organisations in existence than there are of national and local organisations. This level of organisation does, however, offer a potential bridge between the national and local levels.

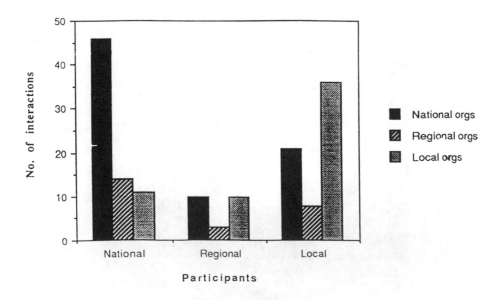

Figure 7   *Policy discussion interactions between tourism organisations*

There was a general feeling of satisfaction with day-to-day operations in the industry amongst participants, with 73% of the standard of service indicators being good or better and 26% being fair or worse.

Policy discussion

Interview participants were also asked about their interactions with various organisations for policy discussions and for the purposes of future planning. Figure 7 shows the patterns of interaction for policy-discussion purposes. As with day-to-day interactions, there appears to be a clustering of interaction between national level participants and national level organisations, and between local level participants and local level organisations, which is more pronounced than in the case of day-to-day interactions.

National level participants have relatively little policy discussion with local level organisations. Local level participants have more policy discussions with national level organisations than the reverse. However, this is to be expected, given the centralised nature of policy formulation, whereby the Department of Tourism and Trade formulates policy and Bord Fáilte, the national tourism organisation, is the principal channel for the industry's input into policy formulation. Once again, there is scope for the regional level to act as a link between the national and local levels or organisation, since although there are very few organisations at this level, there were relatively high levels of interaction with them from national and local level participants.

Participants' perceptions of the effectiveness of their policy discussions with others in the industry are not as favourable as for day-to-day interactions. When rating effectiveness on a scale of 1-5, 64% rated the effectiveness of policy discussion at 4 or better, but 36% rated it at 3 or less. The state sector, with its central role in the formulation and implementation of tourism policy, was the focus of dissatisfaction here.

The overall conclusion of the survey is that, while participants are content with the day-to-day operations of the industry, there is a deficiency in the policy formulation process and there is also a degree of duplication of marketing effort, indicating the need for greater co-ordination of this area.

RECOMMENDATIONS

Local level

The policy discussion process at local level was regarded as much more effective than that at national level, and the effectiveness of the two main organisations at local level (ie., Kilkenny Tourism Council and the Tourist Information Office) was rated above average.

On the basis of this, and on the basis of the literature on tourism organisation which asserts that local level input is important to the overall development of the industry, there is a strong case for the adoption of policy-making structures through which policy proposals coming from the local level and from those with 'hands on' experience of the industry form the basis of policy decisions.

There is a need to develop structures through which the local level input can be integrated into the policy-making process in an effective and co-ordinated manner and in such a way as to avoid fragmentation in the policy-making process.

Local tourism groups geared towards policy formulation and development planning could facilitate the compilation of local proposals for policy. These groups, perhaps based at county level, would incorporate the interests of the various sectors of the tourism industry within the county and would bring these together with representatives of the Local Authority and any locally-based state agencies. These groups would have input into broader local development issues, through multi-sectoral local development forums, and into the tourism planning process at a higher level of organisation, most likely at regional level.

Regional level

The potentially pivotal role of the regional level of organisation was apparent from the interviews. There may be a case for adopting an approach which would facilitate the integration of tourism into broader development at this level. This type of approach would be consistent with the EC policy which favours integrated development programmes over individual development projects. If the RTOs in their present form were to be integrated into multi-sectoral Regional Development Agencies, each of which would have a Tourism Unit, integration into the broader development agenda would be expressed in a structural framework. For overall

44

development, the Regional Development Agencies would have a governing body with responsibility for policy formulation. The interests of the tourism sector would have representation on such a body, along with representatives from other sectors.

In relation to tourism policy specifically, the Tourism Unit at each of the Regional Development Agencies would have its own governing body which would be comprised of representatives of local authorities, state agencies, voluntary associations, local tourism groups and the private sector. Such a forum would provide a focus for the co-ordination of the proposals coming from local level, both for the purposes of the implementation of these at regional level, where appropriate, and for the purposes of expressing these proposals at national level. It is envisaged that the Regional Development Agencies would have statutory representation in the policy—making process at national level for all sectors. In relation to the tourism aspect of their role, this would probably be best represented under the auspices of a National Tourist Authority.

National level

Turning now to the national level, while participants expressed satisfaction with the routine day-to-day operations of the organisation structure in general, there are nonetheless areas which could be better co-ordinated and perhaps more efficient. One such area identified in the study is the co-ordination of marketing effort. It was found that there is extensive duplication between participants liaising with organisations at all levels in an attempt to co-ordinate marketing operations. Perhaps the existence of a forum at national level for national level organisations—The state and private sectors—to discuss their respective strategies could be beneficial in eliminating unnecessary duplication.

The case for an increased input into policy formulation from those actively involved in the industry and who have practical experience of the business, rather than continuing with the present arrangements under which policy is formulated by bureaucrats with little 'hands on' experience of the industry, has already been mentioned. This would be consistent with the EC policy which favours partnership between all levels and agencies, and the reformed structures at local and regional level would facilitate the involvement of all levels and sectors of the industry in the decision-making process.

The establishment of a policy-formulating body or a National Tourist Authority, which would be comprised of representatives from the Tourism Unit of the Regional Development Agencies, the Department of Tourism and Trade, other government departments, Bord Fáilte, the private sector here and foreign agents, would facilitate policy formulation by those with 'hands on' experience of the industry and a more co-ordinated approach, which would avoid the mismatching of the product and marketing efforts. The proposed tourist authority would assume responsibility for all policy and planning decisions and would be the focus for the integration of regional and local level proposals into the final development policies. The National Tourist Authority would provide a forum at national level where the specific needs of different regions, local areas and sectors within the industry would gain expression and from where a concrete policy for development would emerge.

The role of Bord Fáilte could be clearly redefined to enshrine the implementation of policy as its primary function and to strengthen its focus on marketing abroad by eliminating any routine tasks which could be performed at regional level.

In summary, the proposed structures would be based on a bottom-up approach to policy formulation and planning, which would integrate all levels and sectors of the industry. There would be a clear distinction between the roles of policy formulation and policy implementation, and the integration of tourism into the broader development agenda would be facilitated.

REFERENCES

Drea, S (1992)
The Organisation of Irish Tourism. Maynooth: St Patrick's College, unpublished MA thesis.
Pearce, D (1990)
Tourism in Ireland: questions of scale and organisation. *Tourism Management* 11(2), 133-51.
Price Waterhouse (1987)
Improving the Performance of Irish Tourism. Dublin: Stationery Office.

Gender and Employment in Irish Tourism

PROINNSIAS BREATHNACH

INTRODUCTION

Tourism has been targeted by the Irish government as a sector offering good prospects not only of generating foreign exchange but, more importantly, of providing much needed job opportunities at a time of incessantly rising unemployment levels. Tourism has been identified in this respect both for its strong growth performance internationally and its labour-intensive nature.

The government's plans for tourism development were encapsulated in the *Operational Programme* for tourism for the period 1989-93, which was agreed with the Commission of the European Communities in December 1989 as part of the Community Support Framework under which Ireland receives EC structural funding (Ó Cinnéide and Walsh 1991). This programme provided for a total investment in the tourism sector of some IR£300 million over the period of the plan. The programme envisaged a doubling of incoming tourist numbers to 4.2 million, an increase in tourism revenues of IR£500 million (about 75%), and the creation of 25,000 additional tourism-related jobs (an increase of one third). These were very ambitious targets, given that global tourism has been growing at an average rate of only five per cent in recent years.

The first two years of the *Operational Programme* did produce vigorous growth in tourist numbers and revenue, and particularly in investment (Tansey Webster and Associates 1991; Dunne 1992). However, there was a slight decline in numbers in 1991, due principally to a slump in the North American market (attributed mainly to the impact of the Gulf War), although aggregate revenue continued to expand.

Overall, tourism (domestic and overseas) accounted for about 7% of both Gross National Product (GNP) and total employment in Ireland in 1990. However, in the period 1985-1990 tourism contributed some 37% of net employment growth in the economy. Tourism also makes a very important contribution to the Irish balance of payments, accounting for 7% of total

Ullrich Kockel (ed), *Culture, Tourism and Development: The Case of Ireland*, Liverpool University Press 1994, 47-60.

exports of goods and services in 1990 and, perhaps more importantly, over half the overall net current account surplus in that year (Tansey Webster and Associates 1991).

Irish tourism has an important regional dimension, in that tourists are attracted disproportionately to the more rural and remote western part of the country, where incomes are generally below the national average. Table 4 shows that the western regions, with below-average incomes, attract above-average levels of tourism revenue, with the result that tourism makes a much greater contribution to personal incomes in these regions than it does in other regions.

Table 4   *Regional distribution of income from tourism (1990)*

Region	Share of Tourism in %	Share of Population in %	Per Capita Income Index*	Tourism Revenue as % of Total Personal Income
East	29.8	40.9	112	3.7
Midlands	7.2	10.2	86	4.7
Southeast	9.6	10.9	90	5.6
Southwest	22.1	15.1	99	8.4
Midwest	9.7	8.8	95	6.6
West	12.8	8.3	87	10.1
Northwest	8.7	5.9	85	9.9

* Ireland = 100

Source: Tansey Webster and Associates (1991) and *Census of Population 1991*

Given the emphasis being placed by the Irish government on tourism as a means of income and employment expansion, and the resultant growing importance of the industry in the national economy, there has been a surprising dearth of critical analysis of the implications of tourism development. Such issues as the nature of the employment provided by the tourism industry and the social, cultural and environmental impacts of tourism development have been largely ignored (but see Deegan and Dineen 1991).

This essay seeks to fill some of this gap by critically examining the structure of employment in the Irish tourism industry, drawing on detailed surveys carried out by the Council for Education, Recruitment and Training (CERT), the state agency responsible for the training of personnel for the industry. This examination highlights the numerical importance of women workers in the industry, which contrasts with the generally low participation rate, by OECD standards, of Irish women in the labour force (Callender 1990). The high profile of women workers in tourism employment is linked to the low levels of skill and the high levels of seasonal and part-time work in the industry. Given that tourism, therefore, is characterised by a large proportion of poor quality employment, questions must be raised concerning the wisdom of devoting substantial levels of public resources to tourism development in Ireland.

EMPLOYMENT STRUCTURE IN THE TOURISM INDUSTRY

Because of its highly heterogeneous nature and the fact that it overlaps with many other economic activities, employment in the tourism sector is not easily quantifiable. However, in the case of Ireland, detailed surveys carried out by CERT provide an excellent database for analysing the structure of employment in the industry (CERT 1987; 1988; 1991).

In 1987, an estimated 57,000 people were engaged directly in providing tourism services; however, because many of these were employed part-time, or were simultaneously providing services to non-tourists (retailing, catering, etc.), this figure converts to 38,500 full-time equivalents (CERT 1987). This figure accords well with other estimates of employment in the industry (Tansey Webster and Associates 1991). When one includes indirect employment (supplying goods and services to the industry) and further employment induced by the multiplier effects of tourist expenditure, total tourism-related employment for that year rises to 63,000, representing about six per cent of total employment and 10% of service employment.

Table 5   *Employment structure of the Irish tourism industry, 1987*[1]

Sub-Sector	As % of Total Employment	Women as % of Sub-Sector
Accommodation	49	70
Catering	11	38
Transport	16	[2]18
Tour Operators	6	76
Administration[3]	5	[4]44
Leisure/Recreation	6	50
Retailing	[5]8	[6]40
TOTAL	100	54

Notes:
[1]   Unless otherwise stated, all data derived from CERT (1987).
[2]   Based on national gender division for transport sector.
[3]   Refers to public servants involved in tourism administration.
[4]   Based on overall gender division in civil service.
[5]   Refers to full-time equivalents.
[6]   Based on national gender division in retailing.

Table 5 provides a breakdown of tourism employment by sub-sector and gender. While the CERT surveys offer much detail on the gender division of labour in most areas of tourism employment, it is not complete. It has therefore been necessary to estimate the gender division for some sub-sectors from other sources. The proportions given in the table therefore should be regarded as roughly approximate rather than precise.

In 1987, as Table 5 shows, women accounted for some 54% of all those employed in Irish tourism. This is significantly in excess of the proportion of total services employment accounted for by women (44%), and almost twice the female proportion of the overall workforce (31%). If one excludes the male-intensive transport sub-sector (mainly involved in bringing tourists into the country), women account for 60% of tourism employment. For accommodation, which accounts for one half of tourism employment, the proportion rises to 70%.

WOMEN'S EMPLOYMENT IN THE HOTEL SECTOR

It is clear, therefore, that tourism is an atypical sector in the Irish economy, in that it is characterised by a predominantly female workforce. In order to explain this, a closer examination will be carried out of the accommodation sub-sector, in which women workers are particularly prominent. This examination is based on a detailed survey carried out by CERT (1988) of employment in hotels and guesthouses (hereafter simply the "hotel sector"), which account for the great bulk of employment in the sub-sector. The hotel sector is particularly oriented to the tourism industry, with 80% of employment being tourism-related (CERT 1987).

Table 6 provides a breakdown of employment in the hotel sector into employment categories, and gives the female proportion of employment in each category. Just over one half of all employment is full-time permanent, with a further one eighth being permanent but part-time. The remaining one third of jobs are seasonal (both full-time and part-time) or casual.

Table 6   *Structure of employment in the hotel sector*

Employment Category	As % of all Employment	Women as % of Category
Full-time Permanent	52.1	59.2
Part-time Permanent	12.5	79.4
Full-time Seasonal	13.6	73.5
Part-time Seasonal	2.4	88.2
Casual	19.4	n.a.
TOTAL	100.0	66.0*

* Excluding casual

Source: Computed from data in CERT (1988)

Excluding casual workers (for whom no gender breakdown is available) women comprise two thirds of all employment in hotels—over twice the overall female participation rate in paid employment in the country. However, the female proportion is lower for full-time permanent jobs (59%) and higher for all the other categories: part-time permanent (79%); full-time seasonal (74%); and part-time seasonal (88%). This employment structure is very similar to that noted by Bagguley (1990) for the British hotel and catering sector.

The domination of part-time and temporary employment by women is a common feature of advanced western economies. The fact that these employment categories constitute such a large proportion of total employment in the hotel sector—almost a half compared to just 16% in the national workforce—therefore goes a long way to explaining the disproportionate representation of women workers in the sector. However, the fact remains that women are also disproportionately represented among full-time permanent workers in the sector.

The second key explanatory factor in accounting for the high level of female employment in the hotel sector is the low level of skill required of the sector's workforce: less than one third of all workers may be regarded as skilled in the sense of having received at least some formal training. Even among full-time permanent workers, only a minority (44%) have any formal training. Skill levels are particularly low (only one seventh of all workers having had formal training) among part-time, seasonal and casual workers, the great majority of whom are women.

In all work categories, men are more likely to be skilled than women. And the higher the skill level of an occupational category, the more likely it is that it is full-time, permanent and male. Of managerial positions (8% of all employment in the hotel sector), 90% are full-time permanent and three quarters are formally trained, but only 40% are held by women. By contrast, less than half (44%) of unskilled 'accommodation assistants', i.e., chamber maids (9% of all jobs), are full-time permanent, and all of them are women. Similarly, over 90% of waiters/waitresses (21% of all hotel employment) are women, and less than 30% of jobs in this category are full-time permanent.

GENDER SEGMENTATION IN THE HOTEL SECTOR

There is considerable variation in female representation as between the different 'departments' of the hotel sector. Women are particularly prominent in the Accommodation (99% of all workers) and Restaurant and Banquet (86%) departments, but are a minority in Management (40%) and the Bar and Nightclub (48%) departments. The remaining departments, Kitchen (61%) and Reception and General (57%), occupy intermediate positions.

Within departments, there is also a high level of gender segmentation by occupation. Of Kitchen staff, the vast majority of head chefs (skilled) and porters (unskilled) are men, while almost all kitchen assistants and wash-ups (both unskilled) are women. While staff in the Restaurant and Banquet departments are predominantly female, the job category of 'head waiters/ waitresses' is mainly made up of men. Within the Reception and General department, those working as receptionists or accounts clerks are almost entirely women, while porters, 'doorpersons' and maintenance workers are almost all male. In Management, of 161 managing directors and general managers, only one is a woman.

However, there are some occupational categories where segmentation is not so apparent. Almost one half of the categories of chef (other than head chefs) and barperson consist of women (although in the latter case, women are much less likely to be full-time permanent employees). And, while there are virtually no female managing directors or general managers, of those with the simple grade of 'manager', 44% are women, with the proportion rising to 49% for assistant/duty managers and exactly one half for trainee managers. This could mean improving opportunities for women to progress to top management positions in future years. Alternatively, it could mean that women gradually get squeezed out as they move up the managerial ladder. Hicks's (1990) findings appear to support the latter interpretation.

FLEXIBILITY IN HOTEL EMPLOYMENT

Much attention has been devoted in recent times to the growing trend towards increasing flexibility of the workforce (especially in the manufacturing sector) in advanced economies (Atkinson 1985; Schoenberger 1988). This includes both numerical flexibility, whereby workers are taken on and let go on a ready basis by employers, and functional flexibility, whereby individual workers carry out a range of different tasks in a particular workplace.

In contrast to manufacturing, however, labour flexibility is a long-established feature of the hotel sector. In Britain, while functional flexibility emerged in the 1960s in response to labour shortages, it tended to be superseded in the 1970s by increasing numerical flexibility, mainly in the form of part-time and seasonal work (Bagguley 1990). While part-time work is more conducive to functional specialisation than functional flexibility, it has many attractions for employers. These include the ability to adapt to daily and weekly fluctuations in customer demand and the ability to avoid social insurance contributions, holiday and sick pay, etc. for part-time workers. The fact that part-time and temporary workers are more difficult to organise by trade unions is also seen as beneficial by many employers. There is also the fact that part-time and seasonal work appears attractive in particular to many women (especially married) workers. Thus a survey by Dineen (1989) found that, in 1987, the majority of female part-time workers in Ireland preferred working part-time, mainly because of family responsibilities.

According to Bagguley (1990), in Britain, functional flexibility is particularly common among management staff in full-time jobs. In Ireland, CERT (1988) found a very high, and growing, level of functional flexibility outside management grades, with 73% of hotels and 88% of guesthouses reporting flexible practices in non-management grades. The main area of functional flexibility involves movement between restaurant, receptionist and bar work. Since the latter two categories are predominantly female in content, it can be concluded that most functionally flexible workers in the hotel sector are women. The same observation applies, of course, also to numerically flexible workers.

CERT (1988) also found that functional flexibility is particularly concentrated among non-Grade A hotels. To a certain extent this is due to greater scope for functional specialisation in the larger Grade A establishments. However, it is also noteworthy that trade unions are strongly established in the Grade A sector, but are almost entirely absent from the lower hotel grades. Irish hotel workers are mainly organised by SIPTU, the dominant union for general workers. SIPTU has negotiation agreements with 54 Grade A hotels representing three quarters of all rooms in the Grade A sector (SIPTU 1991). However, less than half the hotel rooms in Ireland are of Grade A standard, and trade unions are almost entirely absent from the other grades, where functional and numerical flexibility are particularly prominent.

REGIONAL DISTRIBUTION OF HOTEL EMPLOYMENT

CERT (1988) also provides information on the regional distribution of hotel employment. Table 7 relates each region's share of hotel employment to its share of total employment. A ratio of greater than one in the right hand column indicates a disproportionate concentration of hotel employment in a region. The table shows that hotel employment is particularly strongly concentrated in the western half of the country. This corroborates the findings by Tansey Webster and Associates (1991), noted earlier, that tourism makes a disproportionate contribution to personal incomes in western regions. This is undoubtedly significant, in that these are the most underdeveloped regions in the country, with below-average incomes and inferior employment opportunities compared with the east of the country. Of particular relevance in this context is that, in the past, employment opportunities for women tended to be relatively poorer in the West (Gillmor 1985). Tourism, with its disproportionate tendency to provide work for women, therefore contributes in an important way to expanding work opportunities for the female labour force in this part of the country.

Table 7   *Regional distribution of hotel employment (in %)*

Region	Hotel Employment (1988)	Total Employment (1986)	Ratio
East	29.0	43.7	0.66
Midlands	5.5	8.8	0.62
Southeast	10.9	10.4	1.05
Southwest	21.8	14.7	1.48
Midwest	11.4	8.9	1.28
West	12.1	8.1	1.50
Northwest	9.4	5.4	1.74

Source: CERT (1988); *Census of Population 1986*

On the other hand, given the unskilled and frequently part-time or seasonal nature of employment in the hotel sector, it is clear that the disproportionate concentration of this employment in the West does not augur well for the prospects of closing the average income gap with the East, where high quality service employment is heavily concentrated. Hotel employment, therefore, does provide a considerable level of employment in areas where job opportunities of any kind are in short supply, but at the cost of exacerbating inter-regional income disparities.

EMPLOYMENT STRUCTURE IN OTHER TOURISM SECTORS

CERT (1991) provides detailed information on employment in a wide range of tourist-related activities outside the accommodation, catering and access transport sectors. Most of the activities in question (referred to hereinafter as the 'miscellaneous tourism' sector) relate to leisure and recreation, but some other activities, such as internal transport and other tourist support services, are included. In employment terms, the most important activities involved are golf, craft centres, car hire, language centres and historic houses. Most of these activities also cater for non-tourists (e.g. golf, theatres), so that not all the jobs involved can be attributed to tourism. However, from CERT (1987) we can estimate that around 60% of the employment concerned is tourism-dependent. This in turn amounts to almost 20% of all direct employment in tourism in Ireland in 1990.

Data on the gender make-up of employment is available for sub-sectors accounting for three quarters of all employment in the miscellaneous tourism sector. It is from these sub-sectors that Table 8 has been compiled. A comparison between Tables 6 and 8 shows that the nature of employment in the miscellaneous tourism sector is rather similar to that in the hotel sector. CERT (1991) does not provide for a "casual" employment sector, but a comparison of the two tables suggests that such jobs are mainly subsumed into the "part-time seasonal" category in the miscellaneous tourism sector. Thus, in both the hotel and miscellaneous sectors, about one half of all jobs are full-time permanent, with a further 35-40% in the seasonal/casual category.

Just over half of all the employment in the miscellaneous sector is taken by women. This participation rate, while considerably less than that for the hotel sector (66%), is nevertheless in excess of the female participation rate in services employment in general (44%), and considerably in excess of the proportion of women in the overall workforce (31%). As with the hotel

56

sector, women are under-represented in the full-time permanent category and over-represented in the part-time/seasonal categories; however, the divergences from the overall average female participation rate are not as marked as in hotel employment, where women are overwhelmingly dominant in the latter categories.

Table 8   *Structure of employment in the 'miscellaneous tourism' sector*

Employment Category	As % of all Employment	Women as % of Category
Full-time Permanent	49.9	48.0
Part-time Permanent	10.4	54.9
Full-time Seasonal	22.1	55.8
Part-time Seasonal	17.5	58.0
TOTAL	100.0	52.3

Source: Computed from data in CERT (1991)

Of the 40 separate activities covered in the CERT survey, just seven account for almost 60% of all employment. While the survey does not provide the detailed and systematic analysis of skill levels contained in the CERT (1987) survey of the hotel sector, some general indications can be gleaned from the report. Thus, only one quarter of employment in caravan/camping sites is full-time permanent, and two thirds of this is male, whereas two thirds of seasonal employment is female. Most jobs in this activity are unskilled.

By contrast, over four fifths of employment in car hire is full-time permanent, and this is mostly male. This coincides with a high level of good quality employment in sales, maintenance and administration. Golf courses portray an even division between full-time permanent and other forms of employment, but in both cases, some two thirds of employment is male. In historic houses, the bulk of employment is either part-time or seasonal, with over 80% of seasonal workers being female, compared with one half of those who are full-time permanent.

Irish language courses provide almost entirely seasonal employment, most of which provides supplementary income for teachers and those providing accommodation (both largely female). Language centres (mainly involved in teaching English to continental Europeans) provide a sizeable amount of full-time permanent employment (about two fifths of the total), although the majority of jobs are seasonal. Teachers are the main occupational group involved, and these, in turn, are mainly women.

Craft production is something of an exception to the general pattern of women primarily being involved in either seasonal or unskilled (or both) forms of employment in this sector. The great bulk (70%) of employment in this activity is full-time permanent, a high proportion is skilled (almost one third are craft workers), yet women predominate (70% of all workers).

Overall, however, it is clear that the general pattern of employment in the miscellaneous tourism sector replicates that of the hotel sector, with women disproportionately represented in the sector's workforce by comparison with other sectors outside tourism, and that this is particularly the case with part-time and seasonal work, which itself is much more common throughout the tourism industry than it is in the economy generally.

CONCLUSION

The foregoing analysis shows that tourism is a highly seasonal and unstable economic sector in which part-time and unskilled employment are common features. Around one half of employment in the industry consists of seasonal and/or part-time jobs, while only a minority of workers have received any formal training. The low proportions of full-time, permanent and skilled jobs in the industry are strongly linked to the high proportions of the workforce consisting of women: some 60% of tourism jobs (excluding transport) are taken by women—twice the proportion for the total national workforce.

Irish tourism is also characterised by high levels of gender segmentation by occupation, and high levels of numerical and functional specialisation. Flexible workers are, again, mainly female. While flexibility presents many advantages to employers, it also has attractions to many women workers, especially those with family responsibilities. Finally, tourism employment is disproportionately concentrated in the Western regions of Ireland. While this significantly enhances employment opportunities for women in these regions, it also exacerbates regional income inequalities, due to the low-pay status of much of this employment.

These findings suggest that serious questions should be raised concerning the high levels of resources currently being invested in tourism development by both the Irish government and the European Community. The relatively high proportion of poor quality employment which typifies tourism ensures that the industry holds out little hope of helping Ireland close the income gap with the EC heartland. A strong emphasis on tourism growth therefore serves to confirm Ireland's peripheral status within the Community, relying on the spending in Ireland of wealth generated in highly productive, advanced economic activities in the core regions of Europe and other parts of the developed world.

The current surge of investment in tourism is, at least in part, stimulated by the need to create jobs, of whatever quality, as a short-term response to the mounting national unemployment problem. This reflects, once again, the tendency of successive Irish governments to allow short-term considerations to crowd out the formulation of long-term perspectives (Kennedy *et.al.* 1988). As both the Telesis and Culliton Reports have argued, Ireland can only create a high-wage and high-employment economy through the development of a successful, indigenously-based manufacturing sector. It can be argued that the Irish workforce would ultimately be better served if the considerable public resources currently being directed into tourism were instead diverted to the pursuit of the latter objective.

REFERENCES

Atkinson, J (1985)
 Flexibility: planning for an uncertain future. *Manpower Policy and Practice* 1, 26-29.
Bagguley, P (1990)
 Gender and labour flexibility in hotel and catering. *Service Industries Journal* 10, 737-47.
Callender, R (1990)
 Women and work: the appearance and reality of change. *Labour Market Review* 1, 18-36.

CERT (1987)

Scope of the Tourism Industry in Ireland. Dublin: CERT.

CERT (1988)

Manpower Survey of the Irish Hotel and Catering Industry. Dublin: CERT.

CERT (1991)

A Profile of Employment in the Tourism Industry: Non Food and Accommodation. Dublin: CERT.

Deegan, J and Dineen, D (1991)

Irish Tourism Policy: employment, economic development and environmental interdependencies. Paper to Fourteenth Annual Economic Policy Conference of the Dublin Economics Workshop, Kenmare.

Dineen, D (1989)

Changing Employment Patterns in Ireland: recent trends and future prospects. Dublin: Irish National Pensions Board.

Dunne, J (1992)

World recession leads to empty rooms. *Irish Times*, 1 August.

Gillmor, D (1985)

Recent changes in the employment of women in the Republic of Ireland. *Irish Geography* 18, 69-73.

Hicks, L (1990)

Excluded women: how can this happen in the hotel world? *Services Industry Journal* 10, 348-63.

Kennedy, K, Giblin, T and McHugh, D (1988)

The Economic Development of Ireland in the Twentieth Century. London: Routledge.

Ó Cinnéide, M and Walsh, J (1991)

Tourism and regional development in Ireland. *Geographical Viewpoint* 19, 47-68.

Schoenberger, E (1988)

From Fordism to flexible accumulation: technology, competitive strategies, and international location. *Environment and Planning D* 6, 345-62.

SIPTU (1991)

The SIPTU better hotel guide. Dublin: SIPTU.

Tansey, Webster and Associates (1991)

Tourism and the Economy. Dublin: Irish Tourist Industry Confederation.

Images of Ireland in Europe:
A Tourism Perspective

BERNADETTE QUINN

INTRODUCTION

This essay examines the image of Ireland and the Irish in Europe from the perspective of the tourist industry. Drawing on the findings of a content analysis study of tourist brochures designed to promote Ireland as a tourist destination, it attempts to define the imagery created and projected by tourism promoters. The essay begins by briefly discussing the growing significance of tourism for the global and Irish economies. Attention then focuses on the concept of imagery and its significance in the promotion of holidays. The main body of the essay explores the image of Ireland and the Irish as identified through an analysis of brochures produced by a range of tourism concerns promoting Ireland as a tourist destination in continental Europe. Finally, an attempt is made to place the discussion in a broader perspective and to consider the implications for the general image of Ireland among Europeans.

TOURISM TRENDS

Travel for pleasure accounts for between two thirds and three quarters of all world travel by volume. The main international tourist flows are concentrated in Europe and intra-European arrivals account for almost half of total international travel (Withyman 1987). At a global level, the tourist industry has in recent years experienced a downturn in fortunes as widespread recession and the Gulf crisis have had serious ramifications for international travel. Long haul travel has been seriously affected as the trend has been to take more frequent, shorter holidays and to do so closer to home.

The tourist industry, which is predicted to become the world's leading industry by the turn of the century, is an economic activity of growing

Ullrich Kockel (ed), *Culture, Tourism and Development: The Case of Ireland*, Liverpool University Press 1994, 61-73.

importance in Ireland. Accounting for 6.8% of Gross National Product (GNP) and 6.3% of total employment, the industry ranks among Ireland's five leading export sectors (McEniff 1991). Ireland's share of all international arrivals and receipts in Europe is small, but is increasing following rapid growth in levels of tourist activity since the mid-1980s. Revenue from tourism receipts increased by 38% in real terms over the period 1985-1990 and 63% in current prices as tourist arrivals grew from 2.54 million to 3.1 million over the same period (McEniff 1991).

The Irish government's approach to tourism can be described as relatively interventionist. In 1988, as part of the *Programme for National Recovery*, the government set specific five year targets for the doubling of foreign arrivals, an increase in annual revenue of IR£500 million and the creation of an additional 25,000 jobs. Preliminary indications for 1991 are that despite a 2% drop in visitor levels compared with 1990, spending per head increased for the fourth year in succession.

Traditionally, for a variety of geographical, cultural and historical reasons, the USA and the UK have formed the main source markets for the industry. Great Britain remains the leading source market, accounting for 48% of all arrivals in 1990 (McEniff 1991). However, perhaps the most notable feature of tourist activity in recent years has been the spectacular increase in the number of arrivals from mainland Europe. Increasingly, the industry is looking upon Europe as a major growth region.

IMAGERY IN TOURISM

For those involved in the tourist industry, the concept of imagery holds particular significance. Purchasing a holiday differs from other consumer purchases in two main respects.

First, the potential holiday maker is unable to sample a wide range of alternative products in order to express a preference before making the final purchase i.e. before booking the holiday. The selection of a holiday, for the most part, is not based on past experience or actual knowledge of the destinations under consideration, but on the consumers' perceptions of the available choices. Potential tourists require information about destinations before they can make a choice and herein lie the promotion opportunities for the tourist industry. Tourism promoters create and project images to persuade the targeted consumer that the destination in question is the most suitable holiday option, and the most likely to fulfil holiday desires. The second significant factor distinguishing tourism products from other consumer products is their highly substitutable nature. In the early stages of the decision—making process the consumer is faced with a vast array of options. In such circumstances, effective image projection attains even greater significance.

Any discussion focusing on the projection of destination images for the purpose of attracting holiday makers must acknowledge the fact that the images people hold of regions cannot be neatly and exclusively classified into 'tourist images', 'sporting images', 'political images', and so on. Images are shaped by a wide variety of sources, ranging from personal experience and 'second-hand' experiences of friends and acquaintants, to general exposure to media reports and other documented sources. Thus, those promoting regions as tourist destinations cannot realistically expect to control the sources of image formation, nor the manner in which targeted consumers perceive projected images. In fact, certain studies (Nolan 1976; Price Waterhouse 1987) have suggested that 'official' national tourist board promotional literature tends to be relatively insignificant in shaping general images of tourist destinations. Irrespective of the research conducted to assess the effectiveness of this and other types of literature, the significance of destination images in the holiday decision-making process is recognised in the tourism literature (Mayo 1973; Hunt 1975; Smith 1983), and is strongly reflected in the vast sums of money spent on the promotion of holidays by the tourist industry each year.

THE SURVEY

Holiday brochures are a fundamental means of promoting destination images, and this study examines tourist brochures produced to promote Ireland as a tourist destination in mainland European markets by Bord Fáilte (the Irish Tourist Board), Irish tourism companies and European tour operators. The Irish tourism companies selected for the study are Aer Lingus, the national airline, and Irish Ferries, a shipping company. Most of the tour operators included in the survey are French, although one is German (Dertour), one Italian (I Viaggi del Ventaglio), and one Swiss (Internautic Cruise Service). With respect to methodology, the content analysis involves what can be termed a literal and an interpretive analysis of brochure material. At the outset, the thematic features appearing in the brochures were identified, and then quantified in terms of frequency of occurrence, the amount of space accorded to expression, and the intensity of manifestation. The visual and verbal presentations were then examined more rigorously, and the intricate system of identified meanings analysed.

In spite of the varying origins of brochures—domestic and foreign, commercial and non-commercial—there was remarkable similarity in the projection of a number of essentially broad and intangible concepts, namely: attractive scenery and an unspoiled environment; friendly people and a relaxed pace of life; a wealth of cultural heritage; and an impressive array of available sporting opportunities.

The most overwhelming promotional message is that Ireland is a world apart from modern society (from where, it is assumed, visiting tourists come) and offers vast open spaces of unspoilt 'genuine' landscapes, inducing complete relaxation and the chance to rediscover old world values. From the very outset, the Bord Fáilte brochures establish the natural environment as being the essential basis from which other elements derive their appeal. This in itself cannot be regarded as a particularly surprising finding, nor can it be attributed to any features unique to the Irish tourist product. The promotion of the natural environment is a basic component of any tourist product. Dilley (1989) illustrated this in his analysis of 21 national tourist board brochures by determining that landscape themes accounted, on average, for 32% of all themes covered. The present study found 39% of Bord Fáilte brochure space to be devoted to the visual projection of the landscape theme. All commercial brochures analysed here, both Irish and foreign produced, accord similar significance to the promotion of Ireland primarily as a green and unspoilt destination.

Not only has the Ireland of the tourist brochures managed to preserve its countryside in an unspoilt state (unlike, by implication, many of its European counterparts), it has also succeeded in preserving the traditional fabric of society. This concept is most strikingly communicated in the commercial brochures where settings frequently comprise whitewashed cottages with thatched roofs, stone walls, old farming implements and rakes of turf. The visual presentation of architecture in the brochures was categorised as either 'vernacular' or 'spectacular': the former referring to elements of the cultural landscape closely associated with the 'common folk' of Ireland (e.g., thatched cottages and stone walls); the latter alluding to connotations of wealth and grandeur (e.g., castles and mansions). Cultural artefacts of a vernacular nature dominated to an overwhelming extent in commercial brochures. In Bord Fáilte brochures, the balance was slightly in favour of spectacular architecture.

Central to the image projected of any society is the portrayal of people themselves. The analysis categorised the visual presentation of people under four headings: welcoming; easy-going; modern; and in traditional dress. Characters presented throughout the pages of the Bord Fáilte brochures most frequently communicate the notion of friendliness and warmth. Typically depicted in the service setting, aspiring tourists are assured that they will be like a personal 'friend of the family' whose hosts will be very sad to see them leave.

Leafing through the Irish Ferries and Aer Lingus brochures, the tourist is given a very clear image of Irish people. The scene for Irish Ferries' first package option—'Leisurely Ireland'—is set by a large photograph depicting two men attired in traditional dark clothing, boots and cap, in relaxed conversation by the roadside. Set in a presumably remote, undulating rural landscape, uninhabited except by some cattle in the distance, the photograph portrays a rurality far removed from any association with the stress of modern living. One man, carrying a walking stick, is travelling on foot, while his companion leans against an old black bicycle. The relaxed stance of both men indicates that the frenzied rush of city life is completely alien to this part of the world, with neither appearing to have any purpose likely to distract them from their leisurely conversation.

Characters like this, portrayed in what can be immediately identified as an easy-going stance, and those obviously attired in traditional dress dominate to an overwhelming extent throughout the brochures. The Aer Lingus brochures targeted at the Danish and Belgian markets carry, on the first double page, an illustration depicting an elderly man accompanied by his dog, leading a trail of donkeys laden down with turf along a bog road. Included because of its presumed appeal for a predominantly urbanised readership, it is distinctive in its portrayal of an old-fashioned, stereotypical Irish native: a middle aged/elderly man, dressed in dark clothing, complete with hob—nailed boots and the requisite cap and stick.

Any semblance of 'modern life', instantly familiar to the predominantly urbanised Europeans targeted by the brochures is carefully disguised. The depiction of 'modern' people as determined by their mode of dress and general appearance is a rare occurrence. This selective presentation of people is entirely in keeping with the almost exclusive projection of rural settings. Just less than 10% of scenes depicted in the Bord Fáilte brochures are urban settings. The notion of towns/cities does not exist to any significant extent in the commercial brochures. Although introduced as a city populated by one million inhabitants, Dublin is portrayed as being unspoiled by the detrimental effects of urbanisation. The overall impression created is that Dublin is distinguished by a relaxed pace of life which sets it apart from other cities. One of the main attractions highlighted is the easy access it offers to the surrounding countryside.

The concept of Ireland as a society where traditions and old world values have remained intact is further communicated in the projection of the country as an island steeped in the events and happenings of the past, to such an extent that historic legacies remain evident and widespread to the present day. The choice of photographs in the Bord Fáilte brochures—the Rock of Cashel, Glendalough, Celtic crosses—simultaneously establish the strong religious element which dominates Ireland's past, and the majestic and spectacular nature of Irish history. Evidence of a rich and cultural past can be found in the country houses and castles throughout the country, many of which are now hotels. All brochures emphasise this accommodation sector, inviting tourists to enjoy a stay in luxurious and romanticised settings, reviving the gracious customs of life in Ireland of old. In so doing, the brochures very clearly define the targeted market as being up-market, relatively affluent, and from higher socio-economic groups.

As already discussed, the attractiveness of the natural environment is the basis of the appeal Ireland offers tourists, and this is aptly demonstrated in the promotion of activities tourists can expect to enjoy while holidaying here. Ireland is projected as the ideal location for outdoor sporting activities. It is described as a 'golfer's paradise' and 'a fisherman's paradise'. Opportunities for cruising, sailing, hiking, cycling and horse riding abound. The 'rediscovery of nature' concept underlies the projection of Ireland as an active holiday location. The natural environment offers a certain authenticity, the opportunity 'to get away from it all', to escape from the monotonous routine imposed by exterior responsibilities and society, and to live life to the full. Holidays in Ireland are presented as being characterised by endless space and unlimited time, and holiday-makers exist to the rhythms of nature alone. This 'rediscovery of nature' theme also signifies the restoration of self, a certain revitalisation brought about by intimate contact with elements of nature.

The task of the tourism promoter then is, to persuade potential tourists of the exceptional desirability of one particular destination as opposed to any other, to such an extent as to effect a decision to purchase. Selling a tourist destination involves creating an image of almost dream-like proportions. As already discussed, for the tourist in the process of choosing a destination, the validity of this image cannot normally be ascertained given the nature of the holiday decision-making process. It will, however, be tested while the tourist is holidaying at the destination, and the decision whether to return in future will greatly depend on the extent to which pre-conceived aspirations are fulfilled.

THE 'REAL' IRELAND

Essentially, tourism promoters agree that Ireland is a holiday destination for the more discerning, well educated and relatively affluent European, who is looking for a relaxing, interesting and comfortable holiday experience. This, it is suggested, represents the industry's view of demand.

To fulfil the perceived needs of this demand the industry has carefully and selectively moulded the product to create the image components that have been described. This 'manufactured image' is then widely promoted in Europe as the 'real' Ireland, and those coming into contact with the brochures, bill board posters, promotional videos, media articles and other representations selling this image of the country are influenced to varying degrees.

While there may be widespread recognition of the persuasive nature of tourism advertising, and thus the probability that images are selective and even exaggerated, the promotional messages portrayed will impact, in some capacity, on those coming in contact with, and interpreting, the images. It is of interest, in this respect, to explore the use of imagery to promote Ireland as a tourist destination among Europeans in the broader context of image formation in general. As briefly discussed at an earlier point in this essay, the images people hold of places cannot be neatly packaged in terms of direct associations, but rather are shaped by a disparate variety of unlimited sources. Thus the projection of place images for tourism marketing purposes cannot be explored and assessed solely within the domain of tourist activity.

Arguably, the most obvious promotional strategy to question in the context of broader image implications is the very deliberate exaggeration of the extent to which traditional modes of life, as epitomised in modes of dress, transport and housing, predominate. Most evident in the commercial brochures, the appropriateness of this approach is surely questionable not only in terms of the country's image in other areas of economic and cultural activity but in the context of effective destination marketing. The overly dramatised projection of old-fashionedness is incongruous with the simultaneously projected image of Ireland as a tourist destination offering lively and varied holiday activities. It also seems inconsistent with the concept of Ireland as a culturally stimulating destination.

There is little doubt that the atmosphere of 'quaintness' effectively communicated in the Bord Fáilte brochures acts as an appealing force. Located on the periphery of Europe with a low population density and a reputation for a relatively pollution free environment, Ireland has much to offer the tourist seeking authenticity in the lifestyle of others, or an experiential holiday experience, to use Cohen's terminology (Cohen 1979). However, the over-exaggerated portrayal of Ireland as a country totally out of step with the pace of modern life, as evidenced in commercial brochures, requires closer assessment. Here the 'real' Ireland is equated with 'the gay sound of beer tankards clinking in the pubs' where 'life flows along to the rhythms of nature'. Beyond the immediate realm of tourist activity, such an image exists in direct opposition to that projected by alternative economic concerns as they attempt to stress the advanced nature of Irish society. Ultimately, the projection of contradictory images implies a degree of falsehood, and consequently, an inevitable lack of faith in the projected images.

There exists the challenge of creating a balanced image, distinctive in appeal yet avoiding over-dramatisation. A longitudinal analysis of Bord Fáilte's European brochures from 1970s to the present aptly demonstrates how the national tourist board has modified the 'official' projection of Ireland. Early brochures present an Ireland where tourists can 'forget the stressful hustle and bustle (of city life)', and relax and 'recharge their batteries', and where donkeys and sheep are the only road users. While such references no longer play the same prominent role in Bord Fáilte's promotional vocabulary, the brochure analysis concludes that this approach continues to dominate among commercial operators.

It is interesting to place the study's findings in the context of research conducted on tourists' pre- and post-visit conceptions of Ireland. From the European perspective, market research conducted by Bord Fáilte (1985) and the Irish Tourist Industry Confederation (ITIC) (1989) in the West German, French and Italian markets demonstrates that above all, Ireland inspires an image of beautiful scenery and an unspoiled environment. However, this appears to be the only well defined positive image that Ireland consistently projects. Market research has repeatedly identified a reaction of boredom among the pre- and post-visit impressions of continental Europeans. Surveys record references to Ireland as 'boring', 'all nature and nothing else', 'few possibilities to visit museums and learn about historical and cultural aspects', and 'a lack of activities and lack of entertainment' (Bord Fáilte 1985). Dublin has more recently been described as an 'old and dull place' and 'a boring city' (ITIC 1989).

A comparative analysis of brochures produced by the Scottish Tourist Board (STB) for similar European markets reveals the promotion of a virtually identical tourist product. The STB portrays Scotland as 'Europe's last great wilderness', and emphasises the beauty of an unspoilt natural environment. In addition to this, however, it projects Scotland as offering 'the energy and vitality of the city' and devotes relatively greater attention to promoting towns and cities as places worth visiting. Survey findings from 1985 (Bord Fáilte) reveal that among an Italian sample, Scotland enjoyed a sharp image identified through Edinburgh and the Highlands. In contrast to this, Ireland had merely imprinted an image of 'green and rainy landscapes'.

It can be argued that the images of Ireland projected in the brochures do little to improve these negative images. The emphasis on nature and rurality is overwhelming, and efforts to disguise the existence of any form of extended urban society in Ireland is blatant. Night-time entertainment options, for example, are virtually absent in the Bord Fáilte brochures. It seems ironic, given Dublin's literary and cultural heritage, that references to museums, galleries and theatres associated with the city's famous writers are virtually non-existent. Instead the brochures focus almost exclusively on traditional pub life. Similarly, although cultural heritage is a prominent theme throughout the brochures with the portrayal of architectural styles and allusions to traditional livelihood, it is not projected as being easily accessible to the tourist, who is, in all likelihood, a first time visitor. The characteristically 'soft-sell' promotional approach adopted gives the impression that an atmosphere of olden days pervades the entire country, yet rarely are specific cultural attractions such as the Newgrange site or Bunratty Folk Park referred to.

A fundamental problem for the Irish tourist industry in its attempt to promote Ireland in Europe has traditionally been a very real lack of knowledge and serious misconceptions about the country. Potential visitor surveys conducted by Bord Fáilte in continental European markets have identified 'war/violence' as one of the images most commonly held in almost all markets surveyed. Generally speaking, such images are more prominent among those who had never visited Ireland. While Bord Fáilte claims that the acute lack of awareness of Ireland prevalent in continental markets in the mid 1970s has now been partially overcome, the extent to which this is the case is difficult to determine. A report by the Irish Tourist

Industry Confederation (1989), investigating the image of Ireland abroad, prompted a Bord Fáilte spokesperson to comment that the survey highlighted the fact that people abroad did not know enough about Ireland. In 1986, a survey by the Commission of the European Communities (1987a) showed that Ireland was the EC country least visited by people from other member states. For most Europeans, Ireland remains a country yet to be discovered; only 6% had visited the country in 1986.

CONCLUSION

Following the implementation of the Single European Act in 1993, it can be expected that increased integration within Europe will raise awareness about Ireland in the broad sense, and that this will have implications for the tourist industry. Involving the movement of people across international boundaries, tourism's role in stimulating awareness of other peoples and promoting cultural integration is obviously of great significance.

However, as in other areas of economic activity, there is concern that a Single European Market may eventually have detrimental impacts on the industry. Being the only EC country not joined to mainland Europe after the completion of the Channel Tunnel, a further reinforcement of Ireland's peripherality on the edge of Europe is expected. For the tourist industry, in common with other economic sectors attempting to trade with European countries, the improved efficiency of transport networks will be crucial and travel costs will be a major factor tourism operators will have to overcome.

For the image creators, increased European integration represents both an opportunity to strengthen Ireland's appeal as a holiday destination for Europeans, and a challenge to the standardised and rather narrowly defined projected messages which tend to characterise the promotional approach. In the first instance, it is arguable that an opportunity exists for the industry to utilise Ireland's peripheral location as an asset to be capitalised upon. Geographically separate from the remainder of Europe, its distinctiveness and individuality as a European destination for Europeans becomes more marketable. The notion that Ireland is a place "to get away from it all" can now be justifiably claimed to a greater extent.

As arrivals from mainland Europe continue to increase, the challenge of raising repeat visitation levels becomes an issue for the industry to address. Achieving this requires more creativity in projecting a promotional approach which should be based on a sharply defined, broader range of appeals. Furthermore, as Europeans' awareness of Ireland and the Irish continues to grow because of increasingly integrated activities in all spheres, the continued effectiveness of images based more on fiction than on fact will become for the tourist industry, an issue of concern.

The progressively upward growth trends in visitor arrivals from continental Europe would seem to indicate that the image of Ireland and the Irish created by the tourist industry is proving successful. I would support this to the extent that the indisputable basis of the Irish tourism product is the appeal offered by its natural environment. However, I would strongly argue that the majority of tourism promoters have yet to take full advantage of the potential Ireland offers to visitors. Adopting the approach of selling Ireland as a predominantly old-fashioned society out of step with modern life elsewhere in Europe is inefficient for two main reasons. First, for the country as a whole it is quite simply untrue, and notwithstanding the already accepted persuasive nature of tourism promotion, it is at best unhelpful and at worst potentially detrimental to Ireland's image in other sectors of economic, political and cultural activity. From the viewpoint of market demand, research has clearly and repeatedly shown that Europeans represent a sophisticated clientele whose holiday expectations will not be fulfilled by a singular emphasis on Ireland's rurality. Finally, in purely speculative fashion, from the perspective of the Irish themselves, the stereotypical projection of Irish people in the brochures cannot be welcomed by today's prominently urbanised population.

REFERENCES

1.   **Survey of travel brochures**

Bord Fáilte brochures for European markets:
  Belgium, Denmark, Finland, France, Italy, Netherlands, Norway, Sweden, Switzerland, West Germany
Brochures of commercial companies for European markets:
  IRISH FERRIES—*France, Italy, Netherlands, Scandinavia, West Germany*
  AER LINGUS—*Belgium, Denmark, Finland, France, Netherlands*

Non-specialist foreign produced brochures:
Republique Tours, Tourmonde, Fram Voyages, Air Vacances
Specialist foreign produced brochures:
Dertour, Internautic Cruise Service, Republique Tours, I Viaggi del Ventaglio

2. Secondary literature

Bord Fáilte (1985)
We've been to Ireland! A report on a survey of visitor impressions. Research and Development Department (unpublished).
Bord Fáilte (1988)
Survey of Travellers 1987: overseas visitors. Research and Marketing Planning Department (unpublished).
Cohen, E (1979)
A phenomenology of tourist experiences. *Sociology* 13, 179-202.
Commission of the European Communities (1987a)
Europeans and their Holidays 1986. Luxembourg: Official Publications.
Commission of the European Communities (1987b)
The European Community and Tourism. European File 9.
Dilley, R (1986)
Tourist brochures and tourist images. *Canadian Geographer* 31(3), 19-23.
Dyer, G (1982)
Advertising as Communication. London: Methuen.
Hunt, J (1975)
Image as a factor in tourism development. *Journal of Travel Research* 13(3), 1-7.
Irish Times (1989) 24 February.
Irish Tourist Industry Confederation (1989)
Doubling Irish Tourism: a market-led strategy. Dublin: ITIC.
Mayo, E (1973)
Regional images and regional travel behaviour. Research for changing travel patterns: interpretation and utilization. *Proceedings of the Travel Research Association Fourth Annual Conference, August 12-15, 1973,* 211-18.
McEniff, J (1991)
Republic of Ireland. *International Tourism Reports* 4.

Nolan, S (1976)
Tourists' use and evaluation of travel information sources: summary and conclusions. *Journal of Travel Research* 14, 6-8.

Quinn, B (1989)
Imagery in Tourism Promotion: a case study of Ireland as a tourist destination in continental Europe. Maynooth: St Patricks College, unpublished MA thesis.

Smith, S (1983)
Recreation Geography. New York: Longman.

Withyman, M (1987)
Destination Europe—survey of European countries as destinations. Travel and Tourism Analyst. London: EIU.

Price Waterhouse (1987)
Improving the Performance of Irish Tourism. Dublin: Stationery Office.

Part 2

Issues in Heritage and Tourism

Conflicts In Heritage and Tourism

PATRICK DUFFY

INTRODUCTION

For the purposes of discussion, I am defining heritage in broad terms to incorporate both natural and cultural heritage. Certainly heritage in this sense has been linked with the earliest phase of rich upper class tourists clamouring to gaze in awe at the terrible wonder of Snowdonia or Killarney in the late eighteenth century, or to idly speculate on the function of great monuments like Stonehenge or the Rock of Cashel. Heritage has always been one of the principal engines that has kept the wheels of tourism turning.

What else should tourists do but waste time on idle speculation and admiration: sightseeing, scenery, and touring have remained the corner-stones of the industry for two hundred years. As Fintan O'Toole (1993) has said, 'tourism is a useless endeavour, an immense amount of activity undertaken for no palpable gain' (to the tourist, that is). And this perception of tourism obviously has repercussions on the manner in which heritage, as a potential tourism resource, is exploited. Even the seemingly purposeful activity holidays of the past twenty years do not change this viewpoint.

From the coming of mass tourism in the thirties, especially in America, there has been a determined and dedicated exploitation of heritage as a tourism resource. The Blue Ridge Parkway, developed in the 1950s, must ring many bells for us:

Driving along it is a beautiful and exhilarating experience... Control over the cultural landscape has been a matter of instruction and public relations. The new culture of tourism instructed tourists in how to appreciate nature from the car; farm agents, social workers, doctors, and the Parkway's local newsletter, the *Mileposts*, coaxed destitute Appalachian peoples into modern national life. In the early 1960s, 'Hillbilly Shows' were performed for tourists on the edges of the road. Men in crooked hats and women in long, flowered dresses with

Ullrich Kockel (ed), *Culture, Tourism and Development: The Case of Ireland*, Liverpool University Press 1994, 77-86.

holes in them played music and demonstrated whisky stills and other putative trappings of a culture in dissolution... (Wilson 1992).

Tourism in Ireland has exploited Irish heritage from the outset. There was a kind of instinctive exploitation of the thatched cottage image in response mainly to American ethnic tourism. But in the past decade, at least, it looks like the full might of the industry is coming to bear on heritage.

The Operational Programme for Tourism, Bord Fáilte's development of storyline themes, the financial support for National Heritage Areas and environmentally sensitive areas, all reflect a systematic and planned exploitation which can be justifiably labelled the heritage industry.

The heritage and tourism debate has at its simplest two opposing viewpoints which derive from two fundamental philosophical attitudes to the meaning of heritage: that it has a utilitarian (or economic) value to society on one hand, or that it is intrinsically valuable on the other. In terms of natural heritage or cultural heritage, for example, bogs or vernacular buildings should be conserved because of their significance for communities and landscapes.

This dichotomy of attitudes is uncannily repeated in every discussion of heritage and tourism, and in most of the recent controversies around the country. And the mutually exclusive approach of the two points of view lends some bitterness to the debate. One side argues for development and conservation for the sake of jobs, the other for conservation for its own sake. So ultimately what we are looking at are the credentials of the heritage industry. These have been brought into sharp and fairly sudden focus by the greatly enhanced European Structural Funds, because these funds, through the operational national programmes, have inextricably welded tourism and heritage together in both the popular mind and in many developments and proposals for development schemes around the country.

ORIGINS OF THE HERITAGE MOVEMENT

Interest in cultural heritage in Ireland up until recently was largely confined to a small minority, popularly represented by local historical societies and small groups with interests in folklore and local traditions. The Irish Georgian Society and An Taisce for a long time had a very limited membership; indeed the limited popular appeal of their interests is reflected in the labels 'belted earls' and 'the blue rinse brigade' which were disparagingly attached to them by some canny politicians in the seventies. Their interests were generally elitist/exclusivist, not too concerned with the raising of popular consciousness—or, if they were, they did not have the know-how to preach to the masses. Indeed, the conservation/heritage movement today is still trying to counter the negative legacy of these earlier days.

In the sixties and into the seventies, there was a slowly growing interest in the landscape heritage. Events like the discovery of the Viking settlement at Wood Quay and other activities in Dublin gave a kick start to the cultural conservation movement and were measures of rising interest among the community at large. But in general, interest in heritage in Ireland is probably at a comparatively low level still, in spite of the fact that one of Ireland's greatest resources is its environmental heritage. 'Apathy' would best summarise popular attitudes: insensitive developments, untidiness, litter, uglification and destruction of archaeological legacy, are all testimony to apathy and ignorance. I suspect that the high profile of some heritage items is more a reflection of the articulateness of the lobby than of widespread interest in them.

I think what we are seeing today is an interest that is largely generated by utilitarian motives in response to the promise of large amounts of outside money, and in response to the potential earning capacity of heritage as an industry. The heritage industry has arrived, and heritage or scenery is a commodity that can be sold to tourists!

So, what we probably have to evaluate at this stage is the burgeoning heritage industry in Ireland, and the nature of developments that have taken place in response to it. Fintan O'Toole, journalist, has put his finger on the economic pulse beating in the heritage industry: heritage is a windfall which can be turned to account—the (Blarney) stone is just a bit of rock, the mud (of Ballyporeen) is just a piece of ground, and heritage becomes the magic ingredient which turns it into what economists call an 'added value product' (O'Toole 1991). Today, the new-found interest in heritage embraces dozens of examples of groups all over Ireland, which have been set up in the last few years involved in such things as restoring seventeenth century town houses and medieval castles, or building replicas of medieval or later settlements, or collecting folklore or genealogical archives.

The heritage movement may, therefore, have suspect origins, though undoubtedly many people and communities who have discovered their heritage in response to some exogenous fund or grant have quite genuine attitudes towards it. This outside impetus, however, may contain the seeds of concern about the direction being taken by the heritage movement, because much of the funding results in a tourism-driven approach to heritage, developing projects which might have appeal or potential in the tourism industry, rather than ones that have been motivated by any great indigenous interest in heritage. And what could be more counter-productive or demoralising from the point of view of encouraging indigenous interest in distinctive local cultural or natural heritage than developing it as a means of squeezing more 'bucks' or Deutsche Marks out of people engaged in the leisurely and 'useless' endeavour of tourism? The latest round of the Structural Funds provided millions of pounds for tourism-related heritage projects, most dramatically illustrated in the state-sponsored development of controversial interpretative centres throughout the country (Meldon 1992).

It is not difficult to see how things have gone this way; some of the characteristics which help to keep the wheels of tourism turning are the very central elements of our landscape heritage. There are many unique aspects to Ireland's landscape and settlement—it is predominantly rural, agricultural and, therefore, contrasts directly with the urban-industrial cultures of the European core. Because the Irish agricultural economy has been relatively underdeveloped for so long, landscape and settlement have been comparatively unchanged in a European context. Unlike, for example, the Netherlands or South East England, much of the Irish landscape is untouched, and remains, today, one of the most authentic countrysides in Europe.

However, the very poverty of the country has called for economic development, especially in its rural regions. Tourism has always been seen in Ireland as an important source of foreign earnings and increasingly as an opportunity for an alternative income or income supplement for rural communities. It is in this context that the Structural Funds are increasingly important in offering incentives for rural heritage tourism. The ultimate aim of the industry is to match Ireland's heritage and landscape opportunities with Europe's tourist and leisure needs. And heritage lies at the core of Ireland's tourist potential: recent surveys have shown, for example, that two thirds of European tourists in Ireland participate in historic visits and visits to stately homes and gardens. A large majority of tourists opted to come to Ireland to experience its heritage (Ó Cinnéide 1991), so the industry aims to create "a strong 'brand image' of Ireland as a quality heritage destination, with unique heritage attractions" (Bord Fáilte 1992).

HERITAGE TOURISM

So what we are talking about is the potential for tourism and the tourism industry to transform the landscape and its natural and cultural heritage, and whether this is a good or bad thing, and how much should it be controlled?

The negative side of a tourism-driven approach to heritage is that, through the *Operational Programme for Tourism*, a very large amount of money became available in a short period of time to undertake heritage-type developments. Indeed, under the European Structural Funds it appears that the only way to get money for heritage projects was if they were tourist-related. Many projects were rushed into, generating much opposition and controversy and, for whatever reason, most of the money was given to new developments/constructions with heritage themes, rather than conservation of existing heritage items. There are a great many examples of those around the country. Interestingly, in the case of the interpretative centres, the on-going controversies epitomise the nature of the conflicts in heritage-related tourism: one side supports the projects for economic and social reasons (i.e. jobs, which will certainly follow to a greater or lesser extent), and the other side opposes them for cultural or ecological reasons (damage to the integrity of the cultural or natural heritage). One side is interested in the development of heritage for tourism—not for any intrinsic value which heritage has for the community, or its identity, and probably without much reference to the sustainability of the product. The other side wants conservation and protection of the heritage, and in its extreme expression is opposed to development. Indeed, the words of the economist J.K. Galbraith—"a conservationist is a man who concerns himself with the beauties of nature in roughly inverse proportion to the number of people who can enjoy them"—might justifiably be aimed at some attitudes in recent developments in Ireland.

Some projects have been largely shaped by the needs of tourism—again, this would include interpretative-type projects, such as replica heritage buildings and heritage parks which aim at a wide and varied tourist market, and try to entertain as well as educate. In general, one could say that most aspects of settlement and landscape morphology represent important chapters in the history of local areas, ingredients which give every parish and community its particular stamp of identity. Emphasis on tourism-potential sees heritage in a more utilitarian light, so that the settlement or artifact or site is often made to adapt to the needs of the visitor rather than reflect the integrity of the heritage. Tourism is mainly about holidays, entertainment and having fun. For the average tourist, heritage is a recreational, not a serious interest, and this reality must shape the way that tourism exploits heritage—back to the 'useless endeavour' syndrome!

Part of the industrialisation of heritage, in pursuit of the tourist, is the development of interpretation at its present sophisticated level. Certainly it is good that people and communities should understand their environment and its heritage, be informed and educated about its significance, on the basis that understanding through education (interpretation, if you like) will help people to appreciate, respect and ultimately preserve what they have inherited from the past. Heritage interpretation is one facet of this process. John Feehan speaks eloquently about this:

> There is the need for a blossoming of community awareness of the nature and importance of landscape heritage...to rekindle and nurture its own sense of the value of the multitude of features that define it... for enrichment of local community understanding of landscape heritage... (Feehan 1992).

The problem is perhaps that the interpretation of the heritage, and so the use of the heritage, becomes 'industrialised'. It comes to be seen as part of the tourism sector—something for the tourist—as opposed to being a crucial part of the community's own distinctive identity. And once it becomes part of tourism, it tends to become a product with little beyond a commercial marketable value. F.H.A. Aalen, in concluding a recent essay on heritage and the need to understand and conserve, felt obliged to give it an economic sweetener: "conservation makes commercial sense. Abundant evidence shows that the traditional countryside is a substantial economic asset because of its visual and historical attraction for tourists..." (Aalen 1989).

Emphasis on 'marketing the product' or 'product effectiveness' may lead to oversimplification, or worse, to the bogus history which the 'industrialisation' of heritage encourages, represented, for example, by the American consultant who, when investigating the tourist potential of Carrickfergus Castle, concluded that the place was 'built all wrong'. Hewison, commenting on what he characterised as the Laura-Ashley-isation of England, has illustrated the ultimate expression of the heritage industry aimed at entertaining the visitor: an anaesthetised version of the past, in which the exhibits are often more real than the reality they seek to recall (Hewison 1987). It has been said that so developed is the heritage industry in many parts of the world, that urban conceptions of wilderness nowadays subsume the existence of picnic tables, toilets, washrooms and the like—pleasant surroundings for recreation and having fun. The Wigan Pier development in Lancashire was a response to financial incentives and opportunities offered by a variety of agencies from Brussels under advice by consultants in tourism; similar developments have occurred with the aid of European Social Fund (ESF) monies in Ireland.

Stephen Smith has a more optimistic view: 'tourism can be a positive force for the preservation of significant local sites, festivals and cultural activities' (Smith 1989). Heritage conservation can be seen as a beneficial effect of tourist interest; many places and sites would continue to moulder away were it not for the spur of tourism. And projects to interpret the landscape and heritage must be better than letting them languish unknown and unappreciated. Indeed, rural 'farm tourism' may be exploiting the landscape heritage in a more environmentally friendly and sustainable way for rural communities than destroying the landscape by pouring fertilisers on it indefinitely! In the end, perhaps, the best attitude may be that the negative/utilitarian exploitation of heritage can be turned to good effect in the long term; in the short term, as Feehan (1992) says, 'the best hope for conservation of environmental heritage may be that it is viewed as a product', so that this, at least, will ultimately raise awareness of its intrinsic value to our indigenous community.

CONCLUSION

In conclusion, one might tentatively suggest an emerging structure in the relationship between heritage and tourism in Ireland. The diagram on the following page (Figure 8) highlights differences in priorities in Heritage Conservation, on the one hand, and Heritage Tourism on the other.

These differences have been brought to the fore by the availability of finances and have resulted in conflicts on the ground between competing interests. The large increase in European Structural Funds, especially, has been particularly significant for elements of the tourism industry because of its commitment to employment and development at local and regional level, while the actual amount of money available for straightforward heritage conservation has been much less. The public sector structure of the conservation agencies, whose priorities are not as commercial or development-oriented as the private sector's and whose bureaucracies suffer from a certain amount of inertia, are not as adept at jumping on the 'gravy train' of Euro-funds as the more tourism-driven private sector organisations—or even the public sector tourist boards. Local voluntary and community groups have also been more successful at obtaining grants for tourist-driven heritage projects than have the voluntary agencies in the Conservation Movement, such as An Taisce, whose principal aim is conservation and protection regardless of commercial considerations.

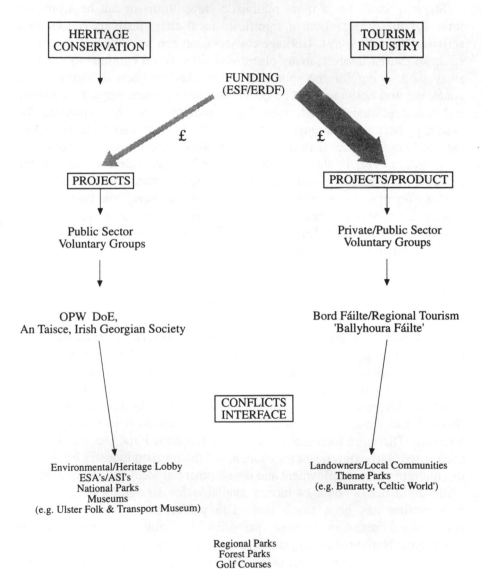

Figure 8   *Conflicts in heritage and tourism*

Both of these broad interests meet in the landscape. Many of the conservation programmes undertaken by the state agencies are quite acceptable to the tourism industry and obviously expand the infrastructure and opportunities available for the industry. National Parks, for example, are good examples of public sector developments which are popular with visitors. Heritage projects, such as folk museums or parks are also popular and successful, while remaining intrinsically educational and cultural in intent. But there are many examples of conflicts which reflect the differing priorities of tourism as an industry and heritage as a conservation policy. Interpretative centres, for example, which have been established by the Office of Public Works with some European funding, might be seen to represent attempts by the state to cash-in on its heritage and move some way to 'marketing the product' in tourism terms. This has caused problems for the conservation lobby. Theme parks, such as 'Celt World' in Tramore, are more unashamedly commercial in their intent. The rash of golf courses and hotels in eighteenth-century houses and parklands falls into the same category, with the heritage of landscape and buildings in this case being minimally conserved and maximally exploited for commercial gain. The battleground for these ideological differences is frequently found in the farms and countrysides of local communities. Here private landowners and individuals in communities often resent attempts by planners and state agencies (supported by articulate local and national lobbies) to implement policies of heritage protection and conservation, which are perceived as restricting local opportunities to avail of financial incentives for heritage tourism development.

REFERENCES

Aalen, F (1989)
Imprint of the past. In Gillmor, D (ed), *The Irish Countryside. Landscape, Wildlife, People*. Dublin: Wolfhound.
Bord Fáilte (1992)
Heritage and Tourism. Second conference on the development of heritage attractions in Ireland. Dublin: Bord Fáilte.

Feehan, J (1992)

Farm tourism. In Bord Fáilte, *Heritage and Tourism. Second conference on the development of heritage attractions in Ireland*. Dublin: Bord Fáilte, 1-2.

Hewison, R (1987)

The Heritage Industry. London: Methuen.

Meldon, J (1992)

Structural Funds and the Environment: problems and prospects. Dublin: An Taisce, 19-26.

Ó Cinnéide, M and Walsh, J (1991)

Tourism and regional development in Ireland. *Geographical Viewpoint* 19, 47-68.

O'Toole, F (1991)

Looking backwards to look forwards. *The Irish Times*, 8 June.

O'Toole, F (1993)

When Mullaghmore becomes more than just a 'hungry hill'. *The Irish Times*, 17 February.

Smith, S (1989)

Tourism Analysis: a handbook. London: Longhams.

Wilson, A (1992)

The Culture of Nature. North American landscape from Disney to Exxon Valdez. Oxford: Blackwell.

Towards Sustainability: Implications for Tourism

JEANNE MELDON

INTRODUCTION

The tourism industry depends on the environment. If the quality of the environment is to be maintained and enhanced while at the same time tourist spending is to be increased, the industry has to be developed in accordance with the principles of sustainable development. But what exactly is meant by sustainable development? Before talking about tourism in particular I want to spend a few moments examining this issue in the context of recent EC policy, since the growth and development of the tourism industry in this country are very much dependent on initiatives from Europe and in particular the structural funds, of which more later. The term sustainable development really came to prominence with the Brundtland Report (Brundtland 1987), which defined it as development strategies meeting contemporary needs without jeopardising the opportunities of future generations to satisfy their own needs.

This principle has become the cornerstone of EC environmental policy and underlies the *Fifth Action Programme on the Environment*, recently adopted by the Council of Ministers. The original Treaty of Rome did not mention the environment. However, the 1970's saw the emergence of a Community policy on the environment, with the First Action Programme. More than 200 pieces of legislation dealing with environmental protection have since been passed by the EC. The Single European Act in 1987 for the first time introduced explicit references to the Community's powers in the field of environmental protection, and established the statutory basis for the requirement to integrate policies for the protection of the environment into the definition and implementation of other EC policies, which forms part of the Maastricht Treaty. The failure of past initiatives to prevent the continued degradation of the environment has resulted in the realisation that a new approach is called for. Passing legislation to protect the environment

Ullrich Kockel (ed), *Culture, Tourism and Development: The Case of Ireland*, Liverpool University Press 1994, 87-96.

cannot be effective unless the requirements of environmental protection are an integral part of all other sectors and policies. It is only when the interrelationship between human activity and the environment is taken into account and the limitations to growth imposed by the carrying capacity of the environment are recognised, that sustainable development will be possible.

The *Fifth Action Programme* is in a sense the blue-print for action on integration and sustainability. In this programme sustainable development is defined as a

> policy for continued economic and social development without detriment to the environment and the natural resources on the quality of which continued human activity and further development depend. (Commission of the European Communities 1992)

The long term success of the key community initiatives such as economic and monetary union will depend on environmental protection and the sustainability of projects in the different sectors including industry, energy, transport, agriculture and tourism. Each of these is dependent on the carrying capacity of the environment, not in isolation but also in terms of their interactions with each other. Sustainable development depends on increased co-operation between different partners who may have different short-term priorities. For example, integration and partnership would help to prevent the kind of conflicts which can arise between tourism and aquaculture (in terms of visual impact and impacts on angling as a tourism product), or tourism and forestry where planting of coniferous plantations has sometimes resulted in the loss of significant scenic views, and tourism and agriculture where intensification of agricultural practices have resulted in damage to the environment in areas with enormous potential for tourism. The lack of integration is well illustrated by the bungalow bliss syndrome. One-off housing in scenic rural landscapes is doing irreparable insidious damage to an essential part of the environmental resource. Planning by politics, lack of enforcement, absence of strategic planning all contribute to the problem.

Looking to the rest of Europe, commentators such as Jonathan Porritt see transport policies as the touchstone for achieving sustainable development (Porritt 1993). Here in Ireland we do not experience the same degree of congestion on our roads and, happily, motorways trundling through scenic areas are still a rarity. At the same time the kind of transport policies which are being pursued may not be sustainable in the long term. Apart from the issue of public transport versus the private motor car, one only has to look at projects as diverse as the infamous interpretative centres, where the conflicts which have arisen are rooted partly in the perceived need to provide access for cars to a fragile environment, and the proposed Glen of the Downs dual carriageway which threatens not only a Nature Reserve but also the scenic integrity of the gateway to Wicklow, one of the most important tourism areas in the country (Wicklow County Council 1992).

THE TOURISM INDUSTRY

The environment is the basic resource upon which the future of the tourism industry depends. Even though a 'green' unspoilt environment is constantly put forward as one of the strengths of Irish tourism, marketing strategies and product development frameworks adopted by the industry do not always reflect an underlying philosophy of sustainable development. Protection of the environment should be the key element, with other factors secondary. Otherwise the success of the industry in the short term will be at the expense of the erosion of the resource in the long term. As Professor Krippendorf, who could be regarded as the 'father' of 'sustainable tourism', has said, it is not a question of how much ecology can the economy stand, but rather how much economy can ecology stand? (Krippendorf 1993). Sustainable development means every improvement in the quality of life—economic welfare and subjective wellbeing—which is achieved with less use of non-renewable resources and less burden on the environment and on people. His plan for action to achieve sustainable tourism requires application of the five R's principle:

- Refuse to pollute;
- Reduce pollution;
- Reuse products and materials;
- Recycle;
- Recover (e.g., energy).

Such an approach may seem somewhat drastic from an Irish perspective; quite clearly we do not have the same problems of environmental degradation that are apparent in other parts of Europe—not to mention the rest of the world. Nor are we experiencing the problems of mass tourism that are experienced by other countries. But why wait until the problems arrive? Prevention is better than cure and the only road to prevention is the sustainable one in all its meanings. The question is whether the policies which are being pursued to expand the tourism industry in this country are compatible with an approach which looks to the long term health of the resource.

Under the current round of Structural Funds, a number of projects have received funding which cannot be considered sustainable (Meldon 1992). The immediate considerations of achieving certain targets in income generation and job creation took precedence over other factors with the result that some of the gain from the investment will be of temporary duration.

The emphasis in the *Operational Programme for Tourism 1989-1993* has been on product development through the creation of new infrastructure to attract further expansion of the industry. This is very evident, for example, in the emphasis on new buildings in the public sector programme, which of course includes the building of interpretative centres. It is quite obvious that such projects are not in keeping with the principles enunciated by Krippendorf. The public concern about these projects runs much deeper than simply the issue of new buildings—it is also about differing approaches to conservation: one which advocates immediate and direct experience of the environment to teach the observer to treasure it in the future; the other which stresses the need to preserve certain fragile habitats from any form of mass tourism or large scale intrusion.

Examples of unsustainable development are also apparent in some of the private sector projects which have been promoted through the *Operational Programme*. These include some of the large scale leisure developments, where the provision of golfing and equestrian facilities has been accompanied by the building of houses or golf villas to provide an integrated leisure facility. In order to attract a certain type of market, the promoters have sought out the most prestigious of Irish country houses and parklands for their developments, with too little concern for the historic and environmental significance of such places. Golf courses in fragile coastal environments are another case in point.

According to the *Operational Programme*, 'preservation and conservation of our cultural and physical environment are absolutely essential to the unique and competitive advantages which the resultant tourism product will enjoy' (Department of Tourism and Transport 1989). However, by adopting a product-based approach, the programme is placing conservation of the environment in a secondary position. Instead, grant aid should be directed towards investment, which would lead to the conservation and enhancement of tourist products that make up the cultural and physical environment.

A clean and unspoilt environment is listed as one of the strengths of Irish tourism, but targets and strategy identified by the *Operational Programme* do not appear to take full account of the facts that

(a)   our relatively unspoilt environment is largely due to our low level of economic development and peripheral location in relation to the rest of Europe, rather than being a result of a conscious planning philosophy or particularly well developed environmental legislation, and this environment is therefore especially vulnerable to change following increased pressures; and

(b)   features which are essential to tourism can be destroyed by tourism itself.

While Bord Fáilte, the national tourist board, is undoubtedly aware of the problems and pressures associated with mass tourism, at the same time it is clear that such concerns have at least in part been overruled by the need to achieve economic development and job creation targets.

THE BORD FÁILTE DRAFT DEVELOPMENT PLAN 1993-1997

Bord Fáilte has recently published a draft plan for 1993-1997. Its title, *Developing Sustainable Tourism*, is significant. It is worth looking at some elements of this plan and examining their compatibility with the philosophy of sustainability and integration of environmental policy and the integration of tourism with other sectors. The plan does take on board the principles of sustainable development in so far as the limitations to growth are recognised and the need to generate higher returns from the industry through an emphasis on quality rather than ever-increasing numbers.

There is a new emphasis in the Bord Fáilte draft plan on conserving the authentic base of the industry rather than sanitising and packaging the product out of existence. This approach is very much welcomed and offers much more scope for long term growth of the industry. Greater attention - and resources—will be given to the reuse of old buildings from derelict cottages to grand country houses. This is in contrast to the past emphasis on the creation of a product based on new structures. There is an emphasis

91

on quality rather than scale, and an acknowledgement of the intrinsic importance of the attractions themselves rather than the facilities designed around them. The logical extension of this philosophy is the need to ensure that any facilities provided to service major natural attractions in particular, must be designed so as to remain subservient. This applies to roads as well as to built structures.

The potential conflict between transport and tourism has already been mentioned even in cases where the objective is to provide access to tourism facilities. In many instances, well surfaced—not wider—roads are required. Good access facilities are important but the way in which such infrastructure is provided and improved is even more vital to the survival of the industry. The biggest need is for adequate co-ordination with other public and local authorities to ensure that the perceived needs of other industries for fast traffic facilities do not take over. Again the Glen of the Downs proposal is a case in point.

The Bord Fáilte plan looks to further expansion of special interest products. Such expansion should be encouraged in a manner which does not permit the demands of product expansion to take over from other considerations—the conservation and in some particular instances, preservation, of the basic resource has to come first.

TOWARDS A STRATEGY FOR SUSTAINABLE DEVELOPMENT

The guiding principles for tourism should be to minimise the overall impact on the environment, to benefit the host community and the locality, and to be sustainable. Tourism must not abuse the natural environment and must respect its architectural integrity.

Decision-making should be local where possible, with local cultural values and societies maintained. Growth should be gradual with the benefits of tourism diffused through many communities, not concentrated on a narrow coastal strip or scenic valley (Lane 1990).

The targets and strategies of the current plan place too much emphasis on the exploitation of Irish scenery, heritage and culture to achieve short-term economic targets. Instead we need to look at how tourism can best contribute to the regeneration of depressed areas and regional economic development, while at the same time funding the management of natural resources.

Approaching tourism from the perspective of the region, rather than through the development of product themes, would help to safeguard and sustain local identity so that the local community would operate an effective 'brake' on development not in keeping with local goals and objectives. Such an approach could help to minimise the conflict that can arise as a result of the intrusion of the speculative developer, whose aims and objectives may be at variance with those of the local community.

Sensitivity analysis and management strategies

Before any tourist strategy is approved for a region, a detailed survey should be carried out, classifying areas or features according to their sensitivity.

For example, sensitivity analysis would identify

- areas or features where there should be no public access of any sort, for example, some designated Nature Reserves;

- areas where no inappropriate development should be permitted, such as large parts of the Burren or the Wicklow uplands;

- areas which should be accessible only to walkers;

- areas where there should be minimal change in existing structures (field patterns, roads, etc.), and where new buildings should be strictly controlled in relation to siting, screening, size, design, and materials used;

- areas where less stringent control is needed, but where any new development should have regard to, for example, vernacular architecture and local materials, and any particular areas such as an Area of Scientific Interest (ASI);

- coastal zones which require particular management strategies to avoid conflict between sustaining the resource and the demands of mass tourism as well as those of other interests such as fish farming.

Tourism management strategies are essential if growth is to be managed according to the carrying capacity of the environment. Management strategies need to be adopted at a local level to ensure that a particular area, identified as a result of sensitivity analysis, would be managed in the manner most appropriate to its needs. Management strategies must also be designed in consultation with the local community including local businesses, planning authorities, environmentalists and the local tourist board. It is heartening to see that integrated community based approaches are already being developed in Ireland, for example, agri-tourism ventures such as Ballyhoura Fáilte (Fox 1992).

The protection of the natural environment and the countryside through land use planning and the management of the rural environment is a key component of the strategy. This can only be achieved through integration of tourism, forestry, agriculture and other socio-economic activities. Tourism would benefit significantly from suitably funded and managed extensions of the ESA scheme for farming, as well as from a much wider application of other agri-environmental measures including organic farming.

Sustainable development can only be achieved by cohesive action through the implementation of comprehensive landuse management strategies which recognise that activities undertaken in any sphere have the potential to interact with the environment and therefore to affect the base on which tourism depends. Part of the plan for action relates to the planning framework. Apart from the factors outlined earlier, planning problems stem from two main sources: exempted development provisions under the planning acts; and inadequacies of the present system of environmental impact assessment.

CONCLUSION

The development of the tourism industry should take place within the framework set by the *Fifth Action Programme on the Environment*, with integration as the key. It is not enough to look at strategies for tourism in isolation. Its objectives and goals must be set in a comprehensive framework for sustainable development.

Why is it important to be aware of how economic policies may be affecting the environment? Why do we need to conserve our resources for the future? The answer is two fold: first, because if we do not act sustainably then the resources on which all economic and social activity ultimately depend will in the long term be eroded, and second, to again paraphrase Jonathan Porrit, ours is becoming an alienated culture, alienated from the land, and from the workings of agriculture: we need the natural world to reconnect ourselves to the natural systems of which we are all a part and on which we all depend. I would suggest that it is this perceived quality of an unspoilt natural environment which is a key attraction for visitors to Ireland and is an element which will become of even greater importance in the decades ahead as the need for an alternative to urban congestion and pollution becomes more profound.

REFERENCES

An Taisce (1990)
Interactions between Aquaculture and the Environment. Dublin: An Taisce.
An Taisce (1993)
Environmental Impact Assessment: theory and practice in Ireland. Dublin: An Taisce.
Bord Fáilte (1992)
Developing Sustainable Tourism: tourism development plan 1993-1997. Dublin: Bord Fáilte.
Brady, Shipman & Martin (1991)
EIS—Wicklow National Park Visitor Centre. Dublin: OPW.
Brundtland (1987)
Our Common Future. Oxford: Oxford University Press.
Commission of the European Communities (1985)
EC Directive on Environmental Impact Assessment (85/337/EEC).
Commission of the European Communities (1992a)
Towards Sustainability: a European Community programme of policy and action in relation to the environment and sustainable development. Brussels: Official Publications.
Department of Tourism and Transport (1989)
Operational Programme for Tourism 1989-1993. Dublin: Stationery Office.

Environmental Impact Services Ltd (1991)
EIS for Great Blasket Island National Historic Park Visitor Centre. Dublin: OPW.

Fox, C (1992)
Community Tourism Initiative: the Ballyhoura experience. Paper given at the Community Connection conference in Enniskillen.

Krippendorf, J (1993)
Impacts of tourism on the environment. In English Tourist Board (eds), *Tourism and the Environment: challenges and choices for the 90s,* London: English Tourist Board.

Lane, B (1990)
Developing Sustainable Tourism in Scotland. Paper given at a conference on sustainable tourism, Edinburgh.

Meldon, J (1992)
Structural Funds and the Environment: problems and prospects. Dublin: An Taisce.

Porritt, J (1993)
Challenges and choices for the 90s. In English Tourist Board (eds), *Tourism and the Environment: challenges and choices for the 90s,* London: English Tourist Board.

RPS Group (1991)
EIS—Burren National Park Visitor Centre. Dublin: OPW.

Wicklow County Council (1991/1992)
EIS—Proposed Kilmacanogue to Glen of the Downs Dual Carriageway. Dublin: ARUP.

Tourism, Environment and Community Development

JOHN FEEHAN

INTRODUCTION

Tourism today is one of the world's biggest areas of economic growth, dwarfing in significance the great pilgrimages of earlier centuries. The foreign earnings generated are of great importance to the economies of many countries, including several developing countries, but the growth of tourism has resulted in environmental degradation and the impoverishment of local culture and ecology (Buckley and Pannell 1990). Even if their welfare is not directly harmed by tourism development, the economic benefits generated by tourism seldom accrue significantly to the communities which need it most: and yet it is their resources which are most directly exploited.

Part of the reason for the uneven distribution of benefit is the kind of tourism paradigm we follow. It is very enlightening to look at the evolution of the prevailing pattern of tourism in historical perspective. The main modes of contemporary tourism can be traced to the beginnings of the phenomenon of group tourism in the eighteenth century. The classical mode was the Grand Tour, in which the 'Great Places'—and Great Hotels to match them—were strung out along a fixed itinerary like beads on a necklace. The values of the classical education of the time and a highly stratified European social world decided what was worth seeing and how it should be seen. The classical dimension began to broaden in the late eighteenth-century with the new and growing interest in romantic landscape and the natural world. With the application of enthusiastic entrepreneurial spirit, the early tourist industry was quick to take advantage of this new market—typified, for example, by the spate of hotels which began to appear in the Grindeswald from 1820 onwards to allow visitors to view and experience the Grindeswald glaciers of the Alps which were re-advancing at this time (Schotterer and Andermatt 1990). It is interesting to note in this

Ullrich Kockel (ed), *Culture, Tourism and Development: The Case of Ireland*, Liverpool University Press 1994, 97-102.

new phenomenon another familiar modern theme: a turning to the natural world to recover something of what was lost to society with the spread of the scientific and industrial revolutions. Our modern tourism has evolved from these early models.

A PARADIGM FOR COMMUNITY TOURISM

We cater very well for the many modern variants of the Grand Tour, but another and essentially different type of tourism now exists also, one which has much more to contribute to rural development, but which cannot be adequately catered for within the 'traditional' tourism framework. The New Tourism is essentially different. Here we have people who consciously want to discover something of what has been lost from daily life in their experience: people who are looking for the hidden Ireland of which so much is being written nowadays, or the hidden Spain of Laurie Lee, or the real Provence or the real Malawi. This kind of tourism may involve very large numbers but they will be spread in an essentially dispersed pattern, for which the heritage centres and the hotel are not primarily designed and are not enough: because the hotel, however excellent, is too removed from the everyday hospitality of the community; because the Interpretative Centre, however excellent, is not real heritage in its natural or cultural context.

A new paradigm is needed for this different kind of tourism. A tourism which has as its priorities environmental conservation and enhancement, the preservation and revitalisation of community cultural values, the promotion of local economic welfare, while at the same time providing the visitor with an enriching sharing in the community's culture, heritage and life, cannot be based on the old paradigm.

We need new models: and there are models for tourism other than the accepted paradigm. They have their roots in a different, a far older tradition than the tourist tradition: in the ancient human tradition of providing hospitality to the stranger. The appropriate model here is a form of accommodation which could be found in any village in an earlier time, and the New Tourist can be seen to be the modern counterpart of those whose needs were best served by this early model. This needs to be looked at reflectively and more thoughtfully than this short article offers, because there are critical lessons to learn about the essence of the modes that can best be accommodated within the rural structure, and equally are the ones which best meet the new and growing opportunity.

COMMUNITY TOURISM AND THE RURAL ECONOMY

A tourism development along these lines has much to contribute to the rural economy. We must look to a time when rural tourism will be a normal farm enterprise, as normal as growing crops and rearing animals. It will be as normal as hospitality, the open door to the stranger, was in rural Ireland until recently. It will be the developed version of it, geared to changed times and new needs and new opportunities, but rural hospitality nonetheless in direct line with an ancient human tradition which in rural Ireland was second to none, and whose decline of late has chilled some of the warmth out of parts of the countryside—few would disagree that the tradition of rural hospitality has suffered considerable erosion and attrition at the same time as the traditional setting and economy which framed them has. The special ethos of Celtic hospitality would be one of the most distinctive facets of the Irish model of rural tourism, but every culture has its tradition of hospitality which would provide the warm flame at the heart of its particular model of rural tourism (Feehan 1992). We need to move to a future where economic hospitality will be a normal option in the small farm economy, and we have to invest whatever resources are necessary to make this a feasible option, especially for the small farms which make up the great majority, and where the need is greatest.

RURAL TOURISM AND THE ENVIRONMENT

The growth of rural tourism is potentially of great significance from a conservation perspective, because it is critically concerned with raising the level of awareness of environmental values among the people who in many ways matter the most, the people who own the land and are responsible for what happens to it. The greatest hope for conservation is that now for the first time ever, environmental heritage has not merely a value as part of the heritage of all of us, but it has a new economic dimension.

Conservation is not simply a matter of maintaining individual sites and monuments as isolated museums or reserves, but rather of maintaining and promoting the diversity and richness of the landscape as a whole. And

John Feehan

although it is necessary to combat individual ignorance or selfishness by taking particular areas within the protection of an effective law, or under the care of the body which is committed with the task of preserving the common heritage of the country, in practical terms such sites can really only be adequately protected within the awareness, pride and sense of care of the entire community whose special heritage they are.

It would be a total misunderstanding to imagine that if we conserve isolated sites and monuments like oases in the middle of an otherwise productive agricultural or industrial desert we are protecting our material heritage. So little is now left that all monuments, and all rare or unique habitats should automatically be inviolate, their protection enshrined in law. But the law reflects the outlook of the community: and few things are more important now than the development and growth of increased awareness among the whole community of the nature and value of the whole fabric of landscape heritage. This fabric is woven of a great multiplicity of features of greater and lesser importance, all of which could never be encompassed or protected by listing procedures, but which can only be protected within the concern of a caring and aware community.

The heritage of landscape not only nourishes and supports our physical well-being; much of our sense of identity, our sense of place and belonging, is rooted in the heritage of our particular local landscape (Evans 1981). We are all well aware of the extent to which environmental heritage has grown in status as a resource for tourism. To a considerable extent it is the realisation that landmarks and monuments are important economic assets which has prompted the upsurge of interest in their preservation, and in their promotion and marketing. But the material relics of the past in the landscape are important not primarily because heritage can be made to generate revenue. What matters most is the fact that through these things we can touch or peep through to the wonder and significance of the past in the most immediate way. The material heritage of the local landscape is of great interest and importance to the visitor, but it should never be forgotten that it is first and foremost the heritage of the local community whose home it enriches. And there is a very real danger that all this new enthusiasm from above will undermine the sense among local communities that this is their heritage and their responsibility in the first place. If that happens, the isolated sites, monuments and locations may survive as oases in the cultural desert, but the landscape context which gives them meaning and richness may not.

That so much from the past has survived in the landscape in the first place is an outcome of local community conservatism, loving care for the

100

past for its own sake, an instinctive understanding that the whole pattern of things was and is important: a sense that one's own place had its story, and that this was an important part of one's individual history, in which to look for meaning and a sense of security and belonging. Everything you found in your own place and with which you grew up was a touchstone which anchored you to some particular stratum in the multi-layered meaning of 'Home'.

CONCLUSION

The preservation of the natural and cultural diversity of landscape is important primarily not for the sake of the values that a central authority imposes, but because of its importance for the community's own sense of identity. Although it is unlikely to be expressed this way very often, what the enterprise is all about, essentially, is finding our place in, and our way through, the universe.

But times have changed, and although change may be the very essence of landscape, the rate of change has so accelerated that patterns created over centuries, features which have survived perhaps for millennia in the landscape, can be obliterated overnight without consideration of their value as part of community heritage, an erosion that progressively impoverishes the richness of living. There is the danger that the community's sense of the primary and deeper value of its material heritage and the broader cultural heritage which is grounded in it, may be smothered under the pressure of imposed values and well intentioned development—and if this happens its real rootedness will have been lost.

Which is why more than ever there is the need for a blossoming of community awareness of the nature and importance of landscape heritage, that can fruitfully echo the possibilities inherent in the broader trends outside itself, to rekindle and nurture its own sense of the value of the multitude of features that define it. Which leads me to repeat my sense of the urgency of the need for enrichment of local community understanding of landscape heritage: an enrichment at least as important as the other dimensions of well-being which constitute the Good Life for which society strives.

REFERENCES

Buckley, R and Pannell, J (1990)
Environmental impacts of tourism and recreation in national parks and conservation reserves. *Journal of Tourism Studies* 1(1), 24-32.

Evans, E (1981)
The Personality of Ireland. Belfast: Blackstaff Press.

Feehan, J (1992)
Developments in education for farm tourism and the inspiration of the Brugh. In Feehan, J (ed), *Tourism on the Farm.* Dublin: UCD Environmental Institute, 93-102.

Schotterer, U and Andermatt, P (1990)
Climate: our future? Bern: Kümmerly & Frey in association with the Swiss Academy of Science.

The Cultural Tourist:
Patron Saint of Ireland?

MOYA KNEAFSEY

INTRODUCTION

Tourism is a phenomenon with important cultural, political and economic implications for the peripheral regions of Europe. In the global economy, tourism and place marketing are seen as potential means of development for areas that have lost out in the process of global economic re-structuring. This essay, based on preliminary research into the growth of cultural tourism in County Mayo in the West of Ireland, is an attempt to introduce some of the themes and ideas which deserve further investigation.

In discussing this research, I venture to suggest that the tourist can be seen as the patron of new forms of creativity and production, such as the commodification of culture, the creation of place and the construction of identity.

These processes are amalgamated in the latest trend in Ireland's cultural tourism development strategy—heritage centres. Such centres have provoked many questions about the best way to develop a sustainable tourism policy in Ireland. For instance, although there has been investment of millions of pounds of European, private and public money to build centres to interpret local culture, critics ask how beneficial these developments actually are to communities in the long run, not only in economic, but also in cultural terms. For instance, who actually sets the agenda for such developments and decides how to package culture? These questions await further research, but for the moment I will try and explore some possible ideas about the growth of cultural tourism and relate these to developments at Céide Fields in County Mayo.

Ullrich Kockel (ed), *Culture, Tourism and Development: The Case of Ireland*, Liverpool University Press 1994, 103-16.

Moya Kneafsey

THE IMPORTANCE OF TOURISM

Since the earliest times, intrepid spirits have yearned to travel and explore, see new places and people, and experience a lifestyle different from their own. To the educated Europeans of the eighteenth century, travel was seen as a necessary therapeutic and instructive occupation, as is illustrated by the numerous travel journals and diaries which were published—such as Arthur Young's Tour of Ireland, 1776-1779, in which he proceeded to describe in great detail the agriculture, countryside and lifestyle of the peasants and gentry alike.

Tourism is a huge industry, accounting for 60-75% of all world travel by volume in 1991 and acting as a major source of foreign currency and income for many third world countries. International tourist numbers are increasing by 4-5% each year, and they currently spend $209 billion a year, generate 60 million jobs and fill 10.5 million hotel beds (Urry 1992). No longer restricted to the upper classes alone, tourism has taken modern Europeans to all corners of the globe, and has created its own interpretation of culture and history in the search for new and exciting experiences.

Tourism plays a major role in the Irish economy, with over three million arrivals—virtually equivalent to the entire population—in 1990. The target for 1997 is 4.7 million (Bord Fáilte 1991). In 1991, the equivalent of 87,000 full time jobs were created, and the contribution to Gross National Product (GNP) was 7.3%. Expenditure by overseas tourists visiting Ireland amounted to IR£910 million in 1992, and Bord Fáilte aims to raise this to IR£1,465 million in 1997. The industry is turning its attention more than ever to the British and mainland European market whilst the American market has stood still.

WHAT IS CULTURAL TOURISM?

The nature of tourism is constantly changing as many people search out new ways of escaping the stresses of modern day living, and new fashions dictate the sort of holiday people should have. For instance, in Scandinavian and European countries, activity holidays now centre on areas that had been previously neglected. Clouds and soft weather are now in as sun worship goes out of favour, and the mild climactic conditions of Ireland are now selling points for this new concept in tourism. The environment, nagging at some peoples' conscience, as it faces perhaps the most serious threats ever, is being seen as a precious resource, and rural areas which have maintained their natural beauty are being seen as havens of relaxation and reprieve for the stressed-out victim of the modern rat-race.

Some tourists today search for unique experiences and activities, and the cultural dimension is being added to the aims of mere rest and relaxation in peaceful rural surroundings. Like the travellers of the eighteenth century, some contemporary tourists are acknowledging the educational value of travel. Increasingly, culture is being seen as a resource, and history has become a saleable commodity. By cultural tourism I mean that a culture—an entire way of life, history, tradition, society and people—is being marketed as a product. However, this is not mass tourism; indeed, the aim of many contemporary 'travellers' is to avoid the better known destinations in search of an experience which seems more 'real' and 'authentic'. The idea is to discover the 'real' Ireland with its traditions and magical Celtic history.

Arthur Young and other touring writers of the eighteenth century could perhaps be described as the first cultural tourists. In this perspective, cultural tourism is not a new wave after all but a reversion to eighteenth-century habits after a relatively brief fad of sun-seeking package tours. The difference is that culture now has become a commodity, and vast sums of money are being generated by it.

THE TOURIST AS PATRON?

The tourist could be seen as a patron of Culture. By this I mean one who gives financial or other support to a person, activity or cause. Within this role, the tourist is the patron of traditional rural lifestyles and ethnic minority cultures which are now packaged in glossy brochures, activity holidays and festivals. The tourist listens to Irish music in the pubs, and buys hand-made Aran sweaters. The creation of identity is a process which is being undertaken with ever-increasing sophistication and professionalism in the West of Ireland. The development and promotion of historic houses, castles, monuments, national parks, museums and interpretive centres is a major part of the strategy for tourism growth, with £26.7 million from the European Regional Development Fund, £7.4 million from the public sector and £5.5 million from private enterprise being invested over a five-year programme to 1993 (Bord Fáilte 1991). The tourist is a patron, or consumer, of these investments, yet some would argue that too much faith is being put into tourism as a way of promoting economic growth and generating jobs. At times it has seemed that tourism is posited as the 'saviour' of certain less favoured areas, not only in terms of income and employment, but also in terms of what Brody (1973) describes as the 'zest and enthusiasm' tourists may bring to a locality. This has led to debate about how best to develop a form of tourism which is sustainable in the long term and of benefit to the host community.

Cultural tourism offers great potential for rural areas, and takes advantage of a fascination with identity and an emotional attachment to the perhaps rose-tinted view of the past which seems to prevail in postmodern society.

THE FASCINATION WITH IDENTITY

A Postmodern explanation perhaps?

The growth of cultural tourism could be linked to what some authors have described as a new epoch, a new stage of development which the capitalist world has entered into. I will try and explain broadly what I see as the relevance of this body of ideas to cultural tourism.

The idea is that the industrialised countries of the late twentieth century have entered a new epoch, described as the Postmodern. This epoch is characterised by a 'sea-change' in cultural practices, and in the 'structure of feelings' (Harvey 1990). It follows, and is a reaction to Modernism, which was generally positivistic, technocentric, and rationalistic, with a belief in the idea of history as linear progress. In contrast, Postmodernist thought is characterised by fragmentation and indeterminacy, and a distrust of universal theories. Postmodernism within academic research features increasing concern within the disciplines of ethics, anthropology and politics, for the voice of the Other. It rejects large-scale theoretical interpretations with universal applications, arguing that the function of these theories was to legitimate the illusion of universal human history. Science and philosophy must therefore rid themselves of their grand claims and view themselves as just another set of narratives.

According to some authors, Postmodernism has emerged simultaneously with the growth of a new middle class, or 'petty bourgeoisie' dominated by those working in service and cultural industries. The emergence of this new group has been tied up with new social movements that have grown up in recent decades, including the Green, Feminist, and Peace movements, and it provides both the consumers of cultural tourism and the audience for cultural phenomena.

With the growth of service industries and the commodification of cultural symbols, a whole group of cultural producers, design professionals, and cultural interpreters has emerged (Featherstone 1990). In addition, there is also the group which Betz (1992), with reference to West Germany, has described as the 'post-industrial non-established' who, disillusioned with dominant ideology and the state, have increasingly turned to alternative lifestyles of anarchism, mysticism, macrobiotics, environmentalism and post-structuralism. For these 'refugees from modernity' (Featherstone 1990), the rural periphery is a romantically attractive destination, along with its traditional music and folk culture. For instance, Ireland is immensely popular with German visitors, who buy up traditional houses and stay there permanently. The motivating factor seems to be a sense of alienation from their own society, and a desire to return to a lifestyle which is perceived as authentic. Thus the contemporary cultural symbols of this new middle class include health food, real ale, real bread, vegetarianism, natural childbirth, wool, lace, cotton, traditional non-western medicines, cycling, mountaineering, and fell-walking rather than contrived, organised leisure (Urry 1990). It is this group who seem to be the main consumers of cultural tourism.

This new middle class inhabits a postmodern world which is characterised by consumerism and commodification of virtually anything and everything (Smart 1991). The rise of postmodern culture is connected to the material and social reorganisation of post-industrial, information or consumer society. The postmodern society, according to Baudrillard, is one in which forms of social organisations based on production relations and power have given way to society organised on the basis of consumption and seduction. Culture is a commodity to be consumed. Many writers have argued that through consumption people are involved in a process of affirming their own cultural identity. As Friedman (1990) argues, individuals are engaged in a struggle for authenticity, a 'desperate negotiation of selfhood', and consumption is an aspect of broader cultural strategies of self-definition and self-maintenance. Consumption is the consumption of identity, a negotiation between self-definition and the possibilities offered by the capitalist market. The clothes we buy, the holidays we take, are a statement about ourselves in a world which is characterised by communication through symbols. Communication through symbols is not new, but the extent to which these symbols are commodified and intrude into our lives, through advertising and fashion, for example, is unprecedented. In a society dominated by the information sector, by the processing of symbols or symbolic objects and by a disposition to leisure and personal development, Bourdieu stresses the cultural as the means adopted by social groups to differentiate themselves.

For example, Featherstone (1992) describes the new trend-setters who make lifestyle and the development of taste their life project. His argument is that the erosion of social differences has led to an offensive by the new middle class to reinstate social differentiation, and it is perhaps this group who are more likely to be attracted to cultural tourism. The craving for distinction finds manifestation through the ornamentation of landscape, the conspicuous display of good taste, and the search for the authentic. Cultural capital has become a powerful currency of exchange within social relations of the postmodern society. Rural peripheral communities at the moment have ample supplies of cultural capital—they are very often seen as the repositories of national cultural symbols, and many of the inhabitants of the cities may be drawn towards these areas as tourists for this very reason. This phenomena can be seen in the West of Ireland which has long been seen as holding the essence of Ireland's Gaelic identity.

The contribution of Postmodernism to an analysis of tourism

Some of the features which have been cited as part of the Postmodern condition can be seen to relate to the growth of cultural tourism. The popularity of cultural tourism could be seen as a response to feelings of alienation in the Durkheimian sense of 'rootlessness', which in turn links in to the idea of a search for authenticity. Tourism has been described as part of a search for a centre (Cohen 1979), or meaning which may be missing in everyday life at home. In addition, cultural tourism employs features of postmodern art and architecture such as collage and pastiche to create specific histories and constructed identities for the tourist gaze. This is what heritage centres do through interpreting and re-creating history and the present. Heritage centres and interpretive centres create cultures and invent traditions through pastiche, eclecticism and spectacle. They objectify cultures and create experiences which enable people to re-live the past through sight, sound, smells, and activities. As Hanson (1989) points out, traditional culture is increasingly recognised as an invention constructed for contemporary purposes rather than a stable heritage handed down from the past. Tradition, as Lindstrom put it, is an attempt to 'read the present in terms of the past by writing the past in terms of the present.'

The more pessimistic interpretations such as that proposed by Levi-Strauss argue that authentic human differences are disintegrating in this commodity culture (Clifford 1988). Tourism, migrant labour, urban sprawl and mass transit have resulted in a sense of 'dis'-orientation. The 'exotic' is uncannily close, and the familiar turns up at the end of the earth. One can no longer leave home confident of finding something new.

The more optimistic theorists argue that culture and identity are inventive and mobile, and they live by pollination and historical transplanting. Rather than globalisation of culture, it can be argued that what is happening is re-invention, revival and re-emergence of tradition and diversity.

So it could be that the move towards more culturally oriented holidays, towards travel instead of tourism, and the appeal of traditional rural lifestyles are bound up with changes in society, and with the needs of individuals who at present feel somehow rootless and are in search of authenticity. Yet there are other factors which could add further explanation to the current trend. There is a need to look at why certain places are promoting themselves in particular ways, and how communities are aiming to meet the interests of the postmodern tourist. Although there is not space here for further discussion, and also a need for detailed research, I think that the motors behind these developments are economic and political and can be understood within the context of European development, and the changing relations between local and global structures, institutions and networks.

CÉIDE FIELDS: POSTMODERNISM IN MAYO?

The starting point for my field research is an examination of the development of Céide Fields Interpretive Centre in northwest Mayo. The Interpretive Centre opened in 1993 and attracted over 60,000 visitors. To illustrate the scale of this development, it should be noted that in 1986 the neighbouring village, Ballycastle, had a population of roughly 200.

Northwest Mayo is an isolated area, which for years has followed the usual pattern of emigration and decline. In August 1776, Arthur Young described the territory on the edge of which the Centre stands as a 'vast, wild and impenetrable tract', and this description is still valid today. The region is generally seen as the back of beyond, and there has often been a sense of isolation from Dublin. There is one restaurant, a few holiday homes and a few B&Bs scattered around Ballycastle. Into the middle of this scene has been inserted a Pyramid. The effect in purely visual terms is quite striking. You drive over the brow of a hill and come upon an intriguing concrete and glass structure which is embedded in the hillside. Immediately beyond the entrance to the building are cliffs which plunge 300 feet down into the Atlantic. Inside is the story of Stone Walls which were built 5,000 years ago by prehistoric farmers and preserved by the Bog. From this discovery has emerged a tremendous effort to put Mayo on the map as a tourist destination and place of unique archaeological, historical and natural heritage. The driving force behind all this is a local man, Seamus Caulfield, who urges 'pride in our roots' and in the fact that farming in Mayo has hardly changed over 5,000 years: 'we know who we are and what we have got; let us start with a new attitude of honest arrogance'.

Céide Fields is billed as the home of the 'first Europeans', and is just one example of the use of identity as unifying factor with political implications. The Celtworld development at Tramore, built with a £1.5m EC grant, is a similar attempt to draw upon the common denominator, the dim Celtic past of the European peoples, whilst at the same time incorporating what tourism minister Seamus Brennan described as the 'wow factor.'

Similarly Venice, in 1991, played host to the most lavish and controversial culturo-historical event of the European year, with a blockbusting exhibition which sought to assert that the Celts were not a mysterious group on the fringes of Europe, but were a civilisation of mainland Europe. Why was there a huge exhibition in Venice which attracted thousands of visitors, at the same time as the development in Céide began? On a more ambitious and glamorous scale than Céide Fields or Celtworld, the 'I Celti' event carried the message that the Celts were a 'unifying European culture' and the subtitle, 'The Origins of Europe', had a striking similarity to the claims of far distant Mayo. The year 1993 also saw the Mayo 'Quinquemillenium', described as the 'focus of the celebration of rural settlement throughout Europe.' The theme of the Celts is bound up with the idea of contemporary European unity and the notion of a pan-European culture. The message of 'I Celti' was that 'we are all Europeans, and therefore we are all inheritors of a European civilisation'. Therefore, it can be seen that cultural tourism plays a vital role in shaping our perceptions of ourselves and other cultures, and the ways in which different cultures relate—or are supposed to relate.

PROBLEMS WITH CULTURAL TOURISM

Tourism has enormous advantages for the economy, being a generator of employment and revenue, and a foreign exchange earner with low import requirements. It is of particular importance to those western rural areas which have suffered the demoralising effects of depopulation and decline. Interpretive centres are evidence that the government is investing in hitherto neglected areas, but some critics are asking whether this is the right sort of investment. What is the point of spending millions on state of the art heritage centres in the middle of the bog when what is needed is accommodation and better roads? Critics question the need to interpret culture at all, an attitude expressed strongly in a letter published by the *Irish Times* on 19 February 1993:

What is this hunger to interpret our land? To whom? For whom?... [P]sychology drugged American tourists must have Ireland simplified for them: a self conscious, history-conscious generation must have Ireland packaged for it.

Strangely enough, American tourists did not form the majority of visitors to Céide Fields in 1990, when the development began. The Irish formed the majority—so perhaps it is they who enjoy seeing their own culture packaged, and not the foreigners. They were followed by English, then American, German and French visitors. Perhaps this craze for interpretation is more than merely a way of encouraging tourism. It may also serve a purpose for the community, acting as a focus for action and contributing towards a sense of awareness and pride in their own heritage.

Yet a heavy reliance on tourism could perpetuate the economic dominance of the periphery by the core, both within Ireland and in a wider European sense. Peripheral communities such as the Connemara Gaeltacht have in the past suffered from a feeling that developmental activities were imposed 'from above' and a cynical attitude to projects carried out on people's behalf emerged. From this there emerged a passivity to economic possibilities which presented themselves in the immediate environment, and an almost dogmatic belief that there was nothing of any significant value in the surroundings, an attitude which still prevails in certain areas today. According to Michael Ó Cinnéide (1987), striking contrasts have emerged between 'core' areas which are foci of economic dynamism, where investment capital and technological expertise accumulates, and peripheral areas which have become increasingly dependent on core areas to absorb their agricultural surpluses, to provide jobs for migrants and assist in the generation of economic opportunities.

A heavy dependence on 'outside' visitors to maintain the economy through tourism could have damaging effects on local self esteem and pride. Here a rather less appealing interpretation of the tourist as patron could be employed. According to the Oxford English Dictionary, to patronize includes to 'support, treat condescendingly.' Irish tourist images are projected at the affluent European city dweller who wants to 'get away from it all' in a rural setting, and it was suggested in the North Mayo Development Plan that Mayo be marketed as a 'leisure park for industrial Europe'. Similarly a Bord Fáilte publication talks about Ireland as 'indisputably the 'playground of Europe'. Tourists from highly developed industrial society 'travel to the periphery from where migrant workers travel to the industrial society' (Kirshenblatt-Gimblett 1988).

The projected image of Ireland reinforces the idea of the country as a retreat from life in the fast lane. As Bernadette Quinn shows in her study of the images of Ireland as a tourist destination, the most important message in tourist promotion is that Ireland is a world apart from modern society, and offers the chance for complete relaxation and a re-discovery of 'old world values.' Brochures often depict whitewashed cottages with thatched roofs, stone walls, old farming implements and rakes of turf.

The representation of Ireland and its people is predominantly rural, with less than 10% of the scenes depicted in the Bord Fáilte brochures set in urban surroundings. An image is created of a destination where the tourist will be in the midst of a beautiful rural setting far away from the city life which she is assumed to have left. What is the impact of such promotional imagery on the actual communities of rural Ireland?

In one sense, recognition of the importance of the environment and distinct heritage must be seen as a good thing. In another sense, rural Ireland is given the character of something of an artefact, a curiosity, and the image of the slow old-fashioned lifestyle could reinforce certain attitudes within Ireland which see anything West of the Shannon as the 'back of beyond'. The presentation of rural areas as behind the times could also be detrimental to continuing efforts to promote industrial development and economic activity besides tourism, such as forestry and horticulture, and hi-tech industries.

In physical terms, such promotion can have a noticeable impact because steps are taken to ensure that the image that is marketed remains, and in some cases, becomes a reality: The environment has come to be recognised as a valuable asset for rural areas, and there have been efforts to increase public awareness of its importance. Bord Fáilte has begun to encourage a more thoughtful attitude to the surroundings. The idea appears to be to create pristine surroundings for the tourist which fit the thatched roof, quaint village image of Ireland. Yet it could perhaps be argued that rules and regulations, and the imposition of uniform design guides, will destroy the very character of Irish villages with their somewhat chaotic and colourful atmosphere, and damage their individuality. After all, neon signs and traffic are features of modern living, and the west of Ireland is not a place frozen in time. It has been influenced to varying degrees by the same industrial forces and economic trends which have affected every part of Europe in one way or another, no matter how remote.

A crucial question is whether it is really possible to preserve a culture. Rural areas are in many ways seen as the repository of a country's oldest and most meaningful cultural traditions in the form of folk crafts, songs, tradition and rural lifestyle. The importance of preserving these areas, which are often on the periphery of the EC, has been underlined by many critics.

An interesting method of using tourists as patrons has been planned in Swedish Lapland (Grahn 1991). The idea is to create a number of 'cultural preservation tourist areas' which would consist of, for example, villages incorporating the surrounding landscape. In order to preserve the region's profile, small local industries must be kept alive in their traditional character through the support of patrons. Sponsoring patrons should be offered opportunities through courses to learn the traditional handicrafts, culinary arts, music and dance as well as about the fauna, flora, geology and languages of the area and about methods of farming, hunting and architecture. Tourists would be considered guests, but at the same time part of a team, with the opportunity to take part in aspects of traditional life such as milking the cows or cutting hay with a scythe. Sponsoring patron tourists would come back year after year and begin to identify with the area, and they would also buy houses in the area through a system of tenant ownership. Possible patrons beside the individual tourist could include private companies, whose employees would be given the opportunity to take part in the activities offered, public institutions, and health organisations which could send mentally disturbed people or over-stressed people for rehabilitation in the chosen area. Patron tourists could buy themselves an interest in the area, consisting of joint ownership in the dwellings and in the entire area. This would give them the right to vote in the elections of the committee of the organization and the right to share in decisions on the future of the area.

This idea raises issues about the 'preservation' of districts of 'high cultural value'. Who decides which areas fall into this category? If patrons are to buy up housing and ownership of the entire area, how does this affect the status of the local inhabitants? Furthermore, is it possible to preserve a culture without really killing its essence or inner spirit (Välkepää 1983)? There is a potential conflict between the needs of the tourist and wider society, and the needs of the people who are supposed to be a part of that particular culture or heritage which is worth preserving.

CONCLUSION

It could be argued that in an informal sense tourist patronage is already happening. For example, in northwest Mayo foreigners have bought up property in the area, and through an interest in cultural activities such as music, they are helping to maintain the vibrancy of such traditions. Yet at the same time, they also bring about changes in those traditions. An example is traditional music. The session, which would have taken place in homes and farms, functioning as an opportunity to learn tunes, exchange stories, dance and talk, now takes place in the pub, and the music is run by a few musicians who are paid by the publican to provide a suitable atmosphere for the tourist. The musicians sit in the corner, where they may be photographed by visitors revelling in this rustic lifestyle, and churn out tunes to keep the guests happy. There may sometimes be a conflict between the musicians, who resent being told by non-musicians what to play, and between the publican wanting to ensure that he gets his money's worth. So we see one example of an aspect of the culture which has changed due to tourism. The music continues, but for a different reason.

However, this is not really a one-sided exploitative relationship. Local entrepreneurs are beginning to tap into this interest in traditional culture. There has been a distinct change in the approach towards the marketing and exploitation of culture. The pageants are organised with a high degree of professionalism, and heritage centres present hi-tech, smoothly running operations which guide the visitor through a seamless experience.

Tourism, then, can play a major role in reinforcing pride in rural areas, which in turn leads to a greater desire to develop traditional skills and abilities, and to share them with others. As one observer put it 'if you're not proud of something, you don't want to share it.' Thus, cultural tourism stands to have a profound effect on rural communities in Ireland and in other parts of Europe, not only in economic terms but in shaping the very character of rural culture in the future. It is these effects that I hope to explore in my further research, and hopefully this will contribute to an understanding not only of the impact of tourism, but of wider aspects of development and the inter-relationship between global and local trends.

REFERENCES

Betz, H (1992)
Postmodernism and the new middle class. *Theory, Culture and Society* 9, 93-114.

Bord Fáilte (1991)
Tourism Opportunities: investing in Ireland's future. Dublin: Bord Fáilte.

Clifford, J (1988)
The Predicament of Culture: twentieth century ethnography, literature and art. Harvard University Press.

Cohen, E (1979)
A phenomenology of tourist experiences. *Sociology* 13, 180-201.

Featherstone, M (1990)
Global culture: an introduction. *Theory, Culture and Society* 7, 1-14.

Friedman, J (1990)
Being in the world: globalization and localization. *Theory Culture and Society* 7, 311-28.

Grahn, P (1991)
Using tourism to protect existing culture: a project in Swedish Lapland. *Leisure Studies* 10, 33-47.

Hanson, A (1989)
The making of the Maori: culture invention and its logic. *American Anthropologist* 91(4), 890-902.

Harvey, D (1990)
The Condition of Postmodernity: an enquiry into the conditions of cultural change. Oxford: Basil Blackwell.

Kirshenblatt-Gimblett, B (1988)
Authenticity and authority in the representation of culture: the poetics and politics of tourist production. In Greverus, I, Köstlin, K and Schilling, H (eds), *Kulturkontakt—Kulturkonflikt. Zur Erfahrung des Fremden*, Notizen 28, Frankfurt/Main: Institut für Kulturanthropologie und Europäische Ethnologie, 59-70.

Ó Cinnéide, M (1987)
The role of development agencies in peripheral areas with special reference to Údarás na Gaeltachta. *Regional Studies* 21, 65-74.

Smart, B (1991)
Modernity, postmodernity and the present. In Turner, B (ed.), *Theories of Modernity and Postmodernity.* London: Sage, 14-31.

Urry, J (1990)
The Tourist Gaze. London: Sage.

Urry, J (1992)
The Tourist Gaze and the Environment. *Theory Culture and Society* 9, 1-26.

Välkeapää, N (1983)
Greetings from Lappland: the Sami—Europe's forgotten people. London: Zed.

The Representation of Culture

DAVID BRETT

INTRODUCTION

The issue of the representation of culture is more than an academic matter. It is an issue around which political forces, frequently malignant, are being organised. I write as someone for whom the experience of living and working in what we must now call 'former Yugoslavia' was a formative experience; as someone around whose house in Belfast no less than seven men and two women have been murdered within a year. In all these cases how one group represents itself and is in turn represented, were and are matters of life and death.

A discussion of tourism enables us to approach these matters on ground that appears to be at least neutral, at best benevolent. But even here we need to be wary. A culture represents to its participants a coherent world picture in which they find their present status and past experience; it is also a system of self-reflections in which the participants may become critically aware of the way in which they are represented. The critical awareness is everything; it permits alternative and variant readings of situations. It defeats ideological orthodoxy without denying the unity of the culture. But my thesis is that tourism represents the world as spectacle—as a representation of representations; and that the relation between the tourist and the toured is, always, a relationship based upon what Said (1978) has described as an 'uneven exchange'. There is a tension between the realities experienced by visitors and by natives; this tension may be internalised by the native in the form of a split consciousness of self—a 'for-others' and 'for-self' between which an authentic self-understanding can come to grief. The tourist, of course, has no such problem; since reality has become a show, a 'sight-seeing' which has objectified and commodified the seen.

I propose to look into the representation of culture as a problem made visible during the process of modernisation. It is not as though such questions did not exist prior to the building of the railways; the Grand Tour was conceived wholly upon representations, and we could easily cite the

Ullrich Kockel (ed), *Culture, Tourism and Development: The Case of Ireland*, Liverpool University Press 1994, 117-128.

romantic search for the picturesque, the sublime and the exotic as being one of the foundations of modern package tours. Indeed, modern tourism may be described as the mechanisation of the picturesque.

But modernisation (with its ease of travel and universal communication), proceeded, and still proceeds, by the erosion of local cultures and the destruction of differences. Tourism is ambivalently linked to this destruction; it looks for the local and the particular which its own preconditions of existence are already eroding.

THE LIVING PICTURE

In the first week of October 1849, the Prince Consort addressed the Lord Mayor's Banquet, and the following passage was recorded by the *Illustrated London News* on 11 October 1849. The Prince was, at the time, conducting his successful campaign for the promotion of the Great Exhibition of 1851. He argued that

> [n]obody will doubt for a moment that we are living at a period of the most wonderful transition which tends rapidly to the accomplishment of that great end to which, indeed, all history points—the realisation of the unity of mankind. Not a unity which breaks down the limits, and levels the peculiar characteristics of the different nations of the earth, but rather a unity, the result and product of those very national varieties and antagonistic qualities. The distances which separated the different nations and parts of the globe are gradually vanishing before the achievements of modern invention, and we can traverse them with incredible ease; the languages of all nations are known and the acquirements placed within the reach of everybody; thought is communicated with the rapidity and even by the power of lightning… The Exhibition is to give us a true test and a living picture of the point of development at which the whole of mankind has arrived in this great task.

The Consort's speech is the primal statement of our dilemma. On the one hand the hegemonic power of modernisation; on the other, human variety. Can one survive the other?

This process of global unification required the creation of a 'living picture'. This part of the Prince's vision was taken up by *The Spectator* in September 1851, in the course of a survey of the spread of the illustrated paper. The Exhibition was 'a representation to the eye', and one which, like photography, 'speaks all tongues'. Pictorial representations, not limited by language barriers, 'may at once convey totally different and totally new ideas to the mind... [which] are universally comprehended... [and] make one participate in the gathered knowledge of all'. The Exhibition was 'performing the office of a large illustrated newspaper'.

Around the Exhibition an entertainment and visual display industry was developing. The *Times* of 21 August 1851 advertised nine panoramas or dioramas on display in central London, plus one huge model of the globe. Visitors arriving by cheap return tickets from the provinces could see vistas of the major European cities, the Hellespont, Niagara Falls and the sights to be seen on an overland journey to India, culminating in a view of the Taj Mahal. The actual tourism of a visit to Hyde Park was reinforced by the virtual or vicarious tourism of the panorama. Amongst all else that is claimed for it, we may wish to see the Great Exhibition as the founding moment of tourism-as-spectacle. To mechanisation is added dissemination.

The exhibits themselves represented cultural differences; there were sections devoted to regional and national manufactures, which were then imaged and disseminated through catalogues and other publications. To visit the different stands was to see the world on display. But these objects had been selected with a view to the European market; thus the manufactures of India were chosen by the East India Company on the basis of what the Company estimated to be the European concept of Indian—a representation that the Company itself had been instrumental in forming. The role of the great trading companies in the commercially directed stereotyping of foreign places is a story yet to be told.

We note in passing that international exhibitions continued and continue to be major vehicles for the ideologically driven representation of cultures. The Italian Exhibition staged at Earl's Court, London, in 1888 included a reconstruction of Venice, canals, gondolas and all. Amongst other examples was the French New Guinea pavilion at the Exposition Universelle, Paris, 1900. Here native architecture, artifacts and raw materials were brought together with examples of the natives. In 1908, in support of the Franco-British Entente, an exhibition at White City included, along with further reconstructions of African villages, the townland of Ballymaclinton, complete with 'genuine colleens' making lace, embroidery and carpets at the doors of their thatched cottages. This is uneven exchange of the crassest kind.

But, and this is the significant historical point, by 1851 the consequences of realised unity were already seen as deleterious to human variety by others closely connected to the Exhibition. A critical reaction to the modernist norm was already under way. Ralph Wornum (1851), writing in the *Illustrated Catalogue of the Great Exhibition*, argued that

> the time has now gone by, at least in Europe, for the development of any particular or national style, and for this reason it is necessary to distinguish the various tastes that have prevailed through past ages, and preserve them as distinct expressions, [because] by using indiscriminately all materials, we should lose all expression.

Human variety has to be preserved as 'distinct expression'. This reaction toward difference, particularity and national variety becomes the opposite pole to industrial sameness. This is the equal and opposite reaction to the force of hegemony. From now on, the representation of culture is enmeshed with the concept of 'distinct expression'. But Wornum was waking up to a problem already far advanced. Consequent upon the romantic quest for the sublime, areas of Europe had already been developed as 'heritage'.

Perhaps the most notorious example is to be found in the promotion of a supposed 'Highland Culture' in the 1820s. This has been extensively studied of late as an example of the 'invention of traditions' (Trevor Roper 1983). But it had been already identified publicly as an 'hallucination' as early as the 1840s, and its principle 'scholarship' exposed as fraudulent even earlier. Nevertheless, the notion of a highland costume and clan tartans continued to be spread by lavishly illustrated volumes, paintings, and by spectacle. The Prince Consort himself, the great modernist, appeared in the show. The pertinacity of the fraud suggests there were very powerful reasons for persisting with it in the face of all evidence, until it became a reality. The clan tartan, the highland costume, the piper, became and remained the iconic representations of Scotland to the world, diffused through imagery.

Throughout the nineteenth century the emergent separate nations of Europe each rapidly defined or had defined for them a concept of national character and national style; and within nations, regions and provinces followed suit, each with their 'distinct expression'. This process continues to this day, within 'emergent' nations. The study of folk costume, and the national costumes sublimated out of peasant dress afford many such examples. With this go such phenomena as the study of folk music, dance and the quest for 'national musical character'.

The degree to which these were pure inventions varied greatly; the Irish Gaelic revival, for example, had a base in historical reality. It was possible to point to a style of decoration and to an architecture and to claim 'national character' with some justification.

These national and regional styles, then, 'represented' their originals to the world at large through imagery—at first through topographical painting, then through the panorama and the illustrated book or newspaper, later on through photography and the picture postcard, and finally through the travel brochure, film and video. And, of course, through opera, dance, music and whatever other forms were capable of carrying the message. Travel for pleasure became a search for the origins of these representations. Where they had no substantial existence they had to be called into being. The search for the original was called 'sight-seeing.'

'Sight-seeing' as a category of social behaviour seems to derive from the practice of viewing the land as 'landscape'; laying an artistic category over an agricultural. In extreme cases, natural sights were viewed through a frame that one carried about on walks, like a non-recording camera. One 'framed' a view of the Lake District, the Alps, the ruins of Rome, and enthused about its picturesque qualities. The relation of this to the postcard and, of course, to the holiday photograph, is obvious without being entirely clear. A process of appropriation through viewing is at work.

This appropriation appears to work, first, by objectification, then by commodification, and then by a form of consumption. The primal process of consumer capitalism has its origins in the romantic concept of the picturesque.

The sights that one viewed were generally wild, sublime, backward and remote in economic level or historical origin: the Highlands, the Alps, castles, ruins. I write 'generally' because there was, briefly, an enthusiasm for the industrial sublime when cultivated Londoners visited Sheffield or Birmingham to view the mills and blast furnaces; and there was another current of urban tourism through which one might visit Paris or London and see their 'sights'. But all of these involved an aestheticisation of the object; the replacement of economic, military, agricultural or scholarly positions by one derived from artistic categories.

Edward Said has described the European study of the 'Orient' as involving an 'uneven exchange'. His study is well recognised as important, but for our purposes I think we must stress the inner-European character of sight-seeing and tourism, and point to the 'uneven exchange' that was involved within the continent.

The typical sights of tourism were 'peripheral': the Alps, the Highlands etc., and the West of Ireland. (And where there may seem to have been an even exchange, as between London and Paris, a little investigation shows the hidden inequality: Paris was represented to London in erotic terms.)

THE AESTHETICISATION OF IRELAND

The aestheticisation of the West of Ireland contains all these elements[*]:

> To dine in London one night and the next at the foot of Slievemore (in Achill Island), with time en route for a comfortable breakfast in Dublin—without a thought about luggage, or more ado than is involved in stepping from steamer to train and from train to road car—must satisfy the most exacting traveller (Midland Great Western Railway 1877).

A chain of hotels was linked by rail and carriage, forming a sequence of centres from which the tourist 'can visit a succession of really interesting and picturesque spots, from which a vast variety of charming and memorable excursions can be made'. It was an area where, according to the 1877 edition of the Midland Great Western Railway tourist handbook, 'many and powerful fascinations ... meet the eye at every step'.

A small literature came into being that extolled Connacht to the hunter, the fisher and the artist, three activities all formative of tourism and linked by the pursuit of the wild.

> The artist by whom this district [Achill] has not been visited, can indeed have no idea of its surpassing grandeur and sublimity; go where he will, he finds a picture ... add to this that every peasant the artist will encounter, furnishes a striking and picturesque sketch, and

---

[*] In what follows here, I am indebted to research by Mary Cosgrove, whose forthcoming doctoral thesis on the artist Paul Henry will contain much relevant material.

as they are usually met in groups, scarcely one will be without this valuable accessory to the landscape (Hall and Hall 1841).

Out in the darkness you see the women labouring and bringing wonder into the rocky darkness of the island with their heavy petticoats of red and blue that you will not surpass for colour in a Titian (Lynd 1912).

Paul Henry stayed in Achill from 1912-1919; he brought to his new locale a mind highly attuned to such evocative and aestheticising writing. His long stay in Paris, his association with Parisian post impressionism and the French artistic cult of the peasant, the enthusiasm for Brittany or Tahiti, and the mentorship of Whistler were all essential stages in an artistic education that met specifically Irish concerns. In his autobiography he portrays his discovery of Achill as a spiritual homecoming.

But the matter was, as we may expect, a good deal more mixed. The London newspaper for whom Henry supplied drawings regularly published feature articles on the pleasures of Ireland. 'Why you ought to go to Ireland', and 'Ireland as a Holiday Resort' are typical titles. As soon as 1912 his paintings were being used to illustrate Robert Lynd's 'Rambles in Ireland' (1912). It was Lynd who persuaded him to go to Achill in the first place; Lynd, the aestheticising travel writer, was also a member of Sinn Féin and an effective propagandist for the movement. His elegant and persuasive prose mixes romantic nationalism with romantic landscapes. Henry, child of presbyterian Belfast, was deeply susceptible to the combination. At the same time he certainly saw himself as a successor to Van Gogh's peasant-painter. He writes in his autobiography that:

I wanted to know the people, their intimate lives, the times of seed-time and harvest. Only after I had gained such knowledge would I be able to paint the country which I had adopted ... I wanted to study the lives of the people and their surroundings as closely and as singlemindedly as the French naturalist Fabre studied the insects of his devotion in the stony fields and vineyards of Provence (Henry 1951).

Well, yes! We need to look at the paintings for any sign of this. And, not surprisingly, we find singularly little. In fact, the human figure largely disappears from the paintings, and some of the best known are evocations of weather and mere stones.

David Brett

Achill for its natives ('for-self') was a place of deep, sometimes extreme poverty; a place from which most of the working population left on regular migrations; a place liable to small but very vicious riots frequently led by those women whom Lynd and Henry described in such glowing terms. The *Mayo News* wrote of 'an impoverished peasantry on an impoverished soil'. None of this appears in Henry's own memoirs other than tangentially. He was either amazingly unobservant, or his omissions are the sign of an unbearable ideological aporia.

The purpose of this example is not a critique of Irish post-impressionism (though I find it hard not to be exasperated by Henry's coyness), nor to try and reduce Henry's work to the level of class-induced self-deception, but merely to point to the violent, not to say the pathological, disconnection between the imagery that Henry (and other painters) were creating of Mayo and Connemara, and the actual life that was being led by the inhabitants. This disconnection was reinforced by nationalist writers such as Lynd, and continued into the official rhetoric of the state-to-be. It is a flagrant case of the ideological imposition of the aesthetic categories over the social, and reminds us of Benjamin's comments on the aestheticisation of politics.

These matters could remain within the domain of art-history, and we could continue to enjoy Henry's paintings with ease, had the painterly language which he, more than anyone else, created not been used, subsequently, for different purposes—a language of profiles, flat veils of atmospheric colour, luscious handling and judicious, very controlled, composition.

I turn now to the brochure 'The Irish Experience: travel holidays 1993' and a frontispiece portraying a group of men launching a currach from the rainwashed strand; behind them a language of profiles, atmospheric colour, luscious paint... This painting, by a John Skelton, is of a grouping very similar to one painted by Henry, but seen from another angle. It is also indebted to Flaherty's 'Men of Aran', a film whose imagery is part of this same pattern of representation. The purpose of this image, however, is to promote thatched cottages which are replicas of traditional Irish cottages, equipped with all the 'old style basics', but featuring modern comforts.

This sort of irony would be no more than facile if it did not point to a much more significant set of questions. Here, or in Tunisia, Portugal, or the Tower of London, we can watch ourselves representing ourselves to the world as the pastiched form of how we were previously represented. A 'for-others' to set aside a 'for-self'. Is there any form of cultural representation which is not, now, a kind of 'airport art'? Critically aware individuals have, for more than a century, sought to distinguish between the 'genuine' traveller and the 'tourist' (usually, of course, including themselves in the former category). Do we now have to stay at home?

In these examples, we have been concerned with the connection between artistic culture of some attainment, and commercial activity of the everyday kind; but there is a middle ground of mediated imagery. What we might call internal tourism. Many examples exist; for convenience I choose a recent documentary series dealing with the arts in Ireland - 'Art on Film'—three films commissioned by the Arts Councils North and South from independent filmmakers. These were latterly reviewed in *CIRCA* magazine by Desmond Bell, in terms that seem exactly appropriate to this paper. The second of these films explored the relation between landscape, local culture and the artist. A major contribution was by the American anthropologist Henry Glassie (who in other respects has done good service). He portrayed the landscape of Ireland as the product of patient farming and neighbourly decentralisation. Well, yes! Subsistence agriculture, landlordism, rack- renting, and latifundia, issuing in famine and emigration. Bell (1993) argues, and I am sure he is correct in this, that the very concept of landscape is a 'mediated relation, influenced by rhetorical constructs like painting, photography, the postcard and the tourist experience'. And what we experience in such films is the remediation of what was already mediated. Culture as spectacle. Please note in this and the previous example, that the 'uneven exchange' has ceased to be that of a 'centre-periphery' kind. The toured are complicit in their re-representation, and have internalised it as their own.

The writings of Frederic Jameson argue that the cultural logic of late capitalism points inexorably toward pastiche as the dominant mode of representation. 'Authentic' experience becomes impossible in the face of multiple, self-propagating and self-reflecting representations. Others, I am thinking here of Jean Baudrillard, have asserted that self-propagating representation actually is the form under which contemporary cultural experience exists; there is nothing outside or beyond the representation of representations.

We are left with a set of questions that are painful and exasperating in equal measure. Are we condemned to be the tourists of our own experience? More pertinently, is any form of tourism possible that does not involve pastiche?

David Brett

One of the melancholy pleasures of living north of the Border is to understand that you live in a region whose very name is disputed and whose representation cannot be other than critical. We witness anguished attempts by the Tourist Board to persuade the world (and ourselves) that we are worth a visit. I assure you: we are! But not in those terms!

Another recent writer in *CIRCA* has looked at the 're-imaging' of Belfast through its urban development. 'A post-modern, consumerist kaleidoscope of images floats uncomfortably on top of the brutalism of terrorist-proof buildings and the symbolism of the past. It is a condition of visual schizophrenia' (Neill 1993). He writes of 'separate cognitive realms': 'Consumer distraction is not a substitute for identity'.

The answer to this must be that identity, particularity, the 'antagonistic qualities' and 'distinct expression' are just that, consumer distraction, an exhibition sideshow; unless informed by a critical spirit. And this brings us back to the start of my paper and the task of representing a culture. I have argued, albeit in broad terms, that the representation of cultures is the first stage in their commodification. The role played in this process by the disseminated image is crucial, since it is the image that provides the source-material for subsequent pastiche. The activity that consumes and is fed by these commodities, is tourism.

CONCLUSION

I hope I have left an escape route from this maze of mirrors. One must resist the temptations of pessimism. I think I have, through the idea of a critical spirit.

Since everywhere—well, almost everywhere—has now become a site of tourism, everyone—well, almost everyone—has become increasingly aware of the commodification process by being its object. (Note here, that I am concerned with inner-European tourism—early, or what we might call primitive tourism is still rampant in the 'undeveloped' world, where its original hegemonic function remains unimpaired.) The original 'centre-periphery' model no longer holds when both capital and information are circulating on a centre-less surface. Is it possible that the 'uneven exchange' of tourism might be replaced by a more equitable 'visiting'? I think we are now witnessing to a critical spirit and seeking to focus it. I detect a sense of human ecology at work, a feeling for limitations that a responsible management of human and natural resources induces.

Allied to this is a critical sense of 'distinct expression'. We are now in a position to investigate the claims of cultural representations, to point to their shady origins and sometimes fraudulent assumptions. This is an urgent intellectual task in what has been called a 'new' but is, alas, a revived 'old' Europe of ethnic hatreds.

The Prince Consort wanted to have his cake and to eat it; he hoped for a unity that preserved differences. We know this to have been a false hope, and that modernisation does not bring about harmony but a state of continual tension between that which is coming into being and that which is vanishing. A critical understanding of the history of modernisation will always see it as a Janus-faced phenomenon. Tourism, as one of its typical activities, partakes of this ambivalence and equivocation; it will always tend to kill the thing it loves—difference. But we now perceive that difference too is problematic.

For a long time now European thought has been haunted by the fear that the very concept of culture has become a pastiche; that we live in a post-cultural age. What I feel is certain, is that an uncritical notion of culture, rooted in ideologically driven representations, cannot be sustained any longer. A culture for the future, and its representation, has to contain its own criticism. I offer this as a problem; not a solution.

REFERENCES

Bell, D (1993)
  Telling Tales: the Irish storyteller in the information age. *CIRCA* 63, 18-23.
Hall and Hall, S (1841)
  Ireland: its scenery and character. London: Jeremiah Howe.
Henry, P (1951)
  An Irish Portrait. The autobiography of Paul Henry. London: Batsford.
James, R (1983)
  Albert, Prince Consort. London: Hamish Hamilton.

Lynd, R (1912)
  Home Life in Ireland. London: Mills and Boone.
Midland Great Western Railway Tourist Handbook (1877 edition)
Neill, W (1993)
  Re-imaging Belfast. *CIRCA* 63, 34-35.
Said, E (1978)
  Orientalism. London: Routledge.
The Times, 21 August 1851.
The Spectator 9, September 1851.
Trevor Roper, H (1983)
  The invention of tradition: the highland tradition of Scotland. In
  Hobsbawn, E and Ranger, T (eds), *The Invention of Tradition*.
  Cambridge: Cambridge University Press.
Wornum, R (1851)
  The exhibition as a lesson in taste. In *The Illustrated Catalogue of the
  Great Exhibition*. London.

Cultural Heritage in an Oasis of Calm: Divided Identities in a Museum in Ulster

ANTHONY BUCKLEY
MARY KENNEY

INTRODUCTION

This article will explore three strategies which have been used for the presentation of culture in schools and museums in the context of Northern Ireland's 'troubles'. The strategies, indeed, have labels which are well-established in the vocabulary of Northern Irish educationalists. They are:

- that schools and museums should be 'oases of calm';

- that schools and museums should provide opportunities for intermingling between individuals of different ethnicities to encourage mutual understanding; and

- that schools and museums should enable individuals of different ethnicities to explore their own and each others' cultural heritage.

We shall first try to give these strategies a basis in an anthropological theory of ethnicity. Second, we shall show how these strategies have been given expression in some work at the Ulster Folk and Transport Museum.

The three strategies are directly related to three interconnected theoretical approaches. All of them emphasise the fact that Ireland (and specifically Northern Ireland) is a modern society. As in other modern societies, the culture of Irish (or Ulster) people is diverse, fragmentary and pluralistic.

The first point will be that ethnic identity is not the only identity that a person has and that different forms of identity are defined in the frameworks provided by specific relationships, situations and 'worlds' (Finnegan 1989). The second, derived from Barth (1969) will be that ethnicity arises not primarily because of the cultural diversity between the

Ullrich Kockel (ed), *Culture, Tourism and Development: The Case of Ireland*, Liverpool University Press 1994, 129-47.

ethnic groups but because of patterns in the way that individuals and groups typically interact. The third will be that individuals typically define themselves in the course of different kinds of discourse and 'social drama' such as narrative, gossip, music, dance, ritual or ceremonial. Some of these cultural forms are the 'property' (Harrison 1992) of a particular ethnic group cared for by individuals and organisations who act effectively as their 'curators'.

The Ulster Folk and Transport Museum has a responsibility to present the way of life and traditions, past and present, of the people of Northern Ireland. It will be argued here that it is correct for such a museum to represent a wide variety of the different worlds in which individuals define themselves; it should also provide opportunities for friendly and practical interaction between individuals of the different ethnic groups; and it should occasionally display aspects of cultural heritage which are characteristic of specifically ethnic identities.

OASES OF CALM: LIVING IN DIFFERENT WORLDS

The idea that educational institutions ought to be 'oases of calm' has long been important in the world of Northern Irish education. Its usually unstated theoretical premise is that people live in distinct and separable worlds.

The idea that individuals live in different worlds comes from a discussion by Ruth Finnegan (1989) of music in the English town of Milton Keynes. Finnegan shows that there exist many different musical 'worlds'. There is the world of brass bands, of folk music, of different kinds of classical music, of jazz and so forth. Each world is quite distinct from all of the others, has its own standards of judging between good and bad music, its own means of learning about music and so forth.

Quite apart from music, the more general point to be made from Finnegan's work is that individuals in modern society (and probably in most 'traditional' societies too) habitually live in countless different worlds, moving easily between them and acquiring in relation to each world a separate identity. An individual, therefore, does not have a single identity, but has in fact many different partial identities each defined by means of his or her relation to a specific world. In a Northern Ireland context, the most relevant fact is that only some of these worlds are definable in relation to ethnicity.

The fact that people do, indeed, live in different 'worlds' provides the pragmatic basis for the long-standing policy of creating, in schools and museums, 'oases of calm'. There is a tradition that the phrase 'oases of calm' originally referred to schools in the battle-torn, nationalist areas of west Belfast in the 1970s. It is said that, at a time when homes were being nightly raided, when rioting was an everyday occurrence, and when explosions and gunfire regularly rattled the windows, one could walk into a school and find peace. In these schools was an orderliness, a cleanliness, and a sense, above all, of calm, only heightened by the devastation outside the school railings. Children who spent their evenings 'bricking peelers' (or worse) would, in the daytime, sit in the school surrounded by vases of flowers and statues of saints.

Whatever the origin of the expression, the practical goal of creating an oasis of calm quickly extended into the state schools and into the world of museums. Schools and museums were to be 'neutral territory'. Into them, the troubles should not intrude. As well as the mere physical exclusion of 'the men of violence', it was also hoped to keep out of the classroom and the museum gallery contentious forms of debate that could 'politicise' these places.

In practice, however, this was not such a great problem. The school curriculum, in fact, exemplifies the division of the cultural universe into discrete worlds, and only some of these are directly related to ethnic division. In a school there are some subjects, notably history, religion, and the Irish language, which might raise sectarian issues. However, in segregated schools it was generally possible to deal even with these issues without raising hackles. For the most part, discussions of physics, chemistry, biology, art, woodwork, geography, literature and so forth can be undertaken without reference to sectarianism or social conflict.

Teachers, therefore, took refuge in the pluralism of the curriculum, and in the ideal of producing 'well-rounded individuals', i.e. people whose identity is defined in relation not only to parochial worlds where ethnicity is relevant, but also to the worlds of literature, science and the rest, where ethnicity has smaller importance. There was a parallel in the two 'national' museums in Northern Ireland, the Ulster Museum in Belfast and the Ulster Folk and Transport Museum in County Down. Of these, the Ulster Museum has a precisely similar breadth of concern as is found in a school. Inside its walls are departments concerned with such subjects as antiquities, art, botany, geology, textiles, or zoology, none of which would have any ethnic connotations.

The Ulster Museum, however, also has a department of local history. In this, though with a different emphasis, it shares concerns with its sister institution, the Ulster Folk and Transport Museum. In fact, neither the local history department of the Ulster Museum nor the Ulster Folk and Transport Museum have been highly controversial institutions. The reason for this again, as in the schools, has been because of the division of the social and cultural universe into diverse worlds.

A major feature of the Ulster Folk and Transport Museum is its open air museum, which depicts a dispersed rural community and a small town in Ulster in about the year 1900. Most of the exhibits in the open air museum have been dismantled and brought to the Museum, 'brick by brick'. As well as the open air museum, there are also galleries suitable for both 'folk' and 'transport' exhibitions. The Museum also stages demonstrations and 'events' aimed at illustrating the way of life of the people of Northern Ireland.

The themes depicted by the Museum over the years have been many and various, and in them the topic of ethnicity scarcely at all arose. The buildings exemplify older forms of vernacular architecture, and the way these have been used by different kinds of people from different parts of Ulster. Another theme has been the variety of agricultural practice. The museum's agriculture department has sought to encourage the breeding and preservation of rare breeds of farm animals. The Museum's textile department collects and displays textiles and their manufacture both for their own intrinsic interest, and for the light which these throw upon the lives of those who made and used them. Crafts, such as blacksmithing, printing, spademaking and woodworking, are regularly illustrated and displayed. The Museum displays all kinds of transport, including shipping—a major aspect of Ulster life—and road transport. Recently, a large gallery has been opened devoted entirely to railways. To nearly all of this, to raise the topic of ethnicity would have been inappropriate. The story of ethnicity in Ulster is not central to most of the worlds which exist in the north of Ireland. There are, simply, many other stories to be told.

The attempt to create 'oases of calm' in the schools and museums in Northern Ireland was, therefore, in large measure made possible through a recognition that the social universe within which Northern Irish people lived should not be divided into sectarian dichotomies. It was, however, a response by teachers and curators to the very extreme conditions of the 1970s when physical intimidation threatened the very foundation of their educational endeavours. As such, it tended to evade (though with some considerable justification) some of the central issues of Northern Irish life. From the mid 1980s, however, a new atmosphere became apparent. Ethnic conflict in Ulster ceased, at least for a time, to be acute and became chronic. Government took steps to encourage reconciliation, and local politicians responded with cautious goodwill. At the same time, educationalists also felt themselves able to take on a more positive role to encourage reconciliation.

SOCIAL INTERACTION:
EDUCATION FOR MUTUAL UNDERSTANDING

If identities are constructed in the context of specific 'worlds', they are also produced in the course of social interaction. Barth (1969) has famously argued that ethnic identity is defined not by the existence of distinctively ethnic 'cultures', but rather by patterns of social interaction which systematically maintain social boundaries. Akenson (1991) has taken up this viewpoint and has argued, using nineteenth-century data, that cultural differences between Catholics and Protestants are comparatively few (see also Buckley 1988a). In the same tradition, Whyte (1986) has weighed the factors in the Northern Ireland situation which sustain social boundaries—segregated religion, segregated marriage patterns, segregated residential territories. He concludes that the most crucial element in the maintenance of ethnic division in Ulster is segregated education. Buckley (1989), without disagreeing strongly, has argued that the lack of intermarriage is more important.

Since at least the 1970s, there have been attempts to provide opportunities for Catholic and Protestant children to intermingle. There are several 'integrated' schools, the most famous of which is Lagan College in Belfast (*cf.* Irwin 1991), where selection procedures ensure that no one ethnic group predominates. Government has declared itself in favour of these schools, and gives them financial support. Nevertheless, by leaving the creation of integrated schools to the initiative of parents, the pace of integrated education has been effectively slowed down.

One reason for the muted nature of government support for integrated education may have been the political opposition which such schools could generate. Another reason has been well articulated in a pamphlet by Wright (n.d.). This is that the commonly stated popular support for integration can sometimes disguise a desire to 'put something across on the others':

Do you know either of the following? Someone with a fantasy of Catholics and Protestants standing reverently before a Union Jack fluttering from the school flagpole; or someone with the fantasy of

Protestant and Catholic children dutifully absorbing a history syllabus which puts Protestants 'right about their Irishness'.

Separate education, he suggests, may itself be a means of managing mistrust, and too rapid an erosion of segregation may destroy the quiet which is currently in most schools.

The main thrust towards intermingling in the classroom comes not within schemes for integrated education, but rather through 'Education for Mutual Understanding' or 'EMU'. EMU was set up in face of a recognition that to force the pace of integrated schools would be unwise. EMU is now one of six cross-curricular themes built into the Northern Ireland Curriculum (Northern Ireland Curriculum Council 1990). Care is taken by those who support it to insist that it is neither 'a threat to particular cultures or traditions' nor 'an attack on the concept of segregated education in Northern Ireland'. Indeed, its critics suggest that, as such, it is ineffectual (e.g., Dunlop 1987).

Central to the EMU strategy has been the cultivation of regular and practical links between maintained and controlled (Catholic and Protestant) schools. Typically, classes from different schools come together on a regular basis for lessons in common, or they will undertake occasional projects often involving field trips or other outings together.

In this work, the education departments of the different museums have taken an active part. At the Ulster Folk and Transport Museum, there are, during school terms, some three 'EMU groups' visiting for 'EMU work-shops' every week. On these occasions, the children are usually divided into small ethnically mixed groups of six to eight children to do practical work involving farming, cooking, candle-making, embroidery, laundry and so on. The children may then be distributed into larger groups to take part in other activities, such as a visit to one of the houses in the Museum's open air collection to complete a 'work book' or a lesson by one of their teachers taken in the Museum's village school.

The schools that participate in these activities are almost always a pair of schools, one Catholic, the other Protestant, which have ordinarily been working together in close cooperation, for months or even, nowadays, years. Classes from these schools will usually visit the Museum on four separate days, and on each occasion, the children will work together in the same small groups. Often their visits to the Museum culminate in a longer visit to the residential unit situated in the urban area of the Museum's open air collection. This gives the children a chance to live together for a few days, working together and making friends.

In cultivating such contacts, care is taken to ensure that the effect will be positive. On the basis of research (McWhirter 1983), the work is designed to encourage practical interdependence and to be part of a long-term relationship between groups of Catholics and Protestants rather than a transitory relationship between individuals.

CULTURAL HERITAGE: CURATORSHIP

The final policy to be considered here is that of encouraging schools and museums, and indeed private individuals and groups, to explore their 'cultural heritage'. The policy has operated through two governmental agencies. One of these, the Cultural Traditions Group of the Community Relations Council, assists individuals and associations in the exploration and portrayal of the 'cultural heritage' of Northern Ireland. The other, the Department of Education (Northern Ireland), is more concerned with specifically educational matters. As with EMU, 'cultural heritage' is now one of the cross-curricular themes intended to permeate every subject in the Northern Ireland schools curriculum.

The idea that encouragement of the idea of 'cultural heritage' (including distinctively Protestant and Catholic heritage) might be conducive to social harmony is, at first sight, somewhat opposed to the practice of schools and museums in the early 1970s. At that time, in trying to sustain 'oases of calm', most educational bodies strove to avoid topics relating to cultural heritage, for fear that such subjects might stir up dissent. In practice, however, the gulf between the past and more recent developments has not been very extreme. The trail, indeed, was already blazed by the museums which, despite the constraint of political fears, had nevertheless continued to present Ulster's 'cultural heritage' throughout the troubles.

At the Ulster Folk and Transport Museum, as was explained above, an 'oasis' was initially created by representing to the public only those Northern Irish worlds which bore little controversial weight. The Museum's aim, however, was never a wholly negative one of 'not stirring up trouble'. On the contrary, under its then director, George Thompson, the Museum had a much more positive vision. Thompson's frequently reiterated purpose was to present to people living in Northern Ireland a vision of what they had in common, a vision around which people of all persuasions could unite.

Anthony Buckley and Mary Kenney

If there has, therefore, evolved a need to alter Museum practice, it is not because the earlier practice was mistaken. It is rather because, in changed times, the earlier vision can now be made more complete. To the vision of a common heritage, one must, therefore, add an additional vision of cultural diversity. The reason this is necessary is that, in reality, Northern Irish society is diverse and plural. If local people are to discover a pride in their own society, then this pride has to be, *faute de mieux*, in a plural society. There is, of course, something of a paradox in asserting, on the one hand, that there are comparatively few elements in Northern Irish culture which are not shared by people on each of the two sides, and, on the other, that there is a need to display and even celebrate cultural diversity. The paradox is solved by showing that, in general, the distinctive elements of ethnic culture tend to be found not among the population at large but among enthusiastic individuals.

In particular, there are a number of different organisations—the churches, the political parties, Hibernians, the Orange Order, Comhaltas Ceoltóirí Éireann, the Gaelic Athletic Association, the Ulster Society and others—which have a quasi-curatorial function, conserving different kinds of intellectual or other cultural property on behalf of a wider ethnic group and enabling this property to be commemorated or reproduced and transmitted to a wider public and to subsequent generations. Although many of these organisations have a widespread following, each one contains small groups of enthusiasts, and even professionals, who have responsibility to keep the culture alive for the benefit of less active members and a more general public. And there are other, less highly organised individuals, storytellers, musicians, dancers, 'local characters' etc, who are occasionally called upon to give performances. All such people act effectively as curators or custodians of the culture on behalf of the wider ethnic group providing, in different circumstances, a focus for ethnic allegiance, for political influence or for occasional but vital social organisation.

In using the idea of 'curatorship' in this way, we are suggesting that museums are in many ways similar to other bodies which, however, are more concerned with the preservation and presentation of specifically ethnic culture. Museum people are familiar with the idea that museums are a 'treasure house, educational instrument, or secular temple' (Baxendall 1991), an idea which has been most graphically elaborated by Duncan (1991). Such ideas, indeed, permeate current debates about the nature of museum curatorship (see, for example, Alpers 1991). Horne mocks his own use of this imagery, describing museum-visiting tourists as 'pilgrims', moving from holy place to holy place. He calls this pilgrimage 'the way of the tourist' (Horne 1984).

Cameron, however, has argued that museums need not always be 'temples'. Instead, he says, some museums move towards another classical form, the 'forum' (Cameron 1972). In a forum, there is no mere reverence for the treasures and symbols of the dominant groups in society. There is, rather, a coming together of diverse opinions for disagreement or debate (Karp and Levine 1991).

The idea of 'museum as forum' in a context of acute ethnic tension is, of course, a risky one. A forum can too easily become not so much a place for civilised debate, as 'disputed territory'. The questions which can too readily arise in debate may include: which people in society are eligible to have their symbols and representations of themselves placed in a museum; and who should be excluded? In such a case, the museum might cease to be a forum and could revert to being, once more, a temple, except that what would be in dispute would be the right to occupy the temple.

In attempting to show the 'way of life and traditions' of ordinary people, the Ulster Folk and Transport Museum has always tried also to show the considerable variety of the worlds within which these people live and move. In so doing, it has tried to provide versions of the past, and sometimes of the present, which members of the public of all kinds could enjoy. In the same way as other 'cultural' bodies strive, somewhat exclusively, to care only for the 'culture' of their own ethnic group, so the Museum's responsibility has been to do this on behalf of people of all Northern Irish groupings.

This is not to say that the Museum has set itself only the evangelistic purpose of 'reconciling the two sides of society'. On the contrary, the Museum has seen itself as representing life in Northern Ireland in all its complexity. As we have suggested, individuals in Northern Ireland, as elsewhere, live in multitudinous different worlds. To explore a large number of these worlds, to present to a general public what the participants in these worlds see as vital and valuable, is to validate the lives of these individuals, and to recognise and to celebrate their identities in each of these diverse worlds.

However, it must be recognised that the earlier tendency of evading discussion of sectarian issues was ultimately unsatisfactory. It might be valid not to overemphasise Ulster's ethnicities: to miss them out altogether, however, is to be untruthful. The earlier policy was a positive response to

137

dreadful circumstances, but it was also one which had to change as circumstances altered. By the mid 1980s it was possible to consider a modified approach based, however, firmly upon the achievements and insights of the past. The Museum, therefore, began gently to move towards the explicit presentation of divisive and sectarian culture. In so doing, it could not afford to court disaster by becoming a 'forum'. It could only hope, in the 1980s and 1990s, to be a 'temple'. This, however, in its context, was not a timid, ignoble or outmoded aspiration, for the temple to be constructed could hope to be one for the whole of society. Alhough it might give recognition to the reality of ethnic cleavages, the Museum could also hope to provide a vision of society in which everyone could take some pride, and around which everyone could, in due course, cohere.

TWO EXHIBITIONS

We shall now consider two exhibitions at the Ulster Folk and Transport Museum which attempted to address directly that culture which provides a focus, in the wider society, for ethnic allegiance, and which also expresses ethnic rhetoric. In so doing, we most emphatically do not wish to suggest that these exhibitions in some way implied a challenge or condemnation either of other present day work at the Museum, or of the work which had preceded it. On the contrary, it would be wholly improper of a museum such as the Ulster Folk and Transport Museum to devote itself exclusively to subjects relating directly to ethnicity, for life in Ulster is much too rich to be characterised within such a narrow framework. Moreover, it is only because the Museum has, throughout the difficult period of the 1970s, established itself as an 'oasis of calm', as a place where Ulster's past was explored with impartiality, that it became possible in the late 1980s to venture into more difficult territory.

The two exhibitions were called, respectively, *Brotherhoods in Ireland* and *Remembering 1690: the folklore of a war*. Both exhibitions arose out of a piece of library and field research undertaken by A D Buckley but supported and assisted by his colleagues, most directly by T K Anderson, C McCullough and P S Robinson, and also by M C Kenney. The research began as a study of the Orange Order but it extended, little by little, to include the Hibernians, the Knights of St Columbanus, the Freemasons, the friendly society movement, the temperance movement, the trade unions, the Roman Catholic sodalities and the guilds. The bodies which were studied were selected because of their manifest similarity one to another. Because of this similarity an all-inclusive name was sought, and eventually, P S Robinson suggested 'Brotherhoods in Ireland' as a title.

The 'Brotherhoods in Ireland' exhibition

Brotherhoods in Ireland was a temporary exhibition presented in the course of 1988. Its storyline was based on the rather abstract ideas of Goldman (1970), namely that actions are complex, and stratified at different levels. Its central theme was that, while in some respects (i.e., at some levels of organisation), the ritual and other actions performed by the different groups were different, in other respects (i.e., at other levels), their cultures were the same. In the apparent diversity of the different brotherhoods was the unity of a common culture.

The exhibition was organised into sections, each devoted to materials relating to different organisations or types of organisation. The sections can quickly be listed:

- introductory section

- the urban guilds

- the Order of Malta (once a crusading order, now a charitable body devoted to medical care)

- the Freemasons

- the Orange and Royal Black Institutions (bodies devoted to upholding Protestantism)

- the Ancient Order of Hibernians (similar to the Orange Order, but devoted to upholding Catholicism)

- the Archconfraternity of the Holy Family (a Catholic sodality)

- the Knights of St Columbanus (an order devoted to upholding Catholic values)

- the Ancient Order of Foresters (a friendly society)

- the Irish National Foresters (a friendly society, now mainly a social club)

- the Independent Order of Odd Fellows (a friendly society)

- the Independent Order of Rechabites (a temperance friendly society)

- the British Order of Ancient Free Gardeners (a friendly society)

- the Loyal Order of Ancient Shepherds (a friendly society)

- the Royal Antediluvian Order of Buffaloes ('the poor man's Freemasonry'—a social club)

- the trade unions

In this array of different organisations, there was, first of all, much diversity. Part of the very purpose of the display was to emphasise the ethnic diversity, and this feature of the exhibition was evident to anyone who had even a slight local knowledge. Several of the bodies, the Orange Order, the Black Institution, the Hibernians, the Order of Malta, the Knights of St Columbanus and the Confraternity of the Holy Family, had purposes which were explicitly related to a specific religious tradition. The other organisations—the trade unions, in general, being a notable exception—had an informal tendency to confine their recruitment to one or the other ethnic group.

The diversity, however, went beyond religion and ethnicity. Some of these bodies were strictly temperate; others were drinking clubs; some were organisations to encourage piety; others had a quasi-political purpose; many had the narrowly practical purpose of organising health insurance. The political ethos of the groups varied considerably. Some were straightforwardly nationalistic or unionist, but other, notably the friendly societies and the trade unions, were ideologically rooted in forms of socialism. They also varied in the social classes from which they recruited. The Order of Malta, in its more exclusive reaches, is restricted to Catholics who can lay claim to aristocracy. The friendly societies (now largely defunct in Ireland) drew their support among the skilled or white collared, as too do the Freemasons, who, nevertheless, also appeal to the well-to-do.

The aim of the exhibition, however, was to show the unity underlying the diversity. The diversity of purpose, ethnicity and ethos between the different organisations, portrayed through the division of the exhibition into sections, was, therefore, challenged by the similarity between the sections. As far as was practical, each section contained an inherently similar set of artifacts:

-   regalia in the form of collars, aprons, sashes, or uniforms

-   lists of officers often with high-sounding titles such as 'Worshipful Master', 'Chief Ranger' or 'Worthy Primo'

-   lists of degrees, again with elaborate titles, such as the Sublime Degree of Master Gardeners', or 'the Excellent and Perfect Prince Rose Croix of Heredom and Knight of the Eagle and Pelican'

-   degree and officers' certificates

-   jewels to indicate degrees and honours obtained

-   wall charts and similar teaching materials for instruction in the significance of the organisation's symbolism

-   banners for use in processions

The point behind all of this was that the diversity which existed in the different organisations was a diversity expressed through inherently similar cultural forms.

It is not for a Museum exhibition to provide an opportunity for commingling between different groups of people. Nevertheless, it seemed to be appropriate, at the formal opening, that the invited guests invited should include members of significantly opposed organisations, Hibernians, Orangemen, National Foresters, Freemasons, clergy and religious of different denominations and others, all of whom had contributed, by advice and also by lending items, to the production of a single exhibition. This exhibition celebrated a tradition, common to each of the two ethnic groups, which was so multipurpose that it was even used to express and provide a focus for division.

'Remembering 1690': the folklore of a war

The second exhibition was constructed, in 1990, to commemorate the 300th anniversary of the Battle of the Boyne. This battle, as everybody in Ulster knows, is annually commemorated by the Orange Order as the moment which established a Protestant ascendancy in Ireland. Its title, *Remembering 1690*, evoked the slogan, 'REM 1690', often written on Northern Irish walls.

This exhibition was, in fact, only one of several exhibitions and events put on, over several years, to commemorate anniversaries of the events of the Williamite/Jacobite Wars. As well as the 1690 celebrations, there were commemorations of the siege of Derry organised, with a remarkable show of goodwill on all sides, not only by the unionist Apprentice Boys of Derry but also by the mainly nationalist Derry City Council. There were official celebrations in Dublin, and the city of Limerick also joined in with celebrations of its two sieges.

In the world of Northern Ireland museums, the Ulster Folk and Transport Museum exhibition was by no means the most important of the 1690 exhibitions. The Ulster Museum in Belfast put on a magnificent, specifically historical display, entitled *Kings in Conflict*. This exhibition recounted the Williamite/Jacobite war as one between three kings, not only William III and James II, but also Louis XIV of France. In this context, the Irish campaign was relegated to a small place in the wars, and much of the Irish folk history was obscured by a depiction of the conflict in Europe. Ireland did, however, feature in the exhibition's most splendid feature, a tableau showing the signing of the Treaty of Limerick in which the faces of actors delivering speeches were projected on to the faces of life-size models. In the Ulster Museum's exhibition, therefore, emphasis was shifted from Ireland to Europe, and from the battle of the Boyne (sacred to Orangemen) to the Treaty of Limerick which concluded the war, and which settled Ireland's fate for the next hundred or more years.

The Ulster Folk and Transport Museum's exhibition was more modest. It dealt with the 'folklore of the war', i.e., with the popular history as depicted in banners, bonfires, trinkets, songs, dances and narratives. Its central materials for display, therefore, consisted of rhetorically divergent representations of the traditional histories of Ireland.

While researching this topic, it was noted that certain organisations had effectively appropriated certain events of the war, becoming unofficial 'curators' of these specific traditions. Thus, the Apprentice Boys of Derry twice annually commemorate the Siege of Londonderry. Similarly, on the Twelfth of July the Orange Order commemorates the Battle of the Boyne. In addition, it was found that events in the south-west of Ireland, specifically the Battle of Aughrim, the two sieges of Athlone and the two sieges of Limerick—in short the 'Fight for the Shannon'—as well as the aftermath of the war had become the 'property' of nationalist traditions. These events were most readily accessible through pictures on banners preserved by the National Foresters and Hibernian movements, both of which recruit among Catholics, and also through Jacobite and nationalist songs and 'Irish dances' which refer to these events.

To tell the story of the Williamite/Jacobite wars through its 'folklore', it was simplest to divide the exhibition into four sections. Two of these dealt respectively with the 'Siege of Derry' and the 'Route to the Boyne'. The other two dealt with the 'Fight for the Shannon' and with the 'Aftermath'.

The first two sections concentrated mainly upon narratives and practices derived from Apprentice Boy and Orange tradition. As well as paintings on banners and drums, the Museum was able to borrow paintings of the Siege by Robert Jackson, a well-known mural painter from Londonderry. Jackson also provided a full-size 'half model' of the effigy of Lundy (some 15 feet high, in full dress uniform, and replete with a moustache of which Salvador Dali would have been proud), as well as other models to illustrate the former practice of burning the effigy from the massive Walker monument (now destroyed by explosion) in Derry. The Museum also borrowed some precious commemorative glassware in the Williamite tradition.

The other two sections dealt respectively with 'the fight for the Shannon' and with the aftermath of the Treaty of Limerick. These stories were told through banner paintings of the National Foresters and the Hibernians, but the sections also included glassware, trinkets, photographs of statues and so on relating both to the battles and sieges and to the Treaty of Limerick.

As well as this, there was a videotape presentation. This too was in two parts. The first half dealt with processions, bonfires, drumming and so forth, relating to the Siege of Derry and the route of King William to the Boyne. The second also had processions, but it also focused upon the narrative, poetry, music and dance in the Jacobite and later the nationalist traditions which commemorated the later stages of the war in the south west.

As this exhibition was being prepared, it was interesting to note that many of the people who ventured an opinion or who were consulted, not least those involved in the teaching of history, thought that the purpose of the exhibition ought to be to correct the mistaken history found in the folk histories.

In general, the temptation to debunk was resisted. Instead, the exhibition adopted a rhetorical conceit that the specific popular histories of the Williamite/Jacobite wars were not incorrect, but were rather incomplete. The exhibition suggested that it was only by putting together the nationalist and the unionist histories that an adequately complete and, indeed, broadly true picture of the war could be presented.

Because of the nature of the ethnic division in the north of Ireland, the Museum daily confronts an especially acute form of the problem identified by Livingstone and Beardsley (1991) of how to include the points of view of several different publics 'without sacrificing … coherence and aesthetic will'. It was not felt to be the Museum's place baldly to declare that these ethnic histories were wrong, nor to claim merely that 'the professionals know best'. Equally, however, it had to tell a limited and coherent story. The exhibition, therefore, sought to affirm the validity of the popular histories of both sides, thereby upholding the honour of the people who espouse these histories. It did not merely disparage the popular histories, nor the largely working class and ethnically-based groups which espoused them. Nor did it try to uphold the honour of one section of society against another. It rather declared, by implication, that each section of Ulster society has as much right to have its importance confirmed as any other.

CONCLUSION

We have suggested here a social-theoretical framework to underpin certain pragmatic policies current in schools and museums in Northern Ireland. Our hypothesis is first, that identity in Ulster is pluralistic, being defined within a variety of different worlds; second, that ethnic identity and ethnic conflict arises through the maintenance of social boundaries in social interaction; and third, that certain cultural forms have become the cultural property of the ethnic group, under the curatorship of organised groups of enthusiasts or professionals, and that these provide a source of rhetorical ideas and act as a focus for ethnic allegiance and social organisation. This framework, we have argued, provides a satisfactory justification for the current educational and museological policies of providing oases of calm where individuals of different ethnicities can both meet together and explore both the cultural heritage they share, and that which is particular to each of the two sides.

It is always appropriate when discussing Northern Ireland however, to add a note of pessimism. There is a limit to what policies of 'cultural heritage' and 'mutual understanding' in schools and museums can achieve, and the limitations ought to be pointed out. Schools, museums and, indeed, many unofficial bodies, among them sometimes the churches, have attempted to bring individuals of the two sides in Ulster into dialogue, and also to create images of a common heritage or common symbols around which the population might be able to unite. This is all very laudable, and indeed such activities, images and symbols might in the long run become building-materials from which peace in Ulster might be constructed. However, we have also argued that it is not the existence or non-existence of divisive or common culture which lies at the heart of ethnic differentiation and conflict in the north of Ireland. Rather it is the use to which culture is put in specific interactions. If it is the responsibility of schools and museums to push in the right direction, one cannot expect such bodies to undertake the task by themselves.

There are, of course, many substantial issues which lie outside the ambit of schools and museums. Schools and museums cannot, on their own, solve the major political conundrum of the Irish border; they cannot heal social inequalities; they cannot remove intimidation, sectarian murder and ethnic cleansing; they cannot, by themselves, make Catholics and Protestants want to give up their preferred 'social distance' from one another. What they can do, however, is to provide neutral territory where members of the two sides can sometimes meet each other and where they can also learn about the things which they have in common and the things which divide them. They can, therefore, provide some of the building materials with which people can hope to construct more harmonious relationships. The kinds of identities which will emerge in Northern Ireland will be in the last resort however, the ones that Northern Irish people negotiate and construct for themselves, in the worlds that they themselves create in their day-to-day social interactions.

REFERENCES

Akenson, D (1991)

Small Differences: Irish Catholics and Irish Protestants 1815-1922. Dublin: Gill and McMillan.

Alpers, S (1991)
The museum as a way of seeing. In Karp, I and Levine, S (eds), *The Poetics and Politics of Museum Display*. Washington: Smithsonian Institution Press, 25-32.

Barth, F (1969)
Introduction. In Barth, F (ed), *Ethnic Groups and Boundaries: the social organization of cultural difference*. London: Allen and Unwin.

Baxendall, M (1991)
Exhibiting intention: some preconditions of the visual display of culturally purposeful objects. In Karp, I and Levine, S (eds), *The Poetics and Politics of Museum Display*. Washington: Smithsonian Institution Press, 33-41.

Buckley, A (1988)
Collecting Ulster's culture: are there really two traditions? In Gailey, A (ed), *The Use of Tradition: essays presented to G B Thompson*. Cultra: Ulster Folk and Transport Museum.

Buckley, A and Anderson, T (1988)
Brotherhoods in Ireland. Cultra: Ulster Folk and Transport Museum.

Buckley, A (1989)
The spirit of Irish sectarianism. *Canadian Journal of Irish Studies* 15, 23-30.

Cameron, D (1972)
The museum: a temple or a forum. *Journal of World History* 14, 197-201.

Duncan, C (1991)
Art museums and the ritual of curatorship. In Karp, I and Levine, S (eds), *The Poetics and Politics of Museum Display*. Washington: Smithsonian Institution Press, 88-103.

Dunlop, D (1987)
Inter-school links: a Limavady experience. In Robinson, A (ed), *Education for Mutual Understanding; roles and responsibilities*. Coleraine: Faculty of Education, University of Ulster.

Finnegan, R (1989)
The Hidden Musicians: music making in an English town. Cambridge: Cambridge University Press.

Goldman, A (1970)
A Theory of Human Action. Englewood Cliffs: Prentice Hall.

Harrison, S (1992)
Ritual as cultural property. *Man* (NS) 27, 225-44.
Horne, D (1984)
The Great Museum: the representation of history. London: Pluto
Irwin, C (1991)
Education and the Development of Social Integration in Divided Societies. Belfast: Department of Social Anthropology, Queen's University.
Karp, I and Levine, S (1991)
Introduction: museums and multiculturalism. In Karp, I and Levine, S (eds), *The Poetics and Politics of Museum Display.* Washington: Smithsonian Institution Press, 1-9.
Livingstone, J and Beardsley, J (1991)
The poetics and politics of hispanic art. In Karp, I and Levine, S (eds), *The Poetics and Politics of Museum Display.* Washington: Smithsonian Institution Press, 104-27.
McWhirter, E (1983)
Contact and conflict: the question of integrated education. *Irish Journal of Psychology* 6, 13-27.
Northern Ireland Curricilum Council (1990)
Cross curricular themes. Belfast: Northern Ireland Curriculum Council.
Whyte, J (1986)
How is the boundary maintained between the two communities in Northern Ireland? *Ethnic and racial studies* 9, 219-34.
Wright, F (n.d)
Integrated Eucation and New Beginnings in Northern Ireland. Belfast: Corrymeela Press.

Tourism and the Irish Language: Problems and Prospects

MÁIRÉAD NIC CRAITH

INTRODUCTION

The relationship between language and identity is extremely complex and has proved the substance of many academic investigations. Many scholars are strongly of the opinion that languages, and particularly minority languages, are instruments of cultural differentiation and central pillars of ethnic identity. In a paper entitled 'Language Law and the Celtic Languages in the United Kingdom', Dr Herbert Gassner (1990), a Croatian from Austria, said that

> justice to the minority is more important than mere convenience. Death of a regional language is also the death of a certain sort of culture.

As a case study, the relationship between Irish language and identity in the Republic of Ireland has much to recommend it. Debates on the relevance of Irish as a symbol of ethnicity or Irish identity have elicited strong responses in the past. One negative reaction to this question was recorded in the *Irish Independent* on 20 July 1985, with the words of K.D. O'Connor, that we no longer feel

> the need to prove we're Irish by waving the three-leaved shamrock of race, language and Catholicism which were an imposition by nineteenth-century nationalists; valid for their time, distinguishing marks upon a dispossessed peasantry, patches of poverty and humiliation.

For the purposes of this essay, I feel it reasonable to assume at the very least the importance of the Irish language as a distinct component of cultural

Ullrich Kockel (ed), *Culture, Tourism and Development: The Case of Ireland*, Liverpool University Press 1994, 149-60.

identity in Ireland, and here I rest my case with Professor Joseph Lee (1989), who argues that

> it is hardly going too far to say that but for the loss of the language, there would be little discussion about identity in the Republic. With language, little else seems to be required. Without language, only the most unusual historical circumstances suffice to develop a sense of identity.

ATTITUDES TOWARDS THE IRISH LANGUAGE

In a 1973 survey on attitudes towards the Irish language (CLAR 1975, cited in Bord na Gaeilge 1986), it was found that

> the central dimension in the attitude system ... characterised the Irish language as a focus for feelings of ethnic or national identity. Irish was perceived as an important validator of our cultural distinctiveness and, as such, something whose maintenance and transmission needed to be secured.

A comparative survey carried out ten years later (Ó Riagáin and Ó Gliasáin 1984) indicated that public support for the language as expressed in the earlier study had been gaining ground over the interim period. However, while there is this strong support at the more abstract, ideological level, in practice the language has long suffered from an association with backwardness and penury; Irish speakers are perceived as

> smaller, uglier, weaker, of poorer health, more old-fashioned, less educated, poorer, less confident, less interesting, less likeable, lower class, of lower leadership ability, lazier and more submissive compared to an English speaker. Basically an Irish speaker is more undesirable.

This view of the Irish speaker is to no small extent a result of the presumed connection between the language and a particular type of rural-based, patriarchal nationalism, and has therefore fallen into disrepute as this form of nationalism declined in popularity. Today, however, attitudes to the language are changing as the use of Irish is growing in urban areas, which provide a very different socio-economic setting.

In recent times a more favourable attitude to Irish has been recorded by the Henley Centre (1991). Research by this centre revealed that 25% of the population, whom they termed 'Young Irelanders', had competent skills in the language. These young people had a very positive attitude towards the language and believed that it would become increasingly important in the future. A further 9%, termed the 'Old Romantics', were convinced of the relevance of Irish to contemporary society, believing that its significance would increase with time. They themselves, however, lacked competence in the language.

While it is not possible in the space of this article to examine in any depth the sociological and sociolinguistic background to this development, nor indeed its wider societal implications, I shall try to assess the implications of a noticeable shift in language use in the context of culture contact from two perspectives:

- To what extent is the Irish language, under these circumstances, an integral aspect of Irish cultural identity that might be utilised as a resource for tourism?

- What are the possible and likely effects on the language and its popular use of different types of tourist-host interaction?

The first question is vital in order to determine the 'commercial' utility and potential benefits of promoting the language from a particular, i.e., tourism-related, angle at present, whereas the second question is more concerned with the wider issues involved in language policy and language planning, which will have a bearing on the long-term prospects of 'exploiting' the language as a heritage resource. Both questions assume that practical and economic issues are relevant to the successful revival and maintenance of Irish in the future. This is a view shared by many socio-linguists. Edwards (1985) says

it is quite clear, I think, that pragmatic considerations—of power, social access, material advancement, etc.—are of the utmost importance in understanding patterns of language use and shift; by extension, they are also the primary determinants of success for any language planning exercise.

UTILISING THE LANGUAGE AS A TOURIST RESOURCE

There is no doubt that, under the present circumstances, the Irish language is an integral aspect of Irish cultural identity that might be employed as a resource for tourism. The present Bord Fáilte Tourism Development Plan for the years 1993-97 (Bord Fáilte 1992) would indicate an acceptance of the Irish Language as a cultural resource, which is marketable as a tourist attraction. It says that

> the survival of Irish as an everyday language in several locations is of great interest to visitors. The language serves to emphasise our distinctive identity in Europe. The opportunity exists to build on this, particularly in the extensive Gaeltachtaí in Kerry, Connemara and Donegal.

Urban versus rural Gaeltacht

This statement in itself is of interest in that it validates the language as a tourist commodity in the scenic, rural historic Gaeltacht, and without doubt these Gaeltacht will always continue as a major tourist attraction. It fails, however, to take account of the extensive growth of the language in recent years in cities such as Dublin and Cork.

While some may regard an urban Gaeltacht as artificial, it must not be forgotten that the original Government designated Gaeltacht areas were themselves defined by artificial boundaries which aimed at preserving the language pockets at a particular point in the recession of Irish towards the more remote western coastal areas.

Furthermore, until a successful policy of positive discrimination is activated in these areas, these historic Gaeltachtaí will further decline. Caoimhín Ó Danachair (1969) has suggested that the wasting of the historic Gaeltacht has already come about in two ways. First of all, he says,

> the area in which Irish is spoken has gradually shrunk, getting smaller and smaller. There are whole parishes in Waterford, Cork, Kerry, Clare, Galway, Mayo and Donegal where Irish was the ordinary language at the beginning of the present century in which there now survive only a few aged native speakers of Irish... The second form of wastage is the declining population within the Gaeltacht districts.

This decline has progressed steadily since the Great Famine and still continues up to and in our own time.

The strategy of reversing the contraction of the Gaeltacht is enigmatic and perplexing. As John Edwards suggests, without positive intervention, these areas will continue to reduce. If however, particular economic aid is supplied, 'there is the danger of creating enclaves which are seen to be artificial, precisely because they are seen to have been specially relieved of certain pressures, by insiders and outsiders alike' (Edwards 1985). The portrayal of historic Gaeltacht in tourist brochures, in as far as there is any such portrayal at all, is essentially one of a predominantly rural backward nature—a quaint society consisting almost entirely of old men drinking Guinness in the bars while their donkeys and sheep freely roam the roads.

Many modern Gaeltacht areas, however, are of an urban nature; easily accessible to visitors and offering all the comforts of a city life. In the words of Joe McMinn (1992),

> [t]his is the language striking back at the very place least associated with it—the city. Irish has developed a new image—very different from the one mocked by Joyce at the end of *Portrait*, of the old, drooling scanachaí who cannot imagine life outside the Gaeltacht.

Some urban districts have already recognised the tourist potential of the language. In Cork, Gael-Taca, which was set up in 1989, articulated the view that a vibrant Irish language 'will play a more important role in tourism policy in the future' (Gael-Taca 1992).

In Galway, for example, Gaillimh le Gaeilge are currently pursuing the promotion of the city as a 'bilingual Celtic city'. The 1992 annual report of this body (Gaillimh le Gaeilge 1992) clearly recognised the benefits which a bilingual policy would afford the city:

> The incorporation of a bilingual policy into the Galway Regional Tourism Plan would protect, maintain and develop the economic benefits that Galway city already receives from the Irish language and would in no small way enhance its position as the Cultural Capital of Ireland. No other city in Ireland has the potential to achieve these aims. Galway competes in increasingly competitive domestic and international Tourism markets. To enhance its appeal in growth

sectors in tourism, it needs to maximise the real and desirable differences that it has in its character, its language, its cultural heritage and diversity.

Demand for Irish

While the socio-cultural implications of this new trend remain a matter for further anthropological research, it must be noted here that these urban Gaeltacht may well have significant market potential for tourism, especially when one considers the vast numbers of people outside Ireland who invest time and money in an attempt to learn and absorb the language.

The Irish language is taught in many universities worldwide from Tokyo to Liverpool, from Harvard to Uppsala/Sweden and to Lublin in Poland—the only university in the world where learning Irish is compulsory for students of the culture in these islands. In Germany, which has long been the third biggest market for the Irish tourism industry, Celtic Studies

with special emphasis on the Irish language—are taught at the universities of Bonn, Bochum, Hamburg, Freiburg and Würzburg (Kockel 1993).

Outside higher education, Irish is taught in adult education centres in most cities in Central Europe and many places elsewhere on the Continent, including Brussels, Amsterdam and Paris. Conradh na Gaeilge branches have been established in many European countries, including Switzerland, France and Spain, and there are also branches in the US, the most recent of which is the Texas branch.

A number of tourism boards in European regions, including, for example, Wales and Scotland, but also non-Celtic language areas such as Friesland, have already recognised a positive correlation between the active promotion of minority languages and the growth in tourism-related development. A recent consultative paper for the Welsh tourist board (Stevens *et.al.* 1992) states that

[t]ourism has an important role to play in the economy helping to provide adequate employment for bilinguals, especially young Welsh-speakers.

The report emphasises the importance of providing economic opportunities especially for young people through language-related tourism developments. It also highlights the increasing demand for tourism products which have a distinctly local flavour, and which reflect an indigenous culture—thus stressing the need for a thoughtful approach to the sensitive "packaging" of localities. It then becomes essential to examine thoroughly the actual, everyday constituents of these useful and convenient buzz-words "cultural identity", and consequently reconsider the image of Ireland and the Irish as projected to the tourist.

Tourist-host interaction and the language

Most types of tourism in Ireland involve, to a greater or lesser degree, social and cultural interaction between tourists and hosts. Thus there are a variety of openings for the 'unobtrusive' introduction of Irish in different contexts, such as bilingual menus or calendars of events. Bilingual placenames could be used very effectively as a stepping stone between the modern names and the meanings preserved in the oral tradition. The following quotation from Brian Friel's play *Translations* gives some idea of the complexity and fascination of Irish placenames (Friel 1984):

> We've come to the crossroads. Come here and look at it, man! Look at it! And we call that crossroads Tobair Vree. And why do we call it Tobair Vree? I'll tell you why. Tobair means a well. But what does Vree mean? It's a corruption of Brian ... an erosion of Tobar Bhriain. Because a hundred-and-fifty years ago there used to be a well there, not at the crossroads, mind you—that would be too simple—but in a field close to the crossroads. And an old man called Brian, whose face was disfigured by an enormous growth, got it into his head that the water in the well was blessed; and every day for seven months he went there and bathed his face in it. But the growth did not go away; and one morning Brian was found drowned in that well. And ever since that crossroads is known as Tobair Vree—even though that well has long since dried up.

The strategy of the adoption of bilingual placenames has already been adopted by Galway city and a placenames committee, officially recognised by the corporation, is actively engaged in the provision of suitable names for new housing developments.

Slightly more challenging to the tourist would be the use of Irish only on posters which are otherwise self-explanatory. To give one example, few tourists in Spain would miss a bull fight announced on a Spanish-only poster; they are well capable of putting together the information conveyed by the picture, date and placename. This scheme is already being used in some Celtic regions of these islands, for instance during Skye Week in the Isle of Skye, and has been successful in increasing tourists' awareness and appreciation of the language as an aspect of living culture, rather than a mere feature of the past. The Scottish Tourist Board now uses Gaelic quite prominently in its advertising.

Particular language events and festivals can prove advantageous to the economy of any variety of settings. 'Éigse Carlow' is an example of the successful promotion of Irish in a festival atmosphere which has served as a major tourist attraction for the town. This festival, which was begun in 1979 as a mere weekend phenomenon, has rapidly expanded into a two week event that has attracted tourists from afar and has involved the active support of many of the town shops, businesses and restaurants (*cf.* Fishman 1991). 'Éigse Uí Ríordáin' is an equally successful Irish language event held annually in Cork City, which benefits both locals and tourists alike. Many other cultural festivals, such as 'Slógadh', 'an tOireachtas', 'Féile Feabhra', or the 'Pan Celtic Festival', regularly prove economically beneficial to their various locations in any given year.

While special language events laid on for the benefit of the tourist may have some attraction in certain circumstances, it would, from a language maintenance point of view, probably be more effective to integrate use of the language into existing events. One fairly successful example of this has been 'Dúchas an Daingin', an all-Irish celebration of local heritage and contemporary culture held in Dingle outside peak season, which attracts a fair number of visitors—many of whom don't actually speak the language, but who come for the language experience. A different form of this is the linking of the language to other holiday activities such as hill walking, painting or field studies (archaeology, botany, etc.), which has been offered successfully by 'Oideas Gael' in Donegal since 1984. In all these various experiments, the language is integrated into "ordinary" activities, rather than being presented as a tourist spectacle. Thus a creative sociolinguistic framework is established in which the language may flourish through association with economic benefits.

The main problem with the encouragement of language use in everyday circumstances at the cultural interface created by tourism is, in the eyes of some observers, the potential change in vocabulary and grammar that may result from this interaction. However, such arguments presume that any change in the language is tantamount to its decline, thus completely over-looking that treating language as a static, sacrosanct fossil is more likely to diminish its usefulness as a means of conversation than creative adaptation to the communicative needs of the present. As Lee (1989) points out,

> [i]t is sometimes asserted that Irish lacked the vocabulary of the modern technological world, and was therefore an 'inefficient language'. The argument, even if true, is trivial. All languages have to regularly improvise new terms. All languages lacked an adequate vocabulary for the economic changes occurring since the mid-eighteenth century. Vocabularies appropriate to industrial society had to be forged in all languages. They were. Obscure languages proved no barriers to industrialisation in nineteenth or twentieth-century [*sic*] Europe.

Languages are in a constant state of flux. In a recent study on the Irish language in the urban Gaeltacht of West Belfast, for example, Dr Gabrielle Maguire (1990) noted that the Irish of the children from Shaw's Road was characterised by an accelerated deviation from linguistic norms. One of the most significant changes in the Irish spoken by these children was the collapse of the initial mutation system. This development had a reductive effect on both the tense system and the gender distinction of nouns. Qualifying adjectives were usually also left unlenited. Despite the loss of initial mutations, however, it seldom caused confusion.

Change in language is not an issue to be avoided. It is merely the breathing of new life into old languages. In the Isle of Skye at present, for example, a Gaelic terminology database is being compiled to ensure that Scots-Gaelic keeps up with the times. The real issue of change is not how it can be avoided, but rather how it can be managed in such a way as to benefit, rather than erode, the language in the process. Considering that the largest number of visitors to Ireland come from urban areas abroad to urban areas here (*cf.* Pollard 1989), the obvious focus for the increased utilisation and enhancement of the language in a tourism context would seem to be the promotion of the use of Irish in urban settings.

CONCLUSION

Meticulous research is required in order to determine fully the extent of the urban Gaeltacht in Ireland today. The bilingual infrastructure which exists in many cities in Ireland both north and south of the border needs to be examined fully in order to ascertain the extent of this asset, a linguistic asset which has the distinct advantage of being located precisely in urban areas, and therefore enjoys the benefits of the main commercial, industrial and administrative centres of the island. Such economic benefits will assure the future enhancement of the language in that it will be associated with prosperity rather than poverty and education rather than backwardness.

In this essay, I have tried to draw attention to the possibility of a new and stronger future for the Irish language—a future which would influence the language to grow, to improvise new terms, and to develop a vocabulary appropriate to an age dominated by economic imperatives. The essay has also given attention to an urban resource, a resource which to date has been underutilised and undervalued. The linking of Irish in a more 'natural' way to urban activities can only serve as a boon, both to the language, and to tourism.

REFERENCES

Bord Fáilte (1992)
   Developing Sustainable Tourism: tourism development plan 1993-97.
   Dublin: Bord Fáilte.
CLAR (1975)
   Committee on Irish Language Attitudes Research: Report. Dublin:
   Stationery Office.

Edwards, J (1985)
Language, Society and Identity. Oxford: Basil Blackwell in association with André Deutsch.

Fishman, J (1991)
Reversing Language Shift: theoretical and empirical foundations of assistance to threatened languages. Clevedon: Multilingual Matters.

Friel, B (1984)
Translations. In *Selected Plays of Brian Friel*. London: Faber and Faber, 377-447.

Gassner, H (1990)
Language law and the Celtic languages in the United Kingdom. *Contact Bulletin* 7(2), Autumn, 1-2.

Gael-Taca (1992)
Gael-Taca Submission for an Irish Language Television Service. Cork: Gael-Taca.

Gaillimh le Gaeilge (1992)
Tuairisc Bliana 1992. Galway: Gaillimh le Gaeilge.

Henley Centre (1991)
Planning for Social Change. Dublin: Henley Centre.

Kockel, U (1993)
HIBERNIOPHILIA GERMANIAE: preliminary explorations of a curious relationship. *Chimera* 8, 73-77.

Lee, J (1989)
Ireland 1912-1985: politics and society. Cambridge: Cambridge University Press.

Maguire, G (1990)
Our Own Language: an Irish initiative. Clevedon: Multilingual Matters.

McMinn, J (1992)
Language, Literature and Cultural Identity: Irish & Anglo-Irish. In Lundy, J and Mac Póilín, A (eds), *Styles of Belonging: the cultural identities of Ulster*. Belfast: Lagan Press, 46-53.

Ó Coileáin, A (ed) (1986)
The Irish Language in a Changing Society: shaping the future. Dublin: Bord na Gaeilge.

O'Connor, K (1985)
Ireland—a nation caught in the middle of an identity crisis. *Irish Independent*, 20 July.

Ó Danachair, C (1989)
The Gaeltacht. In Ó Cuív, B (ed), *A View of the Irish Language*. Dublin: Stationery Office, 112-21.
Ó Riagáin, P and Ó Gliasáin, M (1984)
The Irish language in the Republic of Ireland, 1983: a preliminary report of a national survey. Dublin: Bord na Gaeilge
Pollard, J (1989)
Patterns in Irish tourism. In Carter, R and Parker, A (eds), *Ireland: contemporary perspectives on a land and its people*. London: Routledge.
Stevens, T *et.al.* (1992)
Tourism 2000—A Strategy for Wales: tourism and the community—a paper for discussion. Cardiff: Welsh Tourist Board.

Part 3

Community Impacts of Tourism

Low Income Households and Tourism in Northwest Connemara

MARY TUBRIDY

INTRODUCTION

In the region of northwest Connemara, low income households are finding it increasingly difficult to become directly involved in providing a tourism service. This has happened despite recent shifts in tourism policy, which is placing emphasis on exploiting the natural and cultural heritage for special interest and activity tourism.

Between 1992 and 1993, research has taken place on behalf of FORUM, the Irish rural project in the *Third EC Poverty Programme*, to develop a tourism plan which aims to generate increased socio-economic benefits for disadvantaged groups and low income households. The report (Tubridy 1993) includes a review of the impacts of tourism on low income groups, an inventory of the region's heritage resources, and recommendations for future tourism development entitled *Community Led Sustainable Tourism*.

This article describes the interlinked series of initiatives required to increase the economic and social benefits of tourism to low income groups. These include policy changes among statutory agencies, training initiatives, and financial assistance for new types of products whose development would specifically benefit individuals on low income as well as community based development/tourism groups.

METHODOLOGY

As the research arose from an awareness within the region that tourism had potential for community led sustainable development, the methodology emphasised the participation of the community, and of low income groups in particular. This method can best be described as action research, where

Ullrich Kockel (ed), *Culture, Tourism and Development: The Case of Ireland*, Liverpool University Press 1994, 163-69.

the principal aim of research is to act as a resource for the community and where the resulting plan serves to explain, reflect and record its opinions.

The area covered by the Tourism Plan is delineated by a line running from Leenane, via Recess to Roundstone, effectively all English speaking Connemara. At seven locations within the region (population c.8,000), 'SWOT' (Strengths, Weaknesses, Opportunities and Threats of tourism) sessions were held at an early stage at which the public was given an opportunity to contribute to the discussion on tourism development. Further meetings took place with the six small tourism/community development groups throughout the region, with individuals involved in various types and scales of tourism initiatives and local and national administrators. Other sources of information include a recently published review on the impact of tourism on cultural identity (Edmondson *et.al*. 1993), which is partly based on the results of a baseline survey, commissioned by FORUM, of low income households (Byrne *et.al*. 1991).

TOURISM AND LOW INCOME GROUPS

Accommodation

Byrne's survey revealed that low income households which provide a 'Bed and Breakfast' service share certain distinguishing characteristics. The most important of these is that all are supported by a regular source of earned income. They all have dependent children who help to run the Bed and Breakfast, and most of the women who operating these enterprises have previous experience in a service industry. None of the Bed and Breakfast venues are registered with Bord Fáilte, either because they do not meet the criteria for registration, or because their owners are fearful about the tax and social welfare effects of registration. This effectively excludes low income households from participating in Bord Fáilte marketing activities or in being listed in brochures put together by local community-based tourism organisations.

There is a low level of participation by low income households in the provision of houses to let. A sample survey throughout the region revealed that only 32% of houses to let/holiday homes were owned by local people. Among the 121 low income households surveyed by Byrne *et.al*. (1991), only one had a house to let. While many low income households have land on which houses to let could be built, planning regulations forbid the construction of non-essential one-off housing in the countryside.

In the absence of a source of income from paid employment which would provide low income households with the resources to invest in tourism, there is an essential need for targeted financial support to allow for the establishment, upgrading and expansion of accommodation by low income households. This should include grants for the restoration of old houses, support for the development of small camping sites and the upgrading of accommodation through the installation of heating systems to allow for off-season tourism.

Criteria for registration of accommodation with Bord Fáilte must be reviewed to allow for the registration of small-scale accommodation which can be developed by households on limited means. This means allowing for the registration of houses with one and two bedrooms (instead of the regulation three) and camping sites which have less than the presently stipulated twenty pitches.

Activity tourism

With the exception of cycle hire and deep sea fishing, the expanding area of activity tourism is being exploited by people from outside the region. No low income household in Byrne's survey provided an activity for tourists. Several adventure centres offer a wide range of activities such as walking, mountaineering, sub aqua, sailing, wind surfing and canoeing. All have a common requirement for access to water and land, resources generally owned by the local community, particularly small farmers who are beginning to feel antagonised by this new pressure on their land.

Starting at school, training is required to provide young people living in the region with the skills and interests necessary to develop an activity tourism business. There are many indigenous sports clubs within the region, which, with support (for training, insurance), could provide activities directly for tourists. The integration of local clubs and sporting activities (badminton, fishing, shooting etc.) would generate new products and allow tourism to support community skills and facilities.

The development of activity tourism by low income groups will require grant aid which should be given selectively to landowners and low income groups at attractive rates. Matching funding under the present 50/50 arrangement will exclude low income groups. Grants should also be given to small-scale developments. Under the last round of Structural Funds an equestrian enterprise was eligible for grant aid only if it had a minimum of twenty horses.

The requirement of matching funding could be met more easily if group projects were encouraged. This type of support is particularly important for a type of tourism service which will require land owned by several farmers. Under the last round of Structural Funds, group projects did not receive significantly higher levels of funding. In order to stimulate real community based development, higher levels of support should be offered to group projects and the criteria for groups should be set at five. The perennial problem of public liability insurance is a particular constraint to the development of activity tourism by farmers in Connemara, as few of them have any public liability insurance.

Special interest tourism

Special interest tourism is based around interpretative centres which have recently been built or expanded with the support of Structural Funds: at Letterfrack (The Connemara National Park), at Leenane (Killary Cultural Centre) and in Derrylea (near Clifden) where a local farmer has built a crannog and restored an old cottage. Two individuals offer specialised tours and a festival based on the environment is held in Letterfrack twice a year. Within northwest Connemara, sites of heritage interest are owned by the community and particularly by small farmers. The natural environment of the region is special, dominated by peatlands which have almost disappeared elsewhere in Western Europe.

Training is required to enable the community to preserve, manage and interpret the relevant heritage features of their farms or community landscape for tourism. Resources are also needed for small-scale interpretation initiatives which can benefit individual households. These may include interpretation of the sea among accommodation providers who are situated within easy walking distance of the shore, and the provision of support for stiles, paths and maps to direct visitors to features on their land or within their locality.

Farmers must be given training and financial incentives to manage their land for conservation and public access. The Office of Public Works should play a role in environmental education within the region in an effort to dispel the widely held assumption that conservation implies sterilisation of land, state ownership and the provision of services to tourists.

Training

The state's training authority for tourism, CERT, provides training through formal courses in Galway Regional Technical College, which is one and a half hour's drive from northwest Connemara. Teagasc offers a short night-time course over eight weeks. FÁS responds to requests by community groups for courses which may have a tourism training element.

Both short- and long-term training programmes in tourism and related subjects need to be available on request in the region to both tourism operators and people interested in becoming involved in tourism. This training should be commissioned and co-ordinated by a community based organisation. Training should focus on special interest/activity tourism as well as hospitality skills, languages and marketing. This must also serve to develop a critical attitude to tourism and its role in local development. Training must be complemented by an information and advisory service based in a Resource Centre staffed by at least one full-time Community Tourism Officer.

   The cost of the external training services provided by CERT must be reviewed so that its services are accessible to community and low income groups. All these initiatives imply that resources should be given not only to the statutory agency (CERT) but also to community based tourism development organisations.

TOURISM AND OTHER ECONOMIC SECTORS

Despite the presence of c.300,000 visitors in northwest Connemara each year and the decline in the viability of farming, most of the food consumed by visitors is imported from outside the region. The integration of other sectors of the local economy with tourism should result in more benefits to indigenous producers and processors. This demands an enlightened and innovative approach to development in this region by organisations such as Teagasc, Bord Iascaigh Mhara, the Office of Public Works and the Department of Agriculture.

Environmental management

There is considerable frustration with the management of roads, the water supply, sewerage treatment facilities and amenities of the area, particularly beaches. There is an awareness that this situation is exacerbated by tourists and tourists' cars.

There is an urgent need for investment by central government in northwest Connemara so that the region will have the infrastructure necessary to sustain its environmental quality. This implies that grant allocations from central government would consider not only the size of the local population but also the extent of tourism. Community groups should be given training and access to advice and financial support to help them bring about improvements to local amenities and encourage sensitive development. There is a need for a management plan for the integrated development of the region's principal resource, land, which is coming under increasing pressure from tourism, conservation, forestry and the intensification of sheep grazing.

CONCLUSION

There is a need for a change in approach among tourism policy makers, to shift the emphasis of development towards the unique assets of the region: its scenery and people. It must be recognised that tourism will be sustainable only if it serves to allow for the maximum amount of local control which must be kept informed through appropriate training. This implies that the administration of tourism must be re-structured to allow for greater control of its development at the local level by community based groups. Such a structure linked into the present statutory agency through the County Enterprise Board or Regional Tourist Development Organisation is a logical development of the present informal networking arrangement which already operates within each community. A community based tourism development organisation would have the dual function of co-ordinating training, the development and marketing of tourism services and of representing community interests to other agencies.

The policy regarding financial incentives for tourism needs to be reviewed so that a certain amount is targeted at individuals on low income, not only for social and equity reasons but because the unique natural and cultural heritage of the region is the heritage of this group. Grant aid should be given for accommodation and all the criteria for grant aid should be set to allow the maximum people on limited means to develop a viable and valuable tourism enterprise.

There is a need for changes in the operation of the social welfare system to give greater encouragement to individuals on low income to leave the security of the social welfare net through developing an enterprise. There is, therefore, a case for the present concession whereby individuals, in certain circumstances, can continue to draw social welfare benefits while developing an enterprise, to be extended to all unemployed persons over a three-year period.

REFERENCES

Byrne, A *et.al.* (1991)
North-West Connemara: a baseline study of poverty. Galway: Social Science Research Centre.

Edmondson, R, Fahy, K and Byrne, A (1993)
Tourism and cultural identity. In O'Connor, B and Cronin, A (ed), *Tourism in Ireland: a critical analysis*. Cork: Cork University Press.

Tubridy, M (1993)
A Plan for Community Led Sustainable Tourism in NW Connemara. Dublin: Natural Resources Development Centre/Éigse Ltd.

Recreation Capability Analysis:
A Case Study of Southwest Mayo

MARY O'FLAHERTY

INTRODUCTION

Tourism has been described as an aspect of recreation that can be viewed in turn as an aspect of leisure. Increasingly, tourism researchers and professionals are recognising that recreation and leisure are important motivations in tourism experiences. Modern society's concern for the environment, urban life-style, increased mobility and better education has promoted interest in active outdoor leisure, and thus increasingly there is a fusion of recreation with tourism.

However, with the environment playing a central role in attracting tourists involved in recreational activities, it is essential that in developing the tourist industry we do not kill the goose which lays the golden egg.

To this end, systematic analysis of the attractiveness and potential of a given area can form the basis for

-   comparing present use of resources with their distribution and quality;

-   a means of identifying areas which require development or protection;

-   or designating areas where there is an opportunity to initiate development.

In addition, it can point to the type of recreation use to which the land is best suited.

This essay seeks to outline the methodology employed in assessing the recreation potential of southwest Mayo, and to highlight its value as a planning tool in drawing up a recreation strategy for the area.

Ullrich Kockel (ed), *Culture, Tourism and Development: The Case of Ireland*, Liverpool University Press 1994, 171-82.

Mary O'Flaherty

RECREATION CAPABILITY ANALYSIS

Numerous forms of analysis have been tested; most fall into two categories. The first deals with the evaluation of the landscape and the second assesses the capability of the countryside to accommodate particular ranges of recreational activity (Glyptis 1991). It is the latter—recreational capability analysis — which has been applied to the study of southwest Mayo.

The methodology to be employed in evaluating the recreation potential of the study area is fashioned upon that used by Greer and Murray (1988) in drawing up a recreation strategy for the Mourne Area of Outstanding Natural Beauty. Their methodology, in turn, was drawn from the National Coastline Study in the Republic of Ireland.

The study of southwest Mayo in many ways follows the format of the Mourne AONB report, and for that reason its aims, the methodology employed and the strategy proposed are outlined.

Its study brief entailed the preparation of a recreation strategy which would act as a framework for more detailed plans. Both active and passive recreational pursuits were to be dealt with, particularly outdoor activities. It was hoped that it would provide a model for similar studies in other areas of high amenity and recreational value.

The strategy rationale is based on the concept of integrated development, and for this reason the interlinkages between recreation and other landuses in the area and role in the economy are considered. The strategy itself outlines ways in which the potential of Mourne AONB may be maximized, taking into consideration environmental issues. Three broad policy zones are introduced which form the basis for a locality specific development strategy and management framework.

THE CASE STUDY

Set between Clew Bay to the north and Killary Harbour to the south, southwest Mayo encompasses an area of 2,517 square kilometres. Its landscape is diverse, consisting of upland, lake, lowland and coast. Its upland areas, the Croagh Patrick range, the Sheeffry Hills, Ben Gorm and Mweelrea (the highest mountain in Connacht), give the area its character, but account for its poor agricultural quality. Sheep rearing, forestry and turf production are the dominant landuses. The rivers and lakes are an important resource to the area, particularly in terms of fishing. The Erriff River is one of the main salmon fishing rivers in Ireland, while the nearby Tawnyard Lough is noted for its good sea trout.

Apart from Louisburg and Westport, settlement is dispersed in general, although there is some ribbon development along the main roads radiating from the towns.

Its location on the western seaboard, distance from major urban centres and prevalence of marginal land give southwest Mayo all the hallmarks of peripherality. However, its wealth is its landscape, which gives it a beauty comparable to Kerry or Donegal but which, as yet, remains relatively unexploited.

Breakdown of study area into units and elements

Recreation capability analysis involves a number of steps. An initial survey and study of ordnance survey maps were the basis for the breakdown of the study area into five broad geographical units. These were further sub-divided using criteria such as physiography, visual enclosure, landuse and routeways, for example, an upland area, coastal area or valley (Figure 9).

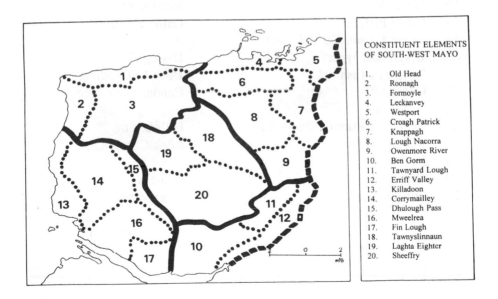

CONSTITUENT ELEMENTS
OF SOUTH-WEST MAYO

1. Old Head
2. Roonagh
3. Formoyle
4. Leckanvey
5. Westport
6. Croagh Patrick
7. Knappagh
8. Lough Nacorra
9. Owenmore River
10. Ben Gorm
11. Tawnyard Lough
12. Erriff Valley
13. Killadoon
14. Corrymailley
15. Dhulough Pass
16. Mweelrea
17. Fin Lough
18. Tawnyslinnaun
19. Laghta Eighter
20. Sheeffry

Figure 9   *The southwest Mayo region*

173

Table 9   *Listing of recreational activities*

National Coastline Study	West-Mayo Study
1. Swimming	Swimming
2. Shopping	
3. Sunbathing	
4. Sightseeing (touring)	Cycling
5. Picnicing	
6. Boating	Wind Surfing
7. Walking/Rambling	Walking/Rambling
8. Court and Organised Games	
9. Sailing	Sailing
10. Golfing	
11. Coarse Fishing	Coarse Fishing
12. Shore Fishing	Shore Fishing
13. Pony trekking	Pony Trekking
14. Camping	
15. Surfing	Surfing
16. Waterskiing	Waterskiing
17. Game Fishing	Game Fishing
18. Horse Drawn Caravanning	
19. Diving (all types)	Diving
20. Deep Sea Fishing	Deep Sea Fishing
21. Canoeing	Canoeing
22. Cruising	
23. Mountaineering/Hillwalking	Hillwalking
24. Rock-Climbing	Rock-Climbing
25. Hunting	
26. Game Shooting	Game Shooting
27. Orienteering	Orienteering
	Motor Cross
	Mountain biking

Activity analysis, classification and weighting

This involves an assessment of the range of activities the study area is likely to support. The aim was to keep the activities within a practical range and, therefore, activities unlikely to gain sufficient participation in this area, or unsuited to the type of resource available, were eliminated. Examples of such are caving and snow-skiing.

The National Coastline Study (Table 9) had an extensive list of twenty seven activities which included both active and passive pursuits. The study also undertook an examination of each activity in order to establish

-    its basic characteristics;

-    its resource requirements;

-    its compatibility/conflict with other activities or landuse;

-    the facility requirements;

-    the status of the activity;

-    the activity appeal and linkages;

-    the normal environmental requirements.

This examination yielded an initial breakdown into three basic categories.

Primary   -   Activities with a wide appeal, low conflict rating and a high popularity rating.

Secondary -   Activities with a moderate range of appeal, moderate conflict rating, and increasing popularity rating.

Tertiary   -   Activities with a specialist or limited appeal and limited (though increasing) popularity rating.

The activities within these categories underwent further testing and grading on the basis of 'Skill' (the level of expertise required), 'Appeal' (the degree of universality of each activity) and 'Organisation' (the extent to which the activity is dependent on man-made facilities, amount of equipment, and a certain level of organisation). This produced the following set of categories and sub-categories (Table 10).

Table 10   *Classification of activities*

PRIMARY	Group A	Universal appeal and involvement. Minimum facility requirement, minimum skill to participate, high linkage.
	Group B	Wide appeal, modest facility, amenity requirements, minimal skill requirements.
	Group C	Wide appeal, dependent on available facilities, considerable level of skill required, equipment content (private) high, organisational content high.
SECONDARY	Group A	(Within category) widest appeal and least organisation, facilities and equipment input, least skill requirement.
	Group B	Wide appeal (though limited in terms of Primary activities), considerable facility/organisational input, some skill required.
	Group C	Appeal limited (by facilities and skill requirement) and high skill and facility content required.
TERTIARY		No grouping indicated or necessary.

Table 11   *Listing and classification of activities*

CODE	ACTIVITY	CATEGORY	GROUP
1	Swimming		A
2	Walking	primary	B
3	Cycling		C
4	Sailing		
5	Coarse Fishing		
6	Shore Fishing		A
7	Pony Trekking		
8	Surfing	secondary	B
9	Game Fishing		
10	Diving		
11	Deep Sea Fishing		C
12	Canoeing		
13	Hillwalking		
14	Rock climbing		
15	Orienteering		
16	Shooting (Game)	tertiary	
17	Mountain Biking		
18	Waterskiing		
19	Motor Cross		
20	Wind surfing		

Arising from this categorisation, a points system was devised which could be applied to each element to establish the recreation potential of the area.

Primary Activities	-	Group A	-	20 points
		Group B	-	18 points
		Group C	-	15 points

Secondary Activities	-	Group A	-	14 points
		Group B	-	10 points
		Group C	-	6 points
Tertiary Activities	-	All	-	5 points

The complete range of activities are classified and graded in Table 11.

Having drawn up a list of activities and a points system to facilitate scoring, it was necessary to examine the activities themselves to establish basic resource criteria. This was then applied to each element to identify what activities were appropriate and possible. For example, canoeing requires water (river, lake, sea), which is accessible by road.

Grading of resource quality

The National Coastline Study took quality of resource and level of organisation and facility provision into account, and awarded bonus points accordingly. For this study, activities involved are of an informal nature, and use the environment in its natural state and, therefore, do not require permanent facilities or organisation (consequently, golf and court games are excluded).

However, it was felt that the quality of resource for a given activity should play some part in the scoring system; consequently, individual elements were awarded bonus points ranging from one to ten, depending on resource quality, based on expert opinion. For each activity three opinions were sought from experts in each activity, who were familiar with the study area. An average score was applied to the relevant element.

By adding all the scores, a total score was established for each element. There was a wide range of scores recorded, ranging from the lowest at 85, to the highest at 315. The scores were grouped as follows:

200 and more points	-	wide range of activities possible
100-199 points	-	medium range of activities possible
less than 99 points	-	limited range of activities possible

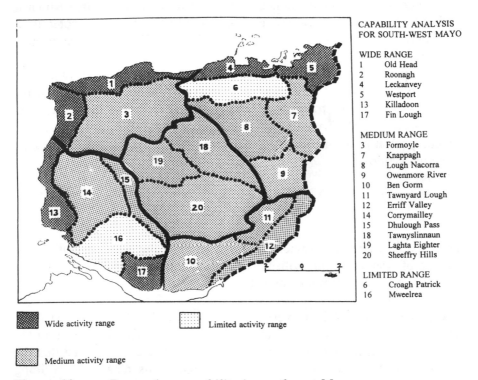

Figure 10 *Recreation capability in southwest Mayo*

Results

Finally, the activity range or capability was mapped according to the above groupings (Figure 10). The findings suggest that the area has considerable recreation potential, with only two elements having a limited activity range. The inland elements have a medium activity range, while the wide activity range is dominated by the coastal elements, as they can accommodate water-based as well as land-based activities.

The area in the immediate vicinity of Westport has a wide activity range, and has potential which is not being fully exploited, reflecting, perhaps, the dominant concern with the development and management of the town itself. The potential of the coastal area of Louisburgh has only recently been recognised. In addition to receiving increasing use from day-trippers, two activity centres have been set up in this area.

The coastal strip from Roonagh pier southwards is a resource which is underutilized. However, before development of such recreation potential is considered, problems of access and unsightly agricultural practices need to be tackled.

The upland areas, most of which possess a medium capability range, are relatively underused. In the main, the analysis points to the fact that the potential value of the foothills of Mweelrea and Croagh Patrick has been overlooked. The Sheffry hills, which form part of the 'Western Way', have severe problems of erosion due to overgrazing, and require immediate remedial action.

CONCLUSION

The capability analysis provides information regarding the distribution and quality of resources. But with regard to the interpretation of the study's findings, a number of points must be highlighted.

The capability survey, by its very nature, is a neutral method of assessment, drawn up to aid graphic representation and hence visual comparison of the various units within the study area. It must also be acknowledged that the pattern, as presented, could easily be altered in its detail by ascribing different scores to individual activities.

The identification of an activity within an element does not necessarily mean that the activity is present within the area at this time, nor is it a recommendation that it should be. In some cases the exploitation of such potential could lead to user conflict or negative impacts on the environment.

However, the recreation capability analysis does provide a solid foundation upon which to build a recreation strategy for the study area. The strategy will entail the application of a spatial framework which will link place with activity, using criteria such as access, recreation capability and distance from urban centre. Implied in such policy formulation are factors such as intrinsic conflict with other activities, ease of development, and best use of resource. The spatial framework will take the form of three policy zones (Figure 11), which are as follows:

(A) Zones suited to large numbers requiring development and facilities to accommodate them.

(B) Areas where recreation could be developed/initiated on a moderate scale, without detriment to the landscape.

(C) Remote or sensitive zones where volume numbers would be inappropriate—suited to specialist activity or those seeking a wilderness experience.

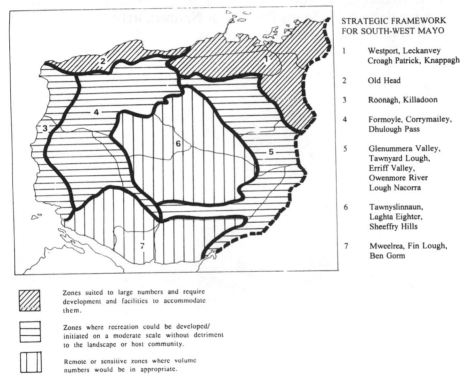

STRATEGIC FRAMEWORK FOR SOUTH-WEST MAYO

1   Westport, Leckanvey Croagh Patrick, Knappagh

2   Old Head

3   Roonagh, Killadoon

4   Formoyle, Corrymailey, Dhulough Pass

5   Glenummera Valley, Tawnyard Lough, Erriff Valley, Owenmore River Lough Nacorra

6   Tawnyslinnaun, Laghta Eighter, Sheeffry Hills

7   Mweelrea, Fin Lough, Ben Gorm

Zones suited to large numbers and require development and facilities to accommodate them.

Zones where recreation could be developed/ initiated on a moderate scale without detriment to the landscape or host community.

Remote or sensitive zones where volume numbers would be in appropriate.

Figure 11   *Area strategies for southwest Mayo*

Additional matters to be considered within this framework are landscape and townscape, accommodation, information and interpretation, and management.

It is hoped that such a locality-specific management strategy will be instrumental in ensuring that the rural community retains its rurality, that the local economy is sustained, and that the environment is maintained.

REFERENCES

Brady, Shipman and Martin, Niall Hyde (1973)
   The National Coastline Study Vol.3: a procedural manual. Dublin: An Foras Forbartha and Bord Fáilte Éireann.
Glyptis, S (1991)
   Countryside Recreation. London: Longman.
Greer, J and Murray, M (1988)
   A Recreation Strategy for the Mourne Area of Outstanding Natural Beauty. Belfast: The Sports Council for Northern Ireland.

Tourism Development at Community Level in Disadvantaged Areas

GEARÓID MAC EOCHAIDH

INTRODUCTION

Over the past ten years or so, community-based organisations have been strongly encouraged to involve themselves in schemes aimed at the creation of jobs and wealth within their localities. This move toward community based or initiated enterprise compares with the earlier social, environmental and recreational role of community organisations. In rural areas community groups, while also pursuing general manufacturing and service job ideas, have been encouraged to investigate projects based on natural resource development. This, in effect, has meant projects involving tourism, farm diversification, and amalgams of both. In the disadvantaged areas of the West and North West particularly, the emphasis has been on tourism projects, largely due to the perceived limitations of farm diversification as a real option.

Tourism has therefore become the main focus for community based enterprise in such communities. Organisations have been encouraged to view the landscapes, natural features, heritage and history of their areas as the basic stuff from which tourism projects can be generated. Grant assistance programmes for tourism ventures have further encouraged and facilitated such a frame of mind.

This essay will examine briefly some of the issues connected with the promotion of tourism development at community level in disadvantaged rural areas. The material presented here is largely based on the situation faced by the Community Connections project. Community Connections is a community development group operating in the West Fermanagh/North Leitrim/West Cavan area.

Ullrich Kockel (ed), *Culture, Tourism and Development: The Case of Ireland*, Liverpool University Press 1994, 183-88.

Gearóid Mac Eochaidh

THE EXPERIENCE OF 'COMMUNITY CONNECTIONS'

There is a strong case for the involvement of the community in tourism development. In many areas group activity is necessary given the absence of individual entrepreneurs. Much of the tourism potential of rural areas is based on natural resources, which are, in effect, the property of the community at large. Benefits should therefore flow, somehow, to the community as opposed to the individual alone.

At this stage, it is perhaps worthwhile to consider the requirements needed for successful tourism ventures. In basic terms there must be a product which can be sold. Landscape alone cannot yield jobs and income. There must be a market for the product, or a good likelihood that a market can be generated for it. The market must be adequately large to make the product viable. The product should be competitive or unique. The product should comprise part of an integrated whole of tourism products, including accommodation/catering, amenities/activities, and services. There should be adequate finance for the establishment of the product or project.

There are social requirements too. At local level there must be individuals or groups which are motivated to undertake tourism projects. These people need certain basic organisational and business skills; if lacking these skills, they should be capable of acquiring them. As individuals or as groups they should have access to the finance needed for the development of projects, either from funding agencies or from personal or community sources.

Areas such as North Leitrim or West Cavan have not traditionally seen many tourists. The tendency of the mass of visitors to the West and North-west has been to keep to the main arteries linking Galway through Sligo to Donegal. Visitors journeying from the Northeast tend to travel directly to the coastal areas of Donegal, Mayo and Galway. At best, North Leitrim and to a lesser degree West Cavan have been areas visited by small numbers of tourists who are based in Sligo or Bundoran/Donegal. There is, therefore, no pre-existing visitor group. There is, also and logically, a very poor accommodation base or structured amenity/activity base for visitors within this sub-region. Tourism here is starting from scratch. There is little or no tradition of tourism.

On the positive side, the area has excellent lakes and fishing, good access to the coast, beautiful mountains and valleys, and much by way of historical and environmental interest. Above all, it is not cluttered with visitors.

However, the population is dropping at a rate which is faster and much more sustained than anywhere else in Ireland. The demographic structure is unbalanced. Over 19% of the population is over 65 years of age. Income levels are low, and there is a very high dependency on social welfare payments. Farm size is small and farm incomes low.

In brief, this area, while possessing natural attractions, lacks a tourism infrastructure, lacks any established tourism tradition, and has a population which for economic and social reasons is likely to have difficulty entering into the tourism business. Local community organisations simply do not exist in many localities. Those that do exist may have little organisational experience, particularly with regard to enterprise development.

The danger in such situations is that haphazard tourism developments will be attempted without first taking into account the reality which prevails at community level. Assumptions may be made regarding, for example, the interest or ability of householders to become involved in something as basic as the bed and breakfast trade. The investment needed to bring traditional dwellings to an adequate standard may prove prohibitive or at least unattractive in the absence of visible tourists. Coordinated marketing of accommodation is unlikely to be feasible where very few operators exist. Specialised tourist amenities such as heritage centres, local museums or interpretative centres will find difficulty surviving in areas of low visitor numbers.

This may appear to be an excessively pessimistic picture of the situation. However, the evidence to date shows that development tends to follow development, and that it is very difficult to establish within a hitherto undeveloped area the blend of tourism goods and services needed to attract and retain visitors and their money. Furthermore, the danger exists that communities may be encouraged to commit themselves to tourism projects without first developing the organisational and business skills needed, or an overview of tourism in the local context.

What, therefore, is required in order to ensure successful development of tourism in areas such as this? Clearly, financial support and sustainable project ideas will be needed. Ideally, such ideas should enhance rather than threaten the natural environment, which is the strongest asset of these rural communities. However, other less apparent steps should also be taken:

- First, and most importantly, agencies promoting and encouraging tourism development need to recognise that local groups will need support other than project finance alone.

- There must be a recognition that groups will need education and training in organisational and business matters, and that groups should not be pressured to undertake projects simply because of the existence of funding opportunities.

- There needs to be support for groups that will enable them to identify and take into account the local economic and social factors which will have implications for any enterprise project.

- Groups and individuals will need to be provided with opportunities to educate themselves regarding all the necessary aspects of tourism development, in order that they can see their own project ideas within an overall context.

- There is a need to provide support for networking and exchange of information and experiences between groups, so that projects are not viewed in isolation from one another.

- Groups should be encouraged to clearly work out the real benefits of tourism projects in the short- and long-term, both direct and indirect.

- Structures will need to be developed to facilitate joint marketing of local tourism products, in order to overcome problems regarding economies of scale.

- Communities need to be supported in developing practical and effective overall tourism development strategies, as opposed to simply concentrating on narrow projects.

Communities have not always been encouraged to work through tourism projects in such a manner. Community Connections has attempted to assist groups come to terms with these issues. As an organisation with affiliated groups spread over North Leitrim, West Fermanagh and West Cavan, we have been able to draw on the more advanced experience of the Northern groups in order to assist the Southern ones. With limited resources, we have been able to organise and run two workshops on sustainable tourism for community groups, at which participants were able to learn from both experts and other community projects. Both workshops revealed a hunger amongst community groups for information and insights into the tourism business.

Having recently secured funding under the INTERREG programme for a relatively modest community development programme, we are now in a position to offer groups the support of our community development and enterprise development workers. Community Connections has been aware, over its short time in existence, of the fact that encouragement and support for community based enterprise has not been balanced to any degree by the provision of community development support. We feel that without this balance little progress will be made.

CONCLUSION

In conclusion, this essay has suggested that many disadvantaged rural areas face difficulties in undertaking successful tourism projects, and that community organisations in these areas need appropriate organisational and educational support over and above those largely financial incentives presently being offered.

Community groups should be encouraged to look at tourism as an avenue for local development, but they must also be encouraged to be critically aware of their own strengths and limits. Development agencies must accept that models of tourism development which have worked elsewhere may need to be changed for the special circumstances existing in disadvantaged areas. Creation of a new industry will need different approaches than those needed in developing an existing one. Some diversion of funding from bricks and mortar projects to the development of appropriate local tourism strategies will be needed.

There will need to be a recognition of the fact that tourism projects, like most enterprise projects, can have a draining effect on the energy of community organisations, and that other areas of activity can suffer, especially in the social field. Organisations will, therefore need to be encouraged not to concentrate all their energies in this one field.

Culture and Urban Tourism:
'Dublin 1991'—European City of Culture

LEWIS CLOHESSY

INTRODUCTION

When it was announced in late 1988 that Dublin had been selected by the European Community to be the European City of Culture for 1991, the cynics emerged in great numbers from the various hiding-places where they had been lingering since the Dublin Millennium disappointed them by proving to be a success.

The idea of the city being awarded a European title, let alone a cultural one, was too much for these informed commentators to resist. All right, they conceded, the Millennium was fine: it was our own celebration and we were not comparing ourselves to anywhere else, so nobody could be too critical. 'European City of Culture' is a different matter: now we will be in direct competition with the other cities who have held, or will hold, that title. Cities like Paris, Florence, Berlin and Madrid. In that company, Dublin will be a laughing-stock, a provincial backwater trying to ape the achievements of the great cities of Europe!

A favourite line of the cynics was that Dublin was not 'ready' to be European City of Culture: its derelict buildings and drug-infested inner city made it a place to stay away from until all had been put right. Perhaps in the year 2010 or so, sufficient cultural life might have crept back into the place to justify giving it a grandiose title. Until then, however...—and at this point, the cynics invariably shrugged their shoulders and turned away.

As always, somewhere at the core of a cynic's argument, there is a valid point: Dublin is a provincial, or as one would nowadays tend to say, peripheral capital. Generally speaking, it does not 'feel' as if it is in the centre of things and many of its streets and buildings do state eloquently that time has passed them by. In spite of huge advances in communications, the place still retains the key characteristics of an isolated community, with all the spite and gossip, and all the shared experience one might expect in a much smaller and more remote place.

Ullrich Kockel (ed), *Culture, Tourism and Development: The Case of Ireland*, Liverpool University Press 1994, 189-95.

One of the worst things a Dubliner can say about someone who has grown too big for his (or her) boots is: 'Sure I knew him/her when he/she used to live near us!' As a put-down, this is in the same league as Groucho Marx's refusal to join any club which would be prepared to accept him as a member, but it does illustrate our civic and indeed national tendency to find high-flown aspiration and achievement somewhat out of line with the decent expectations of the community as a whole.

If, therefore, our self-perception is such that we cannot conceive of ourselves as rightfully occupying the high ground at any stage or in any circumstance, it may fall to others to do our aspiring for us. I believe that this is one of the prime services which the European Community could provide for the Irish. For instance, and whether we like it or not, we carry the obligation of accepting the Presidency of the entire Community for six months every six years and, to our own astonishment and no one else's, we always carry it off brilliantly.

This allows us to believe in ourselves for a few weeks, after which we are free to revert to our peripheral role and attitudes, which are, of course, only confirmed when some bully-boys from the heart of Europe stand by laughing while our unhappy currency is mugged in broad daylight.

THE EUROPEAN CONTEXT

Main Street Europe is a tough place, but the fact remains that we asked to be allowed to walk there. If that means that we take the occasional beating, then we must train for it. This is true of anything we undertake in the new Europe, and, not least, of the topics under discussion this weekend: it's true of culture; it's true of tourism and, therefore, by extension, it is all too true of Cultural Tourism.

I believe that Dublin's term as European City of Culture gave our capital city, and indeed our country as a whole, an opportunity to participate, if not compete, in a sequence of events centred around the concept of Cultural Tourism. Equally importantly, it offered us the chance of coming in, however briefly, from the periphery, just as we had done the previous year when graced with the Community Presidency.

Disregarding the cynics, therefore, our city fathers and mothers bit the bullet of possible Europe-wide ridicule and accepted the dangerous honour of naming Dublin the European City of Culture (or Cultural Capital, as it has been erroneously and persistently called by the media).

190

Culture and Urban Tourism

When the concept of the European Cities of Culture was devised in 1985 by the then Greek Minister of Culture, Melina Mercouri, it was envisaged that, as well as allowing the inhabitants of the selected cities to preen themselves on their contribution to human civilisation, the granting of the title would boost the inflow of visitors from other European cities and countries.

Tourism has, therefore, always been at the heart of the Cities of Culture movement. This was notably the case with Dublin's predecessor, Glasgow, which, as a result of being the 1990 'home' of European culture, has gone from being a city to avoid at all costs to competing vigorously with Edinburgh for the status of Scotland's No.1 attraction.

Why 1991 was chosen as the year in which Dublin was awarded the City of Culture title is a question which can only be answered by a select group of government ministers and bureaucrats. In any event, it proved to be an appropriate choice, even if, as is not uncommon in Ireland, it meant that the organisers were faced with an extremely short planning period, particularly in regard to the need to circulate advance information to overseas tourism markets.

Necessity being the mother of invention, it was decided that the strongest themes which could be developed in a short time to catch the attention of potential visitors to Dublin in 1991 were those which were linked to important anniversaries and to the fabric of the city itself.

Among the anniversaries identified were: the 50th of the death of James Joyce, our greatest novelist; the 200th of the Custom House, Dublin's finest building; the 800th of St. Patrick's Cathedral; the 250th of Händel's arrival in Dublin to conduct 'The Messiah"; and, among European anniversaries, those of Mozart, Vivaldi, Dvorak, Prokofiev and a remarkable number of other composers.

Improvements in the fabric of the city have, in spite of many appearances to the contrary in certain areas, been taking place over the last dozen years or so. In the cultural area, for instance, these years have seen the renovation of the National Gallery, National Museum and National Library, the opening of the new National Concert Hall, the conversion of an old distillery into the National College of Art and Design and the transformation of the Guinness Hop Store, unused for many years, into an exhibition space of great character.

In 1991, this list was extensively added to, with the establishment of the Irish Museum of Modern Art at the Royal Hospital, Kilmainham; the opening of the Dublin Writers' Museum; the refurbishment of the

191

Municipal Gallery; the installation of a new pipe organ in the National Concert Hall; the development of the Irish Film Centre in Eustace Street; the creation of a Georgian Museum on the corner of Fitzwilliam Square, and the restoration of Drimnagh Castle.

Above all of the projects relating to the revitalisation of the city, the Temple Bar scheme stands out as uniquely important. While plans for this project had been on the drawing board for several years, the opportunity to move on these plans did not arise until 1991 when, appropriately in view of Dublin being the European City of Culture, a capital grant of almost £4 million from EC Structural Funds triggered off the commencement of work in Temple Bar.

I should note that the obtaining of the grant was the culmination of an approach to the EC, spearheaded by Professor Frank Convery of University College Dublin, the Dublin Chamber of Commerce, and the Dublin City of Culture office, rounded off by Dublin Corporation, who lodged the formal submission.

The long-term effects of the development of Temple Bar as an arts district in the heart of Dublin remain to be seen. Already, however, the area has a genuine 'left bank' character and is the home of many thriving businesses and cultural centres, and projections are that several thousand people will be working and, indeed, living in the area by 1999. It is, in short, likely to be the focus for cultural tourism in the city by that time.

EVENTS PROGRAMME

When selecting or creating events for the programme of activities during the year, priority consideration was given to how the city itself could form part of these events, by providing a framework or acting as a backdrop. This was consistent with the approach taken throughout the year of considering the city's own fabric as the prime attraction for visitors.

In the course of the year 1991, therefore, major events took place in some of Dublin's most distinctive locations, quite apart from the standard performance and exhibition venues. The most widespread event of the year was the Dublin Street Carnival, greatly enhanced by means of additional grant aid for the City of Culture festivities; the Carnival extended through many streets and on to the river Liffey, culminating in a colourful firework display on the bridges.

Also on the streets was the first-ever crossroads céilí in Dublin, when hundreds of set dancers from around Ireland performed over an eight-hour period in Dame Street for a large and good-humoured audience, composed substantially of foreign visitors.

Just down the road, in front of the Bank of Ireland and Trinity College, two of the most successful outdoor events of 1991 took place: the great folk concert, featuring Dé Dannan, Mary Black and a host of other leading Irish performers, which took place in August, and the appearance of Luciano Pavarotti on screen, transmitted live and large—very large—from his concert at the Point Theatre on the night before New Year's Eve.

In all of these cases, the pleasure of the event was greatly increased by the striking and unusual setting. This was, perhaps, even more true of the 200th birthday celebrations for the Custom House. This great building had just been restored meticulously and beautifully by the Office of Public Works who, no matter what stance one takes on the vexed matter of interpretative centres, have been outstanding guardians of our heritage.

Accordingly, the building itself became the event. The presence of a floating pavilion on the river just in front of the Custom House, full of musicians and dancers in full eighteenth-century costumes and powdered wigs, acted as a foil to the gleaming beauty of the restored building, as three grandstands full of the best and brightest of Dublin's natives and visitors, along with a standing audience estimated at thirty thousand people, enjoyed Händel's 'Water Music' and a spectacular light show, using the façade of the Custom House itself as a screen.

While for me, the Custom House celebration was the most memorable outdoor event of the 'Dublin 1991' programme, it was by no means the largest in terms of attendance. That honour went to the first and, so far, only free rock concert in that ultimate Dublin space, the Phoenix Park. Over one hundred thousand young people, and a few less young ones, like myself, enjoyed the sun and dodged the showers for over six hours as we listened to the soothing noises of the Saw Doctors, the Hothouse Flowers and many other groups.

DUBLIN'S DIFFERENCE

As this sampling of cultural events from the 'Dublin 1991' programme runs the risk of turning into a mere listing, I will cut it short at this point and summarise the strategy adopted to differentiate our capital's term as

European City of Culture from that of our European sister cities blessed, or saddled, as the case may be, with the same honoured title.

It was important to realise, as we did, that we are not recognised as one of the great cultural centres (or even crossroads) of Europe. It would therefore have been futile and ludicrous, justifying all of the cynics' scorn, if we had attempted something of the 'cultural overload' undertaken by Berlin, for instance, who stuffed their Cultural Year from end to end with the world's greatest orchestras, dancers, opera companies, art works, theatre companies, singers, historical artifacts and as many examples of culture, ancient and modern, as you could wish to dream of.

For a different reason, that of trying to blast their way into public awareness, the organisers of 'Glasgow 1990' also went for an 'overkill' approach. It cost a fortune and nearly backfired on a number of occasions, when much-hyped events, such as the enormous 'Glasgow's Glasgow' exhibition and the summer international theatre season, failed to attract anything like the projected attendances.

The final analysis must be, however, that it worked for Glasgow. The evidence for this is contained in the extensive Myerscough Report on the economic benefits to the city of the whole 1990 extravaganza and, of course, in the returns of the Greater Glasgow Tourist Board which show a dramatic and sustained lift-off in the number of visitors.

This was, admittedly, from a very low base and I am advised by Dublin Tourism that, to date, our capital remains comfortably ahead of what we might playfully term its Scottish rival.

Accepting therefore, that spending our way to creating an illusion of cultural centrality in Europe was not on, we had little choice but to base our programme on as extensive a sampling as we could afford of the best from Europe (such as the 'Kremlin Gold' and 'Berlin!' exhibitions and selected theatre and musical performers) woven through an essentially local network of activities, reflecting in large measure what makes us different from other, better endowed cities.

While we were always prepared to accept the superiority of the endowment of other Cities of Culture (how do you seriously compete against Florence, for instance?), it has been an article of faith that the main elements of our own culture which we put on show would be of European, if not world standard, and yet—and this was crucial—of a very different and individual character.

Hence the emphasis placed on displaying our streets, buildings and open spaces; the compilation of the Great Book of Ireland, a 'time capsule' of what gave Irish art and writing its particular quality at this exciting time; and the attention given in the programme to our literary giants, Joyce and Beckett above all, who fused the quirkiness of a Dublin view of life with the main currents of European thinking.

Fintan O'Toole of *The Irish Times* has argued that because Ireland is a peripheral country in Europe, and Dublin, thus, a peripheral city, we should have devised a cultural programme for our term as European City of Culture which reflected this peripherality and, indeed, marginality.

He suggests that the culture of local communities in Dublin is what we should have asserted, rather than giving pride of place to what he saw in 1991 as essentially a cut-down version of a menu more generously available from our European competitors. I am sorry that he seems to have failed to grasp that that was precisely what we were trying not to do and I must accept much of the blame for not conveying this to him and to other media commentators. In parenthesis, I must observe, however, that the presence of media representatives at the two hundred or so 'community' events on our programme, which might be thought to represent the culture of the peripheral and marginalised, was so rare as to have constituted a cultural landmark in itself, when it did occur.

Our objective, then, was to present the culture of the periphery, the culture exemplified best of all, perhaps, in our 1991 programme by the superb National Museum exhibition 'Ór—Ireland's Gold', as being as valid and relevant in today's Europe as a novel by Gunter Grass or a film by Louis Malle.

We may not have succeeded completely in achieving this ambitious aim, and the eternal cynics about whom I spoke so lovingly earlier in this essay would maintain that we have not only totally failed to do so, but have made ourselves look even more uncultured. In spite of them, however, I believe that, in some degree, we have helped to make Dublin less marginal in the thinking of our European neighbours and, perhaps, we have played a role in sustaining and increasing the number of visitors to the city. Dublin not just survived, but surmounted the trauma of the Gulf War, achieving record numbers of visitors and record tourism receipts, not least from continental Europe, in 1991, the year the city became European City of Culture. There is a certain advertisement on RTE television these days which says: 'Draw your own conclusions'. I leave you to do just that.

Appendix

The Culture and Tourism Research Unit at the Institute of Irish Studies, University of Liverpool

The *Culture and Tourism Research Unit* originated from an interdisciplinary research programme on European regional development, initiated in 1990, which focuses on questions of development and change in peripheral regions of Europe from a comparative perspective, promoting experience exchange between these regions. A range of projects carried out under the programme investigate key issues in Irish development within the context of the current restructuring of the economic, political and social organisation of Europe: the Single Market, the opening-up of Eastern Europe, and the creation of a united Germany as the major economic power in Europe.

MAIN ACTIVITIES OF THE UNIT

In summer 1992, the *Culture and Tourism Research Unit* was established to provide an interdisciplinary forum and institutional focus for research on certain key issues identified within this research programme, in particular the management of 'cultural resources' as part of strategies of endogenous regional development.

Development of courses in cultural resource management

With support from the *UFC/HEFC Continuing Vocational Education Development Fund*, and in co-operation with the *European Centre for Traditional and Regional Cultures* and the *European Society for Irish Studies*, a range of innovative short courses are being developed. The courses provide professional training in the management of cultural resources, and can be credited towards an academic and/or professional qualification. They will also be available as a distance learning package.

Ullrich Kockel (ed), *Culture, Tourism and Development: The Case of Ireland*, Liverpool University Press 1994, 197-99

The courses are grouped into five separate units, covering the theory and methods of representing regional culture; legal and socio-economic aspects of cultural resource development; and case studies focusing on aspects of material and non-material regional culture. The testing of course materials commenced in summer 1993, and the first intake of students is anticipated for 1995. The distance learning programme will be offered through regional and national tuition centres across Europe.

Cultural tourism and local entrepreneurship

This project, with support from the *European Society for Irish Studies* and the *Economic and Social Research Council*, examines different structures of, and region-specific approaches to innovative development programmes in Ireland, comparing their experience to that of programmes in other parts of Europe. It investigates the contribution of these programmes to the growth of entrepreneurial culture in peripheral regions, seeking to find suitable ways of improving existing programmes, and to identify vital components of possible alternative strategies.

Ethnic nationalism, language and identity

With support from the *EC Commission*, a pilot study was carried out, in 1990/91, of political culture in three European border regions (Ulster, Euskadi and Schleswig) and its implications for European Unity. Following this study, several issues are currently being followed up.

The effects of the changing territorial and political relevance of borders for regional, national and supra-national government need to be better understood. The purely economic perception of borders as barriers to trade appears to be a rather one-eyed view. In the light of the opening of the internal borders within the European Union, their conceptualisation as 'central places' may well yield new insights into processes of regional development. Cultural territories often do not coincide with the territories of nation states; hence cultural regions frequently cut across national boundaries. This constitutes a major challenge for cultural policy, at the national as well as the supra-national level.

Regional and minority languages play a significant role in the formation of ethnic identities, and there has been a resurgence of lesser used languages over recent years. However, the function and experience of ethnic language schools varies greatly between different regions. Comparative research on language use and ethnic schooling seeks to provide insights into problem aspects of ethnicity with a view to social cohesion, and its relevance extends beyond existing frontier regions, into all areas with multi-cultural societies.

Other projects

There are a number of smaller projects carried out under the auspices of the Unit. Members of the Unit are involved in studies on the socio-cultural impacts of economic restructuring in peripheral maritime regions; evaluative research on 'tourist trail' projects linking the North of Ireland with the North of England and the Southwest of Scotland; and comparative work on emigration from marginal rural areas.

Membership of the Unit

The Unit brings together staff and postgraduate students from a range of departments within the University of Liverpool. During its first two years, it has developed extensive networks at the local, national and European level, reaching from the West of Ireland to Estonia and Slovenia. The work of the Unit is led by Dr Ullrich Kockel (Irish Studies) in collaboration with Dr Máiréad Nic Craith (Irish Studies) and Dr Dominic Keown (Hispanic Studies), and the development of courses in cultural resource management is co-ordinated by Ms Sarah Stamper. There are a number of associated researchers in the Institute of Irish Studies, the Departments of Geography and History, and the University's Centre for Manx Studies. External members of the Unit come from the City of Liverpool's Department of Adult Education, from University College Cork (Ireland), the universities of Joensuu (Finland), Tartu (Estonia) and Tübingen (Germany), as well as from independent research institutes, such as ECTARC (Wales), and from research users in the public, private and voluntary sectors. For further details on the work of the Unit, please write to:

Culture and Tourism Unit, Institute of Irish Studies,
University of Liverpool, P.O.Box 147,
Liverpool, England, L69 3BX.